ACCESS GUIDES TO YOUTH MINISTRY

Retreats

**Edited by
Reynolds R. Ekstrom**

THE WORLD OF
DON BOSCO
MULTIMEDIA

New Rochelle, NY

Access Guides to Youth Ministry: Retreats
is published as a service for adults who love the
young and want to share the Gospel with them.

It is a guide to understanding the young and a resource
book for helping them. As such, it is addressed to
parents, parish youth ministers, clergy who work with
the young, and teachers.

Forthcoming *Access Guides*:
Leadership
Early Adolescent Ministry
Spirituality

Prepared in conjunction with
The Center for Youth Ministry Development

Access Guides to Youth Ministry: Retreats
©1991 Salesian Society, Inc. / Don Bosco Multimedia
475 North Ave., Box T, New Rochelle, NY 10802

Library of Congress Cataloging-in-Publication Data
Retreats / edited by Reynolds R. Ekstrom.
p. cm. — (Access guides to youth ministry)
Includes bibliographical references.
    1. Retreats.   2. Youth—Religious life.
        I. Ekstrom, Reynolds, R.   II. Title: Retreats.   III. Series.

ISBN 0-89944-152-1 $14.95

Printed in the United States of America

03/91   9 8 7 6 5 4 3 2 1

Table of Contents

PART ONE

FOUNDATIONS OF YOUTH RETREATS

PART TWO
MODELS AND STRATEGIES

PREFACE TO THE ACCESS GUIDES

A NEW CONCEPT

Welcome to the *Access Guides to Youth Ministry* series. The Center for Youth Ministry Development and Don Bosco Multimedia have created the *Access Guides* series to provide leaders in ministry with youth with both the foundational understandings and the practical tools they need to create youth ministry programming for each component outlined in *A Vision of Youth Ministry*. *Access Guides* have been developed for pop culture, evangelization, and liturgy & worship and justice. Upcoming *Access Guides* will address leadership, family life, prayer, and spirituality. Each of the *Access Guides* provides foundational essays, processes for developing that particular component of youth ministry, and approaches and program models to use in your setting. The blend of theory and practice makes each of the *Access Guides* a unique resource in youth ministry. To help you understand the context of the *Access Guides* series we would like to provide you with a brief overview of the goals and components of a comprehensive approach to ministry with youth.

A RENEWED MINISTRY

Over a decade ago, Catholic youth ministry engaged in a process of self-reflection and analysis that resulted in a re-visioning of youth ministry — establishing the goals, principles, and components of a comprehensive, contemporary ministry with youth. *A Vision of Youth Ministry* outlined this comprehensive approach to ministry with youth and became the foundation for a national vision of Catholic youth ministry. In the years since the publishing of *A Vision of Youth Ministry*, Catholic youth ministry across the United States has experienced tremendous growth.

From the outset the *Vision* paper made clear its ecclesial focus: "As one among many ministries of the Church, youth ministry must be understood in terms of the mission and ministry of the whole Church" (*Vision* 3). The focus is clearly ministerial. "The Church's mission is threefold: to proclaim the good news of salvation, offer itself as a group of people transformed by the Spirit into a community of faith, hope, and love; and to bring God's justice and love to others through service in its individual, social, and political dimensions" (*Vision* 3). This threefold mission formed the basis of the framework or components of youth ministry: Word (evangelization and catechesis), worship, community, justice and service, guidance and healing, enablement, and advocacy.

This threefold mission also gives youth ministry a dual focus. Youth ministry is a ministry within the community of faith — ministering to believing youth *and* to the wider society — reaching out to serve youth in our society. While the experience of the past decade has emphasized ministry *within* the community, youth ministry must also address the social situation and needs of all youth in society. A comprehensive approach demands a balance between ministry *within* the Christian community and ministry *by* the Christian community *to* young people within our society and world.

The *Vision* paper described a broad concept of ministry with youth using four dimensions. Youth ministry is...

To youth — responding to youth's varied needs;

With youth — working with adults to fulfill their common responsibility for the Church's mission;

By youth — exercising their own ministry to others: peers, community, world;

For youth — interpreting the needs of youth, especially in areas of injustice and acting on behalf of or with youth for a change in the systems which create injustice.

Two goals were initially developed for the Church's ministry with youth:

Goal #1: Youth ministry works to the total personal and spiritual growth of each young person.

Goal 2: Youth ministry seeks to draw young people to responsible participation in the life, mission, and work of the faith community. (*Vision* 7)

The first goal emphasizes *becoming* — focusing on the *personal* dimension of human existence. Our understanding of the unique life tasks and social-cultural context of adolescence provides directions for fostering their growth in discipleship and Catholic identity. The second goal emphasizes *belonging* — focusing on the *interpersonal* or *communal* dimension of human existence. Active engagement of youth in the Christian community's life and mission provides an important context for growth and overcomes the danger of marginalizing youth in the Church, segregating them from the real centers of power, responsibility and commitment in community life.

In light of the Church's priority upon justice and peace, the mission of the Church to transform society (*The Challenge of Peace* and *Economic Justice for All*), and the need to engage in a critical assessment of our culture and society, it is necessary to add a third goal to the two goals from 1976. This third goal emphasizes *transforming* — focusing on the public or *social structural* dimension of human existence. This third goal could be framed in the following manner:

Goal #3: Youth ministry empowers young people to transform the world as disciples of Jesus Christ by living and working for justice and peace.

This third goal seeks to help young people realize that living and working for justice and peace is grounded in the Gospel and Catholic social vision and is essential for being a Christian. Youth ministry needs to empower young people with the knowledge and skills to transform the unjust structures of society (locally and globally) so that these structures promote justice, respect human dignity, promote human rights, and build peace.

An underdeveloped, but increasingly important section of the *Vision* paper is the contexts of youth ministry. "In all places, youth ministry occurs within a given social, cultural, and religious context which shapes the specific form of the ministry" (*Vision* 10). This contextual approach seeks to view young people as part of a number of social systems which impact on their growth, values, and faith, rather than as isolated individuals. Among these systems are the family, society, the dominant culture, youth culture, ethnic culture, school, and local church community. In the last several years, youth ministry has become much more aware of the impact of these systems.

A COMPREHENSIVE APPROACH

The framework (or components) describes distinct aspects for developing a comprehensive, integrated ministry with youth. Briefly, these components include:

Evangelization — reaching out to young people who are uninvolved in the life of the community and inviting them into a relationship with Jesus and the Christian community. Evangelization involves proclaiming the Good News of Jesus through programs and relationships.

Catechesis — promoting a young person's growth in Christian faith through the kind of teaching and learning that emphasizes understanding, reflection, and transformation. This is accomplished through systematic, planned, and intentional programming (curriculum). (See *The Challenge of Adolescent Catechesis*).

Prayer and Worship — assisting young people in deepening their relationship with Jesus through the development of a personal prayer life; and providing a variety of prayer and worship experiences with youth to deepen and celebrate their relationship with Jesus in a caring Christian community; involving young people in the sacramental life of the Church.

Community Life — building Christian community with youth through programs and relationships which promote openness, trust, valuing the person, cooperation, honesty, taking responsibility, and willingness to serve; creating a climate where young people can grow and share their struggles, questions, and joys with other youth and adults; helping young people feel like a valued part of the Church.

Guidance and Healing — providing youth with sources of support and counsel as they face personal problems and pressures (for example, family problems, peer pressure, substance abuse, suicide) and decide on careers and important life decisions; providing appropriate support and guidance for youth during times of stress and crisis; helping young people deal with the problems they face and the pressures people place on them; developing a better understanding of their parents and learning how to communicate with them.

Justice, Peace, and Service — guiding young people in developing a Christian social consciousness and a commitment to a life of justice and peace through educational programs and service/action involvement; infusing the concepts of justice and peace into all youth ministry relationships and programming.

Enablement — developing, supporting, and utilizing the leadership abilities and personal gifts of youth and adults in youth ministry, empowering youth for ministry with their peers; developing a leadership team to organize and coordinate the ministry with youth.

Advocacy — interpreting the needs of youth: personal, family, and social especially in areas of injustices towards or oppression of youth, and acting with or on behalf of youth for a change in the systems which create injustice; giving young people a voice and empowering them to address the social problems that they face.

This is the vision and scope that the *Access Guides* series seeks to promote through foundational understandings and practical, pastoral approaches. We at the Center hope that this series will empower you with the knowledge and skills to become more effective in your ministry with youth.

WORKS CITED

The Challenge of Adolescent Catechesis. Washington DC: NFCYM Publications, 1986.

A Vision of Youth Ministry. Washington DC: USCC, Department of Education, 1976.

ABOUT THE AUTHORS

Joanne Cahoon is currently an Associate Staff member of the Center for Youth Ministry Development in Naugatuck CT. She has been a parish coordinator of youth ministry, a high school catechist, and a campus youth minister for over 10 years in the Baltimore area. Joanne holds an M.A. in Religion and Youth Ministry from LaSalle University. Her essays have appeared in the *Network Papers* series and *Access Guides to Youth Ministry: Evangelization* (Don Bosco Multimedia, 1989).

Rebecca Davis is a graduate student in theology at Loyola University, in Chicago. She holds a B.A. in Theater and Speech from Hanover College, and has served as coordinator of youth ministries for two years at St. Mary of the Knobs Parish in Floyds Knobs, IN. Rebecca is a graduate of the national Certificate in Youth Ministry Studies Program, and she was contributing author to *Access Guides to Youth Ministry: Pop Culture* (Don Bosco Multimedia, 1989).

Rev. Robert Duggan is a priest of the Archdiocese of Washington DC. He holds a doctorate in Theology from the Catholic University of America and is presently Director of the Office of Worship for the archdiocese. Fr. Duggan has served in parishes and as a faculty member of the North American College in Rome. He has also taught at Catholic University and the Washington Theological Union. His publications include *Conversion and the Catechumenate* (Paulist, 1984), a volume which he edited.

Reynolds R.(Butch) Ekstrom earned a Masters degree in Pastoral Studies (M.P.S.) from Loyola of the South. He has been a full-time staff member of the Center for Youth Ministry Development (1987-1990), and before that served as Associate Director of Religious Education for eight years in the Archdiocese of New Orleans, centering his work and ministry on adolescent religious education. Butch has taught in the Pastoral Institute of Incarnate Word College, San Antonio; at LaSalle University, Philadelphia; at Seton Hall in New Jersey; and in the Institute for Ministry, Loyola New Orleans. He is the author of *Concise Catholic Dictionary* (Twenty-Third Publications), *Access Guides to Youth Ministry: Pop Culture* (Don Bosco Multimedia, 1989), and youth catechesis booklets on faith-themes, *Personal Growth* and *Relationships* (Sadlier). He is co-editor of the *Access Guides to Youth Ministry: Evangelization* (Don Bosco Multimedia, 1989) and *Good News for Youth* series (Don Bosco Multimedia, 1990). For five years, he has been a regular contributor to *Top Music Countdown*, a quarterly ministry journal on contemporary music.

Pam Heil is campus youth minister at St. Francis de Sales High School, in Columbus, OH. With her husband, Frank, she is parent to three adolescent boys and one adolescent girl. Pam received her B.S. in Education with majors in English and Psychology from Kent State University. Her theological studies have been through Ohio Dominican College and the University of Dayton. For the last nine years, she has conducted workshops and presented lectures to youth on human sexuality. She has completed work on her national Certificate in Youth Ministry Studies.

Jeffrey Kaster is the diocesan consultant for youth in the Diocese of St. Cloud, MN. He has been involved in youth ministry since 1975 as a volunteer leader, a parish coordinator of youth ministry, and director of a total youth ministry program. Jeff holds an M.A. in Theology from St. John's University, Collegeville, MN. He now teaches courses in youth ministry and retreats at St. John's. He also authored the booklet, *Youth Ministry*, published by Liturgical Press in 1989.

Dr. James C. Kolar has worked with youth and young adults since the early 1970s. Married and the father of five children, Dr. Kolar centers his work and ministry today at the Community of Christ the Redeemer in St. Paul, MN where he is active as leader of the renewal community there.

Dennis Kurtz is currently the director of youth ministry in the Diocese of LaCrosse, WI. He is now completing a Masters degree in Theology at St. John's University in Collegeville, MN. Dennis has served as the Teens Encounter Christ (TEC) program's Region VI coordinator and as president of its national board of directors. He is the present coordinator of the Region VII Youth Ministry Coalition. He resides in Eau Claire, WI.

Robert McCarty is presently coordinator for youth ministry training in the Archdiocese of Baltimore. He earned an M.A. in Religious Education from LaSalle University and holds a certificate in family therapy from Temple University in Philadelphia. Bob has served as a parish director of religious education, a youth minister, and as counselor and minister to delinquent youths. He has also worked as director of a retreat center in the Baltimore area. Bob's essays have appeared in *PACE* magazine and in the *Readings In Youth Ministry II* (NFCYM, 1989). He has written and produced a video and manual on adolescent suicide, *I'll Carry You*, and has co-authored *Training Adults for Youth Ministry* from St. Mary's Press.

John Roberto, M.A. Rel. Ed., is Director and co-founder of the Center for Youth Ministry Development. He is the managing editor of the DBM-CYMD publishing project. John has authored *The Adolescent Catechesis Resource Manual* and "Principles of Youth Ministry" (*Network Paper #26*), and served as editor for the *Access Guides* on *Evangelization*, *Liturgy and Worship*, and *Justice* and for *Catholic Families: Growing and Sharing Faith*.

Charles Shelton, S.J., currently teaches at Regis College and lives in Denver, CO. He taught social science and has done adolescent counseling at Regis Jesuit High School in Denver and was for a time on the campus ministry staff of St. Louis University. Fr. Shelton received an M.A. from St. Louis University and his M.Div. from the Jesuit School of Theology in Berkeley, CA. His doctoral studies in clinical psychology were done at 'Loyola University of Chicago. He has published many articles, essays, and volumes on adolescent growth/spirituality issues, including the much-acclaimed *Adolescent Spirituality* (Loyola UP, 1983) and *Morality and the Adolescent* (Crossroad, 1989).

Dr. Michael Warren is the prolific author and editor of many articles and books in the field of youth ministry, including *A Future in Youth Catechesis* (Paulist Press, 1975), Readings and *Resources for Youth Ministry* (St. Mary's Press, 1987), *Youth and the Future of the Church* (Seabury Press, 1982), *Youth, Gospel, Liberation* (Harper &Row, 1987), and most recently *Faith, Culture, and the Worshipping Community* (Paulist Press, 1989). Dr. Warren has been widely published in respected educational journals, like *Religious Education* and *The Living Light.* Since 1975 he has been a faculty member in the Theology department at St. John's University, Jamacia, NY.

ACKNOWLEDGEMENTS

"Twenty-Five Years of Youth Weekends" by Michael Warren, appeared originally as "Twenty Years of Youth Weekends" in the book *Youth Gospel Liberation* (Harper & Row, 1987), and is reprinted through the courtesy of Dr. Michael Warren.

Portions of "Moral And Psychological Foundations" by Charles Shelton S.J., were excerpted from "Moral Development in Adolescence: Issues And Possibilities," *Occasional Paper #6*, published by the Center for Youth Ministry Development, 1986. Portions are also reprinted from *Morality and the Adolescent: A Pastoral Psychology Approach* by Charles Shelton S.J. (New York: Crossroad, 1989). Reprinted by permission of Crossroad Publishing.

"Evangelization Through Youth Retreats" by Dr. James C. Kolar, appeared originally in *Evangelizing Youth* (Wheaton IL: Tyndale House, 1985), and is reprinted by permission of Dr. James C. Kolar.

Portions of "Spiritual Direction in Youth Retreats" by Dennis Kurtz, were excerpted from "Spiritual Guidance for Adolescents: Three Perspectives," *Network Paper #30* published by Don Bosco Multimedia, 1989.

"Conversion: The Underlying Dynamic" by Robert Duggan, is reprinted from *Catholic Evangelization Today* edited by Kenneth Boyack (New York: Paulist Press, 1987). Reprinted by permission of Paulist Press.

"Retreats for Adolescents: Practical Guidelines" is reprinted by permission of the Office of Youth and Young Adult Ministry, Diocese of Sacramento, CA.

Part One

Overview

Foundations of Youth Retreats

In developing this volume on youth retreats we have tried to create a unique resource. This book will go beyond the boundaries of the usual manual on retreats for young people. It is not, you will quickly note, simply a compilation of retreat outlines. It is more than the usual listing of retreat themes, appropriate for younger and older adolescents, or for certain liturgical seasons, with brief suggestions on how to implement them. Such manuals have their value and their places in our ministry libraries. The *Access Guides to Youth Ministry: Retreats* is meant to help you probe the roots of retreat ministries for adolescents, the important, central place such retreats have held in the recent renewal of faith-formation ministries for youth, the best strategies and approaches developed for such retreats, and insights on how you can initiate or renew various aspects of a retreat ministry with adolescents in your own parish, school, or regional area.

There are many reasons why retreats have been integral to many youth ministries during the past twenty-five years or so. Retreats provide youth with a much-needed experience of community and relationship, through relaxation, fun, prayer, and Christian challenge, in safe, structured environments, with others who care about them. Retreats help young people grow in faith. Depending on how they are designed and implemented, adolescent retreats can be evangelizing experiences. They can catechize youth. They can offer much-needed spiritual guidance to the troubled, the hurting. Always, youth retreats lead young people toward meaningful prayer and worship. The best of youth retreats move beyond a limited ministry of gospel comfort and care for the young. (Warren 13) In recent years, especially, many retreat teams have tried to emphasize to youthful retreatants that the gospel also calls and challenges us all to work for justice, to seek reform of those things out of whack in our world, and to be persons who serve others, gladly, as did the One we freely follow.

Over the years, we have discovered that retreats for youth are not ends in themselves. Certain ministry activities help us prepare adolescents for them. And, importantly, certain types of ministry and outreach must be carried on, after retreats, as follow-ups with young people. These help them uncover the full fruits of their retreat experiences and enrich the faith moments and spiritual relationships they may have encountered through us.

Human development, social change, and faith-growth are dynamic, multifaceted processes. Those of us engaged in work with adolescents know this intuitively. Francis Ianni has noted, recently:

> The lives of adolescents hold a fascination for all of us. We have an enduring faith that the future of our world rests with the young, and so we look to this period of life more than any other for an evaluation of current society and the probable social future. As adults we assign to these younger members of society the role and the responsibility both to carry on our accumulated knowledge and to learn from our mistakes. Much more than childhood or even early adulthood, adolescence is viewed as a period of promise and preparation, and yet it is also seen as a time of special problems. (Ianni 1)

We reach out to young people because we care about them, about what they can and will become. We believe that they can grow and change. That they will develop, change, and make choices, despite their vulnerabilities and immaturity. That society can change too. That we can intervene in the lives of young people, and in the world at large, call for conversion, and hope that, through our ministries, Christian light and Christian faith will empower us all.

Underlying all that is said in this book, about why we try so hard to help adolescents mature in faith, or how the young grow through phases of moral- and faith-development within retreat-focused ministries, is the conviction that at the heart of adolescent spiritual growth is a deep, personal relationship with Jesus and the desire to identify, freely, with those who follow him. To this day, short and extended youth retreats alike should be focusing youth on the Lord and the call to walk his way. In his book *Adolescent Spirituality*, cited many times by contributors to this *Access Guide*, Charles Shelton (also a contributor to this volume) says:

> Through our travels with adolescents, we have come to see that their own discovery of Jesus' call is grounded in their own experience, as it is influenced by developmental issues that are threaded throughout these developing years. We have also seen adults exercise a pivotal role in the adolescent experience, for it is through adult-adolescent relationships, that young persons can capture in a fuller and richer sense what it means to "come, follow me" down the road toward Christian adulthood. (Shelton 342)

The relationship forged, the community life and fun experienced, the prayer and worship celebrated, and the gospel proclamations enthusiastically made, have guided adolescent retreats to a central place in the ethos of youth ministry since the mid-1960s. With Michael Warren we can recognize that, "Persons examining the development of youth ministry in the United States in the past thirty years soon recognize the remarkable contribution made by the renewal of youth retreats."

OVERVIEW OF PART ONE:
FOUNDATIONS OF YOUTH RETREATS

Part One of this volume opens with a short, pointed reflection by **Michael Warren** on the history, the roots, and the critical developments in the adolescent retreat movement in the United States. Noted as one of the most respected, incisive of thinkers and writers in all of Catholic youth ministry, Dr. Warren also offers several timely challenges and proposals to retreat ministers. In particular, he proposes that we reclaim, and then faithfully proclaim, an authentic understanding of Jesus, and his radical gospel, in order to challenge the many types of adolescents we encounter to work for social transformation, eagerly, and long after their immediate, intense retreat feelings have waned.

Part One also presents essays by **Butch Ekstrom** and **Charles Shelton** on the theological foundations of the good news shared with adolescents and on key insights from the fields of moral-development and psychology. These point out some of the why's and how's involved in calling young persons to Christian growth and conversion. As a complement to these theological reflections, and the foundational concepts drawn from moral- and psychological-development studies, **Robert Duggan** in his perceptive Chapter 5 essay, "Conversion: The Underlying Dynamic," speaks eloquently to the ultimate goal of all the evangelizing and other faith-growth methods we use in reaching out to persons of all ages, but especially youth.

A three-part Chapter 4 examines the ways in which retreats for adolescents can minister, directly, to various personal and faith needs. A veteran of many years of work with youth and young adults, **James C. Kolar** narrates experiences which indicate how retreats can evangelize the young. **John Roberto** presents a number of practical ideas on how to make youth retreats events which catechize participants. The former national chairperson of the Teens Encounter Christ retreat movement, **Dennis Kurtz**, draws from his wellspring of experience to discuss how retreats can be spiritual guidance opportunities for adolescents. Part One concludes with an insightful essay by **Joanne Cahoon** describing ways that retreat ministers can nurture their own spiritual growth even as they reach out to young people in their communities.

WORKS CITED

Ianni, Francis A. J. *The Search For Structure: A Report On American Youth Today*. New York: Free Press, 1989.

Shelton, S.J., Charles. *Adolescent Spirituality*. Chicago: Loyola University Press, 1983.

Warren, Michael. *Youth and the Future of the Church*. New York: Seabury, 1982.

Chapter 1

Twenty-Five Years of Youth Weekends:
A Revised Appraisal

Michael Warren

Persons examining the development of youth ministry in the United States soon recognize the remarkable contribution made by the renewal of youth retreats. The renewal broke the tradition of silent monastic retreats, in which youth participated mainly as listeners and worshippers, with some opportunities offered for individual counsel. After over a quarter century of development during which emerged such varied weekend models as Teens Encounter Christ (TEC), Search, Antioch, The Christian Awakening, and Christians on Retreat (COR), it seems appropriate to examine and assess these weekends of Christian living. A good place to begin such an assessment is with a brief history of the origins of some of these programs.

In 1961 the first English-language Cursillo was held in the United States, having been brought from Spain four years earlier by the United States Air Force cadets who had been stationed there. (McLaughlin 94-101) In Spain, the Cursillo had been started by Bishop Juan Hervas as part of an experiment with ways of bringing the gospel to men, who in his culture tended to think of religion as a matter more appropriate to women. He called his program the Cursillo de Christianidad, The "Little Course In Christianity." It was a "little course" because it was given for a short weekend and tried to deal with the heart of the gospel. His Cursillo stressed uncomplicated explanations of Christian faith with clear examples from everyday life. A good part of the weekend also involved ordinary Christians giving personal accounts of their own struggle to live the gospel. These were witness talks, living testimony from everyday folks. They were given in a context of community — of a group of persons joined by their common faith in the enduring presence of Jesus' spirit. Their common unity was celebrated in intense moments of prayer and worship, especially in the Eucharist.

The Cursillo had a tremendous impact and spread through Spain like wildfire. If anything, it spread even faster in the United States. Within two years after the English-language Cursillo started, it had spread to 23 states. When the full impact of the Cursillo over the past 30 years has been fully evaluated, we will find it had an astonishing influence on tens of thousands of Catholic adults. The Cursillo enabled many of them to transform their knowledge of Jesus into the deep interiorized personal form of knowledge we call "faith knowing." Some of these adults saw the possibilities of the Cursillo for youth.

Two priests in the Diocese of Brooklyn, Fathers Jim Tugwood and Doug Brown made a Cursillo in late 1963 and immediately adapted the basic format for young people. They recruited a youth team, trained them as facilitators, and in July 1964, in the basement of a high school, ran their first weekend, called simply "The Encounter," meaning an encounter with Jesus whom we call Christ. Clearly based on the Cursillo's theme of letting one's light shine, their program was later called "The Christian Awakening" in the early 1970s, when the word *encounter* came to connote nude group marathons. Their program has spread throughout the United States, and to Belgium and France. It has had a singular influence on Catholic youth work in Australia, New Zealand, and other South Pacific countries. [1]

More than a year before the Brooklyn program started, Msgr. Peter Armstrong, director of the San Francisco Catholic Youth Organization (CYO) program, launched the "Search for Christian Maturity," usually called the Search program. Although the Cursillo was already spreading on the West Coast in March 1963, the date of the first Search program, Armstrong's efforts developed from his experience with group dynamics and totally apart from any Cursillo influence. The initiative for Search came from young people who asked for a weekend design within which they could function as team members. Experience- and community-centered rather than content-centered, Search has been devoted to the needs of youth as they defined them and has continued to adapt to the changing needs of youth in different areas. From the start, Search avoided asking youth for the sort of total commitment to Jesus that might be appropriate for an adult at the end of a Cursillo. These unique aspects of Search, however, do not negate important similarities with the other youth weekend models. [2]

Because it could be tied to a well-organized network of diocesan CYO offices, Search grew fastest of the three emerging youth retreat models. Shortly after its start, dozens of diocesan CYO offices were running

Search weekends. The biannual CYO convention became a special forum for spreading the excitement of Search, which featured a youth-centered rather than an adult-centered team.

Another well-known program is Teens Encounter Christ, which began in October of 1965 in the Diocese of Lansing, MI. The program had been developed earlier that year as a project at the Loyola Pastoral Institute. Possibly because of this background, TEC seems to have begun with a much more elaborately worked-out theory of what it was trying to accomplish than did either Search or The Encounter. TEC has used a much greater proportion of adults on its teams and has also incorporated a strong death-resurrection liturgical theme based on the Easter vigil. (TEC Center) However, anyone who compares the TEC weekend outline with that of a Cursillo will find a dramatic parallel between the two, including the presentations and meditations and activities such as chapel visits and the Sunday night reunion. In recounting the story of TEC beginnings, its co-founder, Fr. Matthew Fedewa, has often explained his debt to the Cursillo. [3]

The most significant aspects of these various team-led, celebrative weekend experiences of the gospel message, are remarkably similar. They have shown the Church that young people are open to the gospel message when presented in the proper context and in language that speaks to them. They have also shown that many young people need a chance to struggle to put their faith into their own words. It is almost as if we have only to whisper the message to them and then stand back so they can learn to shout it. Further, these programs have centered evangelization and catechesis solidly within their proper atmosphere of celebration. These programs have shown that catechesis lends itself well to intense occasions such as these weekends.

Since these weekends have been in operation, what has happened to those who have participated in them? Tens of thousands, perhaps hundreds of thousands, of young people have come to a Pentecost-like insight into the meaning of Jesus' message. Right now, years later, their lives remain transformed by that basic experience. Some are now themselves working with youth because of their experience on Youth Teams. Some are ministering through their work and through their family life, in a conscious desire to be faithful disciples. There are bishops who have learned the secrets of Christian faith in a special manner through working with young people in TEC, Search, Antioch, or the Christian Awakening. There must be many priests, brothers, and sisters in our country who can trace their ministries somehow to their involvements as teens in these programs.

These various weekend programs represent extraordinary achievements that have benefited young people in many parts of the world. Yet we cannot expect that all these programs have completed their evolution. Neither should they be encouraged to rest on their laurels as if what they have achieved so far is the last word. There is much more to be done, and my purpose here is to prompt some discussion of what the "more" might be.

As far as I know, there has been no serious effort to update the youth weekends of Christian living. Apart from some minor adjustments, the basic weekend programs are the same as they were in those exciting days of experimentation in the mid-1960s. [4] However, the world is not the same, neither the wider sociopolitical world nor the theological world. It is interesting to contrast the endless and sophisticated revisions in catechetical school materials for young people over the past two decades with the relatively unchanged materials of youth weekends. Because printed catechetical materials for youth have finally taken up the 1968 call of the Medellin Conference to pay more attention to social issues, we now have some fine texts on social justice for youth in schools. However, the world reflected in the content of TEC, Antioch, Search and Christian Awakening is still the relatively asocial world of 1964. Because I fear our weekends can easily overlook key features of the world of our day, I invite us all to ask ourselves the following questions.

What happens when youth ministry conveys a clear impression that the matters of moment for youth are all personal and interpersonal matters? What happens when our agenda with youth deals only with such issues as becoming self-directed, developing a sense of one's own individuality, developing a healthy and Christian sexual self-understanding, developing a capacity to respond to God in prayerful ways, and coming to an appreciation of the personhood of others in one's family, one's friends, and in all those one meets in the course of a day?

To be sure, we all recognize how essential these matters are for living as a Christian in our time. However, these matters are still not sufficient as a full presentation of the gospel. To limit our work to these matters is to give the impression that they encompass all that is needed to be a follower of Jesus in our day. But they are not a full loaf. They are insufficient to nourish the spirits of young people. A youth ministry program that deals predominantly with the self is not a complete presentation of the Christian message. Such programs inadvertently deny youth access to questions that must be faced by followers of the one we call Lord. The arms race, social injustice, and violence among youth are matters of importance for young people and yet they are given little, if any, attention on our weekends.

With respect to the arms race, the young who participate in youth weekends have potentially a much longer future of coping with a world on the brink of annihilation than do their elders. This is one reason for helping them pay attention to this world. Another compelling reason is that the heart of Jesus' message stands opposed to these weapons that can destroy all life. Further, militarism establishes patterns of social injustice that are counter to the gospel. "In a world where 500 million people (the minimum estimates of the World Bank) are seriously underfed, we build Trident submarines at over a billion dollars apiece, so that we can add 14 of them to the 2,055 missiles and planes that launch 9,200 nuclear weapons." (Meehan 426) We find the results of these patterns on our own streets, where the homeless wander and sleep. We also find these patterns in places like El Salvador, where "one percent of the population has been murdered in the last four years, almost all by the paramilitary death squads tied to the Salvadorean Government" supported by the United States. (Chapin and Clark 269) Violence among youth is another problem. However, many working with the young overlook this problem of violence. Our weekends are run as if it did not exist. Are we hurrying past this world, even diverting our attention from it, as we make our journey from Jerusalem to Jericho?

Can any program deal with all these matters on a single weekend? Common sense says no. But to run a weekend program on Christian living and to ignore the wider world is a mistake with long-range effects. It situates the gospel in an out-of-this-world context. Shutting out this wider world makes it difficult, if not impossible, to connect the gospel message with matters that should be the most pressing ones for Christians in our day.

Instead, we can take the main themes of our weekends and deal with them in a different mode, like taking a melody line from Mozart or Chopin and putting it to a different beat. Think about this for a moment. Where does the power of the particular presentations made during these weekends come from? The special significance of any presentation comes from the way it is introduced, the examples used to ground the message, and the specific applications that extend its significance to the lives of youth. I call this process *backgrounding*, that is, setting up a horizon within which we view the gospel. This backgrounding needs to reflect more of the wider social world in which we live. Otherwise we give an impression that the gospel affects only one's private world, that it is a matter of personal choice only and ultimately a matter of personal decision and will. Gustavo Gutierrez suggests that such an approach does not go far enough: "In our relationship with God and with others there is an inescapable personal dimension: to reject a fellow human being — a possibility implicit in our freedom — is to reject God as well." (Gutierrez 97) Notice how Gutierrez re-names the personal dimension of faith. Instead of using "personal" to mean the self, that is, "we" or "I," he suggested that the proper understanding of the personal in faith also looks to the person of the other.

The gospel is a matter of choices, *but not only of choices*. The great evils of our day arise not from personal malevolence but from structures and systems that are evil. The arms race and the resulting militarization of whole societies are one such evil system. We live in a different and more dangerous world from that of 1965. In 1964, the cruise missiles — able to reach their targets in six minutes — did not exist. Also, today many people are more keenly aware of systemic evil. Now our task is to allow this new awareness to influence consciously these programs for youth.

Many believe that concern for the social or systemic dimension of the gospel is something that should be dealt with on some later weekend, not on the occasion of the first evangelization which summons young people to conversion. They feel that it is important to introduce the young to the person of Jesus, to let them encounter Him, and then, after they are well-grounded in prayer and communion, to deal with matters of social justice. Such thinking claims that these aspects of the gospel are consecutive, that personal relationship with Jesus as Lord is to be followed by the call for justice. The bishops of the Roman Catholic Church, however, have taken a different position on this question. At their 1971 Synod in Rome, they clearly stated that "action on behalf of justice and participation in the transformation of the world fully appear to us as a constitutive dimension of the preaching of the gospel...." Concern for justice is not a follow-up to effective evangelization; there is no effective evangelization unless this concern is part of it, at least in a backgrounding way.

However, this same synod had some important things to say about education, which might have a bearing on weekends of Christian living.
The still predominant method of education today favors a narrow-minded individualism. A great part of the people are actually swallowed up in a boundless overestimation of possessions. The school and the mass media stand now even under the power of the established "system" and so they can only form persons in the way they are needed by the "system" . . . not new persons, but only a reproduction of the traditional types.

The bishops then describe the proper way of education, according to the radical demands of the gospel.

The right education demands a transformation of heart; fundamental to this is the admission of sin in its personal as well as its social forms. Education must emphasize a totally human way of life in justice, in love and simplicity. It must awaken the capacity of critical reflection on our society and on its current values; it must stimulate the readiness to reject these values when they no longer contribute to helping all persons come to their rights. (Gutierrez 401-2)

So I am proposing that weekends of Christian living could do with a re-examination of their presentations and meditations, to see if they could be recast or adjusted to pay greater attention to important aspects of our current world. Perhaps now after 25 years it is time to take another look. Such a re-examination does not have to be done hastily. It could involve many concerned persons working together over an extended period. Such a project could be a marvelous process of self-initiated learning for those who choose to undertake it.

Another matter I wish to propose is a re-examination of the Jesus we are presenting. I have been concerned about the vision of Jesus presented in many different programs for middle-class youth. This Jesus tends to represent the dominant concerns of the moderately well-off and privileged. (Brown 84-101) The dominant concern of the middle-class tends to be greater comfort, and thus the middle-class Jesus is presented as the one who comforts. Overlooked is the Jesus who not only comforted but who also confronted and challenged. The middle-class Jesus is not the "man for others"; the middle-class Jesus is the man *for us.* Jon Sobrino points out that this is not a new problem.

In [19th and early 20th century] liberal theology Jesus represents in its sublimest form the good that is to be found in human beings. He thus becomes, in his own historical context, the supreme embodiment of the virtues of the middle-class citizen of the late nineteenth century in whom life and culture, throne and altar, existence and virtue are all in harmony. (Sobrino, *The True Church and The Poor* 25)

The challenge of such a presentation of Jesus is that of accepting him as a sign of God's love for us. It is essential to understand Jesus as God-with-us and as God's special gift to us. Accepting Jesus as God's love embodied is an important first step on the road to discipleship. Yet to go no further is to remain with a middle-class and ultimately false image of Jesus.

The gospels remind us in many ways that Jesus calls us to embrace the poor and the weak and those who do not fit. In the gospels, Jesus continually calls attention to the social situations that needed to be changed and to the people who suffered in these social situations, the poor. Who are the poor, as presented in the gospels? One writer describes them as follows:

> Although the term "poor" in the gospels does not refer exclusively to those who were economically deprived, it does include them. The poor were in the very first place the beggars. They were the sick and disabled who had resorted to begging because they were unemployable and without a relative who could afford to or was willing to support them.
>
> There were of course no hospitals, welfare institutions or disability grants. They were expected to beg for their bread. Thus, the blind, the deaf and dumb, the lame, the cripples, and the lepers were generally beggars.
>
> Then there were the widows and orphans: the women and children who had no one to provide for them and, in that society, no way of earning a living. They would have been dependent upon the almsgiving of pious societies and the temple treasury. Among the economically poor one should also include the unskilled day-laborers who were often without work, the peasants who worked on the farms and perhaps the slaves.
>
> On the whole, the suffering of the poor was not destitution and starvation except during a war or a famine. They were sometimes hungry and thirsty, but unlike millions today, they seldom starved. The principal suffering of the poor, then as now, was shame and disgrace. As the steward in the parable says, "I would be too ashamed to beg." (Lk 16:3)
>
> The economically poor were totally dependent upon the "charity" of others. For the Oriental, even more so than for the Westerner, this is terribly humiliating. In the Middle East, prestige and honor are more important than food or life itself. Money, power, and learning give a person prestige and status because they make the person relatively independent and able to do things for other people. The really poor person who is dependent upon others and has no one dependent upon him/her is at the bottom of the social ladder. That person has no prestige and no honor. That person is hardly human. That person's life is meaningless. A Westerner today would experience this as a loss of human dignity. (Nolan 22-23)

Whereas the gospels are filled with Jesus' passion for the poor and for justice for the poor, sometimes our own accounts of Jesus' life omit this central concern. But we cannot understand the message of Jesus unless we understand the biblical idea of the Kingdom of God, which was a call for justice. (Sobrino, *Christology at the Crossroads* 41-78) The biblical idea of the reign of God, also called the Kingdom of God, especially as preached by Jesus, assumed that something was wrong with the order of things and must be corrected. Change of heart is essential for righting wrong, but so is change of structures, change of public policy, change of systems that are evil. The basic wrong Jesus' preaching sought to correct was the lack of loving kindness and goodness, the lack of love for one's sister and brother and neighbor and for the stranger and the weak and the beaten-down. What made the preaching of Jesus so dangerous was that he challenged systems. He called for a new order that sided with the poor, replacing greed with sharing. Jesus' idea of the Kingdom shouts for correcting something that is out of kilter in society. In Jesus' preaching, change of heart is to be tied to change of structure. When the powers-that-be realized this side of His preaching, they decided to get rid of Him.

I propose that weekends of Christian living for youth need to reclaim this Jesus, the man who was eliminated because He exposed the greed of the rich. They need to reclaim the Jesus who called so strongly for nonviolence and love of enemies that some of His later followers resigned from military service as soon as they became Christians. [5] These weekends need to reclaim the Jesus who called for the transformation of social structures. To ignore this Jesus is to distort the paschal mystery. What is obviously involved here is another stage in the development of weekends of Christian living, a stage that will pay greater attention to the world in which we live and will prepare youth for a lifetime of paying attention to issues of justice, a stage that will present a portrait of Jesus more faithful to the historical person who was "terminated" because of His challenges to unjust structures.

Years ago the youth retreat movement discovered the genius of the dialogue format on weekends and handed over the discovery to youth leaders worldwide. However, in my judgment, the movement has not utilized the full possibilities of that discovery. Why have we not developed second-level weekends for young people wanting to go deeper into the mystery of Jesus? Could we not, for example, develop weekends for members of our weekend leadership teams, to assist them coming to a deeper understanding of Jesus, including the complex period in which He lived, His teaching, and the communities that followed Him? For the young people who leave our weekends eager to translate their experience into daily action, do we not need second-level weekends dealing specifically with social issues and with ways of helping their peers understand and deal with these social issues? A common problem of all these weekend programs is the tendency of the participants to want to hold on to their original experience and then recapture it by coming back to other weekends. Someone has called those who are frantic about such repeat experiences "weekend junkies." These young people want to go back. We need to encourage them instead to go on, to go deeper, to take up more courageously the challenge of the gospel. That encouragement may take the form of further weekend experiences at a much deeper level.

Most weekend programs acknowledge that they are not the total answer. The above suggestions do not ask them now to seek to become "total" programs. Instead, they suggest the possibility of going a bit farther in their ministry with youth. None of these new directions needs to be decided overnight. Yet, with some planning, weekends can be designed around themes such as peacemaking and nonviolence; the Jesus who was criminalized because of his call for social change; and around issues such as world hunger, weapons production, or the more just distribution of wealth. When young people from these weekends of Christian living become involved with even younger people in order to help them understand such issues, then we will have launched a new day in youth ministry. We may then have a new range of achievements to celebrate in the name of Jesus.

ENDNOTES

[1] The information given here on the Christian Awakening is, as far as I know, not documented. It comes from my own knowledge of the events and from conversations with leaders in Australia and New Zealand.

[2] This information on Search was given me by Msgr. Peter Armstrong and Fr. Michael Harriman, Youth Director, in San Francisco, in detailed telephone conversations. I am indebted to the kindness of both.

[3] James Brown, "TEC in Perspective," a videotape, 27 July 1983 — distributed by the Youth Ministry Office, Diocese of Green Bay, WI.

[4] It may be significant for leaders of youth weekends to know that Bishop Juan Hervas and other early Cursillo leaders were adamant that nothing should be

changed in its format, "not a single iota." An extensive critique of that stance, as well as of the pre-Vatican II theology of the Cursillo, appears in Antoninus Feeney, "A Critique Of The Theology Underlying The Cursillo" (M.A. thesis, Catholic University of America, 1971).

⁵ A subtle study of the tradition of nonviolence in the early church is Knut Willem Ruyter, "Pacifism And Military Service In The Early Church," *Cross Currents* 32.1 (1982): 54-70.

WORKS CITED

Brown, S.S., Raymond. *The Churches the Apostles Left Behind*. New York: Paulist, 1984.

Chapin, Jim and Jack Clark. "El Salvador: Paralysis." *Commonweal* 4, May 1984.

Coles, Robert and George A. White. "The Religion of 'The Privileged Ones.'" *Cross Currents* 31.1 (1981): 1-14.

Gutierrez, Gustavo. *We Drink from our Own Wells*. Maryknoll, NY: Orbis/ Dove, 1984.

McLaughlin, John. "I Made a Cursillo." *America* 110 (January 18, 1964): 94-101.

Meehan, F.X. "Disarmament in the Real World," *America* (December 27, 1980): 423-426.

Nolan, O.P., Albert. *Jesus Before Christianity*. Maryknoll, NY: Orbis, 1978.

St. Louis TEC Center. "Introduction and Explanation of the TEC Experience. St. Louis: Teens Encounter Christ.

Sobrino, Jon. *Christology at the Crossroads*. Maryknoll, NY: Orbis, 1978 ,

_____. *The True Church and the Poor*. Maryknoll, NY: Orbis, 1984.

Chapter 2

Theological Foundations of Youth Retreats

Reynolds R. Ekstrom

Michael Warren hints at something important in his fine discussion of developments in adolescent retreat ministries during recent decades. The 1970s and '80s proved to be very exciting times to be involved in the Catholic youth ministry renewal movement. These years served up many opportunities to discover and to reclaim sound approaches to youth outreach, to evangelization, to adolescent catechesis, to worship, to justice education and service, to peer ministries, and to many other ways by which we help young people grow in faith. We began to see, more clearly, the impact that our mainstream culture, the mass media, family challenges, and the demands of living in multicultural communities are having on the transmission of faith to the young. Greater insight filtered through via our one-to-one encounters, our parish ministries, our school programs, our neighborhood activities, and particularly in the lifestyles undertaken in our households.

Voices both hope-filled and discouraging could be heard in the 1970s and '80s. Many can still be heard (or read) to this day. Certainly, the youth ministry renewal, as a whole, has given encouragement to many who care for young Christians. The practice of providing intensive faith-growth experiences for adolescents through retreats, in evening-, daylong-, overnight-, and multiday-formats, obviously, has been one of the most vital, most frequently utilized elements in the entire, revitalized youth outreach and pastoral care process begun, in recent decades, in U.S. parishes and Catholic schools.

A basic, profound presupposition in all active youth ministry is that the hearer of the Christian message is a person who can understand and freely respond. The fundamental reality of any person in history, any

hearer, is his or her personal experience. In our knowledge, our relationships, our questions, our memories, our limitations, our hopes, our deepest
longings of the soul, our listening, and our freedom to make choices, hearers of the Christian word come to experience or, in other terms, confront a
radical dependence on others: other people, other things, and, ultimately, an
Other, a mystery revealed yet concealed to us. A contemporary theologian
claims,

> The dependence upon God is that which establishes my reality, not
> what denies it. We are infinitely different from God — with the abso-
> lute difference that creation has brought about — and we never merge
> amorphously with God.... Human beings are finally what bespeak
> God, not only in the depths of their endowments but in the radical
> direction of their lives. For to be human is to be radically directed
> towards God through knowledge and love. It is within this transcen-
> dence of knowledge and love, within the experience of the personal,
> that even wordless nature is caught up and borne back to God.
> (Buckley 47)

Beyond words, beyond definitions, beyond self-understandings,
beyond daily experiences, humans glimpse their radical need for that holy
Mystery, one which we either must accept or refuse and deny, in a fundamental way. (Carr 19-29) As hearers of words of good news, Christians
mature and develop as creatures of God by reflecting on who and what they
can become in and through Jesus Christ.

Key visions and practical documents have provided direction, in
recent years, like blueprints, for those initiating or revising-and-revitalizing
their efforts to share the word of the Other, in their ministries, with adolescents, young hearers of the Word. In 1972, the U.S. bishops developed a
pastoral message on Catholic education, *To Teach as Jesus Did*. It emphasized that the Church's mission to young people is to transmit an essential
message for them to hear (didache), the revelation of the Mystery, to invite
them to the life of community and relationship shared by Christ's hearers
(koinonia), and to call them to engage in service freely (diakonia), as
Christians dedicated to transforming humanity and creation, and as people
consciously directed toward God. On youth ministry, *To Teach As Jesus
Did* explicitly remindedus that:

> Christians should be sensitive and discerning in their approach to the
> young, who through their baptism and confirmation have been incor-
> porated into full membership in the Christian community. This com-
> munity does have solutions to many of the questions which trouble
> today's youth, but it cannot realistically expect young people to
> accept them unless it, for its part, is willing to listen to their problems.
> Thus it must not only strive to teach the young but to learn from
> them.... (*TTJD* 36)

Critical, recurrent themes have been resounded, many times, in recent decades, in many of our key resource statements. Each human being has a history and a destiny. Each can decide who he or she can be and what he or she will become. Each deserves the dignity and respect due all those created in the likeness and image of our Creator. This includes adolescents. In our mainstream culture, youth are treated, typically, as objects, persons to be used, to be left on their own, without rights or ideas, persons to be seen not heard. Yet, they are human persons, loved by God, radically directed toward a God who wants relationship with them; their gifts and potential, their freedom to hear and to respond to Mystery, should be nurtured, valued, honored.

As Thomas Groome has noted often, everyone has a right to speak his or her own word, to name his or her own reality. The journey of each person to God "is a sacred one... in its own way, [it] is unique." (Groome 263) All persons, young and old, are called to be "makers of history." In our creaturehood, in our freedom to act, and in our drive to find life's meaning, we can make personal choices and influence the way of the world, as co-creators with the Other. Groome has said, each human being, gifted by the Creator, "can reach a Christian consciousness that causes [him or her] to engage in the world to make present the Kingdom already and prepare the material for its final completion." (Groome 264)

These recurring themes spring from contemporary, fundamental theologies. Beyond youth ministries, or more specifically beyond adolescent catechesis programs, which aim, solely, to produce "good Catholics", we have learned to develop pastoral care approaches which try to aim young people toward personal wholeness and toward mature, Christian adulthood, as active members of a community, a people of God. We have dimly begun to see,

> Christianity is not an indoctrination into certain conditions or facts or realities which are always the same, but it is the proclamation of a history of salvation, of God's salvific and revelatory activity.... And because God's activity is directed to man [sic] as a free subject, Christianity at the same time is also a proclamation of a history of salvation..., of revelation and the interpretation of it which man himself makes. Consequently, this single history of revelation and salvation is borne by God's freedom and [our] freedom together and forms a unity. Fundamentally, Christianity makes the claim that it is salvation and revelation for every person; it makes the claim that it is a religion of absolute value. It declares that it is salvation and revelation not only for particular groups of people, not only for particular periods of history in the past or in the future, but for all people until the end of history. (Rahner 138; Haight, *The Experience and Language of Grace* 119-142)

In 1976, the landmark document, *A Vision of Youth Ministry*, identified the essential philosophy, principles, goals, dimensions, and hopes for
ministry to adolescents in the later decades of this century. Within the
sweep of this vision, many ministers came to recognize, more lucidly, that
the heart of outreach to youth is found in relationships. Sound youth ministries, like the best of missionary outreach strategies, build and maintain
relationships with those addressed. In youth ministry this is usually adolescents, in order to hear their needs, to be of help to them, and, then, in the
process lead them to a more meaningful relationship with a holy Mystery, a
holy One who has already loved them into being and One who unfailingly
seeks an intimacy with them. The term, youth ministry, has implied, since
the mid-1970s, a multi-dimensional, carefully-crafted, pastoral strategy
designed to nurture the Christian formation of adolescents. (Roberto 8) At
its roots, this ministry was (and is) aimed at sparking adolescent spiritual
growth, a desire to hear more about Jesus, and to enthusiastically respond
to Him, via authentic discipleship. (Shelton 8-11) Thus, it is about Christian
conversion: youth ministries seek to help young people build enough trust,
in an Other and in the community which follows his path, that they will
want to become Christian hearers and disciples. The *Vision* document noted
that such ministries focus on

>...the Church's mission of reaching into the daily lives of modern
>young people and showing them the presence of God.... It is a return
>to the way Jesus taught, putting ministry before teaching and people
>over institutions. In this ministry, religious content is a way of life for
>the person ministering and the young person touched, through a
>sequential development of faith, dependent on the readiness and need
>of the adolescent. (*Vision* 5-6)

The *Vision* paper added that every youth ministry ought to be provided with an orientation to persons and fundamental values, as was the
ministry of Christ.

The catechetical directory for the United States, *Sharing the Light of
Faith*, appeared in 1979. It crystallized several insights on strategies for
adolescent faith-development which were creatively articulated in the '70s.
Sharing the Light of Faith, commonly known as the NCD (the National
Catechetical Directory), reiterated the call for a "variety of models" for
youth ministry which integrate "message, community, service, and
worship," corresponding to stages of development and needs expressed by
the young. (*NCD* 18, 141) Significantly, the NCD added,

>The need for a variety of approaches should be taken into considera-
>tion in preparing social, recreational, and apostolic programs, as well
>as retreats and other spiritual development activities. (NCD 141)

Those involved in youth retreat leadership, at the time the directory was published, were, in many instances, already integrating several interdependent faith-growth ministries (evangelization, catechesis, worship, community-building) in their retreat experiences for adolescents. The best youth retreats continue to do so today.

The notions that ministry addresses first and foremost human subjects or hearers, that it speaks to them about their needs and about a lifelong journey toward faith-maturity, and that it is rooted in a call to conversion and Christian community were more easily understood and accepted by those in "youth ministry" circles by the mid-1980s. A key resource for teachers, youth ministry coordinators, DREs, school principals, and campus ministers called *The Challenge of Adolescent Catechesis: Maturing in Faith*, reaffirmed these notions in 1986. Also, it proceeded to indicate how they are integrated as presuppositions in sound youth evangelization efforts, adolescent religious education, retreat experiences, and other youth ministry contexts.

The *Challenge* acknowledged that younger and older adolescents experience crucial turning points in the human journey. They confront the faith tradition handed on by their families and wider faith community and, normally, begin to discover, sometimes with great pain, how to own it, as their own, through deep "questioning and anguished or even frustrating search..." (*Challenge* 6) The *Challenge* proposed that young people respond spiritually to God in the ways they live their lives, that the true heart of Christian faith lies in a living relationship with an Other:

> A social and developmental understanding of the human person
> guides our ministry with youth. Through this ministry we seek to cre-
> ate a climate conducive to the healthy development of adolescents
> and provide them with multiple opportunities for growth in matu-
> rity.... We are challenged to help them explore different understand-
> ings of personal and vocational identity, to voice openly their
> questions..., to develop a sense of accountability in the context of
> relationships, and to cultivate a capacity to enjoy life. (*Challenge* 6)

Handing on Christian beliefs to young people and inspiring them toward authentic, deeper faith responses, in other words toward a life of Christian discipleship, must be rooted in, must spring from, and must be supported by an active Christian faith community. Those who accompany adolescents, sponsoring them and walking with them in their questions and journeys, as the *Challenge* has said, help them establish firmer, personal identities in Christ and likewise, "foster in youth a communal identity as Catholic Christians." (*Challenge* 8; also Groome 15-17, 265-275) The *Adolescent Catechesis Resource Manual* added new clarifications about developments and directions infused into the youth ministry renewal movement, and about some of the fundamental, theological presuppositions which have undergirded it during the 1970s and '80s:

> The breakthrough began by the mid-1970s. New creativity began to respond to the declining picture with a new vision and direction for youth work. New research on church youth began to surface... The new "theology of ministry" and "theology of church" that were emerging in the post-Vatican II era gave theological substance and a new vocabulary to youth work.... Both religious education/catechesis and youth activities were expanding beyond traditional limits to incorporate an awareness of the humanistic, interpersonal, affective dimension of coming to faith. Youth retreats were the common ground for this renewal. In the ferment, the orderly boundaries that had once separated and regulated the relations, goals, and methods of religious education, CYO, schools, scouts, camping, etc., became porous. There was a sense of belonging together somehow, and there were also a lot of partisan feelings about whose tradition, procedures, and leadership made sense for the future. (Roberto 7-8)

It would be a serious oversight, I believe, to consider the dynamic developments in ministry to adolescents, especially the developments on the youth retreat scene, as dissociated from the whole fabric of ministry renewal, in Roman Catholic circles, set in motion in the middle of this century. Given that the world has changed and that human beings and their needs are constantly undergoing change, the pastoral renewal moment we, today, identify as Vatican II urged us to reexamine how we form persons in Christian faith, how we help persons become initiated into full Christian community membership, and how we actively support them in living their lives as ones seeking the Mystery-with-us yet beyond us. The Second Vatican Council called for a renewal of the ancient catechumenate process, a catechetical and liturgical methodology through which Christian initiation and holistic faith-formation can occur, by which we invite persons outside our faith community to deeper, meaningful Christian experience and prepare them for lives of active Christian discipleship. (*Ad Gentes* 13-14; *Sacrosanctum Concilium* 21) What would this holistic faith-growth process toward full Christian initiation encompass?

> * Those who have perceived, initially, the gift of faith and desire to better hear (know) Jesus should be further invited and accepted into Christian community; this "should be the concern of the whole Christian community," especially of the sponsors, so that from the beginning the catechumens (those experiencing further initiation and deeper faith-formation) will feel they belong to the people of God;

* It is not a mere exposition of dogmatic truths nor an indoctrination in norms of morality alone, though catechesis and conscience-formation will be involved;
* It is a period of formation in the whole Christian life;
* It is an apprenticeship: the new disciples in formation are to be joined with the true teacher, Jesus Christ;
* Those in formation should learn to practice Christian values and virtues;
* Also, catechumens should be introduced into the entire faith, liturgy, and loving action (charity) of the people of God;
* They should learn to cooperate, actively, in the building of the faith community, by their profession of faith and their living witness/example;
* In sum, they are already members of the household of Christ ("joined to the church") because they are, in effect, learning to live in faith. (*Ad Gentes* 14)

The renewal and restoration of the catechumenate, a means for Christian initiation reclaimed from ancient gospel-era traditions, was eventually motivated by and explained by the Rite of Christian Initiation of Adults (RCIA) in 1972. The RCIA alludes to a progressive, developing, lifelong conversion undertaken, as those engaged in the formation process (those being "initiated" into the body of Christ) learn what it takes to assume full membership in the Christian body. The official RCIA Study Edition, published in 1988, speaks of doorways, and it hints at internal, personal evolutions, as one steps more deeply into complex Christian experience. Initiation is perceived as a journey, as "periods of inquiry and growth; alternatively the periods may also be seen as preparing" for the ensuing doorway or personal evolution in Jesus. The Christian initiation process, thus, includes:

(1) Inquiry and relationship-building: "reaching the point of initial conversion and wishing to become Christians…";
(2) Learning and living the content/message of faith: "having progressed in faith and (having) nearly completed the catechumenate," those in faith-formation enter intense preparation for deeper faith-commitment;
(3) A life of Christian service and commitment: through reception of the sacraments of initiation, and in the ensuing commitment to Christ, "spiritual preparation" is concluded and new Christians live in accord with the gospel and their baptismal promises.

Naturally, in the 1970s and '80s, many of the young Catholics we encountered had already become full members of the Church through the reception of the sacraments of initiation (Baptism, Confirmation, and

Eucharist). This remains the case in many circumstances today. Some leaders at Vatican II knew something dramatic, however, and people in the vanguard of Catholic religious education and the Catholic youth ministry renewal in the U.S. discovered it, quickly. One can be fully initiated in the faith and, yet, remain somewhat immature in faith. This seems especially true given the mainstream culture, the lifestyles, the pressures, the choices, and the diversity of values and voices we experience, as youth and adults, commonly, in this time. Even those who are already full members among us, youth or adult, could likely benefit from a holistic ministry approach, a faith apprenticeship, to guide them, during our times, in their faith insights, in their gospel knowledge, in their ongoing journeys toward deepest conversion, in Christian counter-cultural awareness.

Some of the essential dynamics and benefits of the restored catechumenate process can and should be applied, indeed, in youth ministry contexts. All that is said about the catechumenate process, and about the needs of catechumens, their basic religious wishes and needs, with proper interpretation and explanation, could be applied to adolescents of the 1990s as well. (Walsh 28-32, 53-61)

Practical experiments, which were sparked, at first, within traditional youth group programs and traditional religious education models, taking cues from *To Teach As Jesus Did, The Challenge of Adolescent Catechesis*, and other documents we have mentioned have called for multi-dimensional approaches to youth outreach, echoes of the doorways or phases of the initiation and Christian evolution process. Advocates have initiated youth ministries which lead adolescents, consciously and progressively, toward deeper faith, deeper questions, and a living response to a Christ they are coming to know and follow. Such ministries should incorporate:

(1) Inquiry and relationship-building: "because God is already in people, one task [an initial step] of the Church is to form and facilitate good relationships that will unveil God's presence." (Kimball 115) We do so because we trust that young people need to, may eventually want to, hear our compelling gospel message and will need to learn about the "how-to's" of Christian life.

(2) Living and learning the content/message of Christianity: young people "need information to help them understand more clearly how to continue relating effectively.... The Church, however, has [also] the content of a tradition, lasting centuries,... the whole salvation story, as well as the local church's story, which should illuminate and enhance the individual's story still in progress. So, content connects all three: my story, our story (local church), and the story (salvation history)." (Kimball 116)

(3) A life of deepening Christian commitment and Christian engagement: through inquiry, contact, and Christian content, those progressing on the journey toward mature faith, even those already fully initiated through sacramental rituals, yet remaining immature in some significant ways about how to be Christian, "will want to dedicate themselves to personal and spiritual growth, and even help others grow as well." (Kimball 116)

The theologian Rudolf Schnackenburg insisted that the true Christian cannot live above or beyond history and real life; he or she must be summoned, by the trends and times, to fulfill the challenges God has assigned to each age. It has been noted by many, in recent times, how young people, frequently, seem very hungry for genuine friends, community, supportive understanding, someone to listen, spiritual experience, and an imaginative reason to go on. Like many of us adults, they want to be touched somehow. Since youth retreats, and other more creative faith-development activities, address these needs in various ways, at times quite well, they have become integral to countless youth ministries in our parishes, schools, dioceses, and other Church organizations. When it comes to adolescents' religious motives, they typically long, as is so understandable of youth, to identify with (to bond with) not so much a something — a doctrine, a church, a Catholicism — as a Someone. (DiGiacomo and Walsh 15-20; Ekstrom 43-60)

James DiGiacomo has written, in a compelling way, about what we have tried to communicate, fundamentally, about the human-divine relationship, through our various styles of youth ministry and religious education and about what we have unfortunately not accomplished. For example, DiGiacomo has claimed:

First, some good news. Those of us who minister to the young have learned a great deal about adapting to their needs. We have developed skills in communicating with the young. We have learned to announce the gospel message not in a vacuum but in ways that speak to the young in their actual situation, in language and categories better suited to their stages of growth, with a more sophisticated awareness of their needs, limitations, and capacities. During these years, youth ministry has come of age; a whole professional class has emerged, and new structures have been developed to reach youngsters where they are, rather than where we would like them to be. Like good missionaries, we have learned how to adapt to the natives, to respect their [youth] culture, to listen to and take seriously both them and their experience…. But there may be bad news as well. Missionaries must not only adapt to the natives they serve; they must also be faithful to the message they have to proclaim. How well are we doing this? Are we helping to produce a generation of disciples, or just turning out a different kind of religious consumer? (DiGiacomo 16)

Prophetic voices in pastoral outreach to youth, like DiGiacomo, have called us to form young people in a "spiritual literacy" and active discipleship, which "goes far beyond the (ability) to rattle off orthodox answers to theological questions or to master lists of commandments,"... and so forth.

Our needs, and the needs of our young people, lie elsewhere. We need a more authentically Christian notion of what religion is all about. We have to help them recover a sense of measuring up to something or Someone, or their religiosity will degenerate into a new narcissism. Adolescents, especially, need assistance in dealing with some perennial questions that still await answers: What is God like, and what does God want from me? Is Jesus any more than a pal? How do I deal with my sinfulness? Can I accept a church of imperfect people and find a place in it? How do I reconcile my desire for spontaneity with a realistic acceptance and even esteem of routine? Do sacramental celebrations have any worth when they do not issue in my immediate, palpable self-improvement? (DiGiacomo 20)

To some degree, a youth ministry project for the 1980s and '90s will be the search to find better answers to these cogent questions. What fundamental insights or goals will, in fact, guide us now in assisting others, particularly adolescents, toward maturing faith as Catholic Christians? What methods, techniques, tasks, and ministry models have we adopted and should we adopt? As we have noted, earlier, one clear, but tentative response has been: "foster in youth a communal identity as Catholic Christians and help them develop their own faith identity." (*Challenge* 8) From our fundamental theological insights flow essential tasks. As Catholic Christians, we choose to:

(1) Strongly affirm all of creation and all of human history, especially the unique part each person plays in it.

(2) Practice a love for a friend and liberator, called Jesus, plus a love for and service to the people, the community of disciples, who follow him.

Why? We strive to sponsor and to guide, carefully, those we encounter in youth retreats, catechetical sessions, broader youth ministries, and in outreach or drop-in places, toward a more holistic Christian lifestyle, or better yet, toward a way of being Christ-like in our world much in need of help and gospel vision. How do we, faithfully, try to encourage young people we meet on adolescent retreats, or elsewhere, in personal faith and a sense of shared faith in Christian community? How do we best introduce them, more deeply, to Someone, as well as some things of our tradition?

How do we minister in a way that communicates, more authentically, what religion is all about? John Nelson has written,

> One way is to consciously try to be both midwife and adoption agency. As midwife, the youth minister is there helping adolescents give birth to their personal convictions and values. The young themselves must parent these children of their minds and hearts. At other times the youth minister's role is adoption agency. She or he presents to them convictions and values already born within the Catholic Christian tradition which he or she represents. We invite them to adopt and make their own these children of our community's mind and heart.... How does one decide, not which role to play [hopefully, the youth minister is always doing both], but which one to emphasize? To switch the metaphor, it may make sense to zig and zag. Like someone trying to navigate a sailing vessel across a body of water with conflicting winds and tides and currents, one decides in a given situation which tack seems wisest, knowing that soon one has to correct one's course with some change of direction. (Nelson 98-99)

Whether you are a man or woman interested in doing better retreats for young people or one who, simply, wishes to provide some other form of Christian service to them in a more effective, faithful way, you might well ask today, Why do we go to such great lengths? Why would we attempt to midwife or to act as adoption agents? Why does our faith tradition, you could also call it "our church," go out of its way to touch youth somehow? What is, really, so critical about introducing them to a deep, lasting relationship with Someone? What's underneath the surface, underneath it all? And why would we hope they would want, much, to be like that Other, that One of mystery and holiness?

What is it that drives us, compels us, to be contemporary evangelizers and missionaries, even there in the many retreat houses, and malls, and schools, and liturgies, and Pizza Huts, and families in which we discover ourselves, surprisingly, trying to help young persons hear a gospel message which we do not want to compromise and which we want to share fully and honestly? How would you go about communicating to adolescents and others, in words and silences and deeds, what religion, at its roots, is all about? There must be something so important about and so fundamental to human experience, and about the possibilities inherent in the human-divine connection in history, that we go to such great pains to reach youth where they are "rather than where we wish they would be."

Why do we try so hard to help others, in our ministries, to confront questions about humanity, about daily life, about life's meaning? Why not just give them all the right answers, as if that could actually get done? Why do we even hope they'll find an answer, albeit tentative, to the pondering point, "What would that God want from me?" In others words, why do we strive, so energetically, even when we feel tired and discouraged and like not going on any more, to show to others the wisdom in being a believer, a follower of Christ, even in being a Catholic? What do we hope that others, freely, will adopt as their wisdom, their truth? What do we hope will be "born in their hearts," as the great doctors of the Church were given to say? And, finally, the question that really strikes me, here, about my own responses to it, and about how you will take the responses it raises for you: what is it, basic to human experience and human needs, in our longings and our genes, in our common humanity, almost like a radical predisposition or a spiritual inclination built in, which makes it possible for young people, or for those older, for us, to even consider and want to respond to the Other about whom we hear and in Whom the original followers of a Way found meaning so long ago?

The words of Bernard Cooke have a special ring for those seeking insight.

> While God['s] creative power sustains the existence of human life, the influence that helps this personal life to grow comes by the divine self-gift. And while God is distinct from us, the reality of divine self-giving happens within our consciousness through God's presence to each of us. God does not stand outside us and send graces to us; God dwells within us personally as a lover in the awareness of the beloved. God is "grace," the great grace, uncreated grace... This divine friend's loving presence provides ultimate hope and support as we encounter the difficulties, decisions, and sufferings of life. The reality of this relationship, as we increasingly accept it, provides a wisdom to guide us in the important decisions that shape our person-hood and destiny... Christians believe that [this] is a growth "into Christ," a deepening friendship with the risen Lord that itself leads to increasing personal relatedness to God and increasing personal trans-formation, that is, growth in the life of grace. (Cooke, *Sacraments* 232-233)

The sharing that we do before, during, and after faith-growth experiences with adolescents, such as retreats, if it is, indeed, Catholic sharing, rooted in and springing forth from a Catholic ministry orientation, will be based on trust that each person has a radical desire for and capacity to accept God, an Other, a true Mystery. That each person can be a hearer of the word of God. In the depths of our being, each of us has been trans-formed by God to be oriented to (earlier we said "radically directed" toward) the Holy and our horizon, in a sense, in search of God. Each of us is a bearer of grace, waiting to hear further word from our Creator,

mysteriously wanting to take the journey. Karl Rahner named this openness
or capacity for the divine. He called it the supernatural existential. (Rahner,
44-89; Haight, *The Experience and Language of Grace* 146-151) The One
who has disclosed Godself, in history, in creation, and in faith tradition, to
human beings past and present, and in Jesus, is also disclosing, in each of
us, a desire for relationship and intimacy with each of us.

> There is no sharp separation, therefore, between the history of the
> world and the history of revelation, just as there is no sharp separation
> between the history of the world and the history of salvation. In other
> words, saving revelation is available within the ordinary fabric of
> human existence.... Thus, every human person is already the recipient
> of divine revelation in the very core of his or her being in that God is
> present to every person in grace. (McBrien 235-236)

Yet, an authentic Catholic Christian ministry proclaims more than
personal, private revelation, or the call to an elect group, or the strident,
misguided warnings about the need to be "born again," as a sole means to
be saved and to be united with God. McBrien notes,

> The "more than" is what we profess in the articles of the Creed: the
> saving activities of God in Israel, in Christ, and in the Church. The
> "more than" is also given in the various persons and events of history
> as well as in the natural created order itself.... (McBrien 236)

In principle, at least, God's offer of love, and God's revelation, is
available to all persons. All are called to salvation, yet revelation and salvation find their proper response in faith. Some people will gladly respond to
the Holy in faith, others will choose to walk other paths and find other ways
to seek meaning and answers. God's self-giving, God's loving self-commu-
nication, which we are here calling revelation, is closed only in the "sense
that Christ, who is the fullness of revelation, has already been present to us
in history." Yet, God continues to manifest Godself to us, though, "in that
God is a living God and remains available to us," and we believe this God
will not, fundamentally, revoke or alter that which we have come to know
through Jesus, the one who has best shown us the way to full life.
(McBrien, 242-243) The documents of the Second Vatican Council remind
us that the Creator has chosen "to share with us divine benefits which
entirely surpass the powers of the human mind to understand." (*Dei
Verbum* 6)

If God remains available to us all and if this Other, mysteriously,
desires a loving relationship with us, even to the point of building into us a
capacity or spiritual drive to know God and to find the meaning to life God
has created, why then would we work, so diligently, so tirelessly, at a youth
ministry, at youth retreats, or an adolescent catechesis? For that matter, why

would we long to help young people or adults form firm Catholic Christian identities? In fact, why would we even think it so crucial to see that we, and others, live our lives as Christians, more significantly, as Catholics?

Of course, the answer lies somewhere in the vision that we propose and in the lifestyles, united in the Other, that we adopt and pursue. In our retreat experiences for the young, and in all the other faith-growth strategies we employ for others, in parish communities and elsewhere, we are suggesting some things fundamental, things we have learned in centuries of faith and tradition and in relationship with the Someone who has loved us into being.

The most basic, fundamental understandings and convictions we try to hand on to young people, and to others, in leading them toward mature Christian experience, include observations about the experience of reality and about accurate Christian knowledge.

THE DIVINE AND HUMAN IN RELATIONSHIP

The Creator has chosen to communicate with human beings. This God is not far removed from nor uncaring about the plight and hopes of human beings. The initiative in the dialogue, in fact, has been taken by the divine. Unexpectedly, our God has called and spoken to Abraham, Moses, the prophets, Jesus of Nazareth, and so many others. It is this Creator, we believe, who has longed to establish a lasting, friendship covenant, who has sought an abiding reconciliation with a sinful people, ancient Israel. It is this God, our God, who sends a special word, in Jesus, that we might all be hearers of his Word of life, that we might respond, freely, in faith, to God's universal offer of life and love, an offer which we might name, also, grace. It is the Christian Scriptures' tradition which, likewise, describes the divine One as standing at the door, knocking, looking for our free faith response, hoping that we will all, eventually, be united in the Word that the divine has sent that we might hear and answer. Bernard Cooke has said,

> Very simply, God speaks first and Christian [faith and] prayer is a response to that divine word. This implies, however, that people must realize how and where God speaks. The Bible occupies, of course, a privileged place as Word of God; but the history of biblical interpretation proves that understanding what God is saying through these texts is far from obvious. (Cooke, "Christian Understandings" 90)

How else do we see God and humanity in relationship and in active communication? Beyond Scripture, ritual worship, sacraments, moral norms, and other, various Christian prayer forms and community gatherings provide significant occasions for proclaiming, hearing, and responding to God's word.

Most basically, people need to understand how the happenings of their lives are truly "word of God." This does not mean that they should come to see these daily experiences as a series of "little miracles" that God is specially working for them — such a view may be pious, but it is erroneous. Rather, they need to be led to the understanding that all created existence is grounded in the divine self-giving, that human life is permeated by God's invitation to accept divine presence, and that the Spirit of God does indeed work wherever human beings are deeply concerned for one another's well-being. (Cooke, "Christian Understandings" 91)

OUR GOD IS A GOD WHO SAVES AND FORGIVES

When we acknowledge that this Someone seeks relationship with us we, essentially, see this loving Creator as a God-for-us. Some think, today, that human knowledge, skills, technology, science, and/or empirical solutions are all we'll need to meet the many problems and demands we face. Others shun such mindsets. They seek shelter and safety in a Christian fundamentalism or congregationalism, turning away from troubling questions, stresses, and vexing relationships, in a pluralistic culture. Still, others find their needs filled, artificially, in acquisitions of power, romance, possessions, pride, and in consumer habits. Thinkers remind us that an adequate understanding of revelation and salvation must lead us toward two questions: How and why has evil, or sinfulness, crept into human experience? and Does God help us in resolving this evil? In other words, is there any way to reconcile a good and loving Creator with the reality of evil in our existence?

A biblical notion of sin recognizes that human beings are very capable, as free persons, in their personal choices, to follow paths of infidelity and basic denial of the radical dependence so fundamental to our creaturehood. Hand in hand with this, our faith tradition acknowledges that, socially, and institutionally, evil — in the forms of injustice, violence, oppressions, and basic disrespect for humans — is embedded, deeply, in our lives and organizations. People today should be led, therefore, to insight on the personal and social dimensions of evil, the sins, which remain barriers to reaching our destiny, our salvation, the reign of God, as individuals and as humanity as a whole.

James DiGiacomo has cautioned us, pointedly, with regard to this, this sharing of insight, this attempt to raise others' religious and spiritual literacy. What about the Creator or the Word, Jesus, we so often speak about with adolescents? What about God's unflagging commitment in love and presence to us? And what about the demands, we perceive, that our God places on humanity, the challenges (not just the comforting sides) of the gospel, and the possibilities for forgiveness of inevitable failures and alienations? He asks,

> In our religious converse with the young, do we talk about Jesus' Father the way he does? In some ways, the answer is obviously yes. Children in today's church learn of God's love and care and of their own worth. But do they hear of a God who makes demands? Or does [this God] come through as a God who wants whatever they want? We rightly teach them, as Jesus did, that God's love for us is unconditional, that [God] loves me no matter what I do. But what some may be hearing is "God loves me so much, [God] doesn't care what I do." … This kind of optimism is appealing but hard to square with innumerable passages in the New Testament where Jesus warns us, in the most solemn terms, of the fate that awaits those who refuse the Father's offer of life. (Are these texts chosen ever as readings in youth liturgy?)… everything is at stake in the way human beings use their freedom. How prominent is this theme in religious education and exhortations of the young? (DiGiacomo 16-17)

Bernard Cooke offers us a nice summary on how God, the Creator, is for us, and how this can or should be interpreted with others:

> … A somewhat new and more understandable approach to "grace" has come to the fore in recent theology: an approach that sees God's self-revealing presence in the consciousness of believers as a radically transforming force that is capable of saving them and through their actions saving others as well. This perspective is, of course, very biblical; the New Testament writings are filled with it….. However, this biblical view needs to be translated into people's understanding of how God dwells with them in today's world, of how God's presence is meant to transform individuals and society, and of what is expected of human beings in response to God's presence. (Cooke, "Christian Understandings" 89)

JESUS THE CHRIST

What do people you know, adolescents included, really think about Jesus? Are their ideas rather diverse, incorrect, incomplete, or vague? A sharp insight into who Jesus is, and of what the experience of Jesus of Nazareth was, remains fundamental to Christianity and our life as followers of this person in history.

Popular views of Jesus Christ, both within and without the church, range from one end of the theological spectrum to the other. Some see Jesus principally as teacher, which he is, but as one principally concerned with communication of doctrine and with its purity of expression. Others perceive Jesus as ruler, judge, and king, which he is…Others know Jesus as the holy man of God, which he is, but it is a holiness that separates Christ from the world, that places him high on some pedestal…. Still others understand Jesus as a liberator or revolutionary, which he is…. Finally, there are those who can accept Jesus as no more, or no less, than their brother, a human being like us in all things. Jesus is our brother, to be sure, but he is also the Son of God, the Lord of history, the only one about whom it can be said that he is of the same substance as the Father, the Almighty. (McBrien 388-389)

Often, there is a lack of common, accurate insight shared among those who identify themselves as Christian. This pertains to who Jesus was or is, what he means to people today, what the resurrection has meant, a central experience in the Christian story. Why is this, seemingly, something that does not much bother many Christian congregations? A sound, well-intentioned ministry will focus on the realities about the historical and the holy Jesus, the risen one, who came to be known, in post-Easter faith, as the anointed, the son of God, the Christ and Messiah. Such focus will avoid a romantic, an all-powerful, a mythic and triumphant-only, imagined Jesus.

While limited, we do have some evidence about who Jesus of Nazareth was, what he was like, what he said, in words and deeds, and what he hoped for. (Theissen 1978; Gager 1975; Nolan 1978; Haight *An Alternate Vision*).

Circumscribed though our accurate knowledge of the historical figure Jesus is, it contains elements that are of immense importance to Christians' down-to-earth religious beliefs. The extraordinary ordinariness of Jesus, his refusal to exercise institutionalized political power, his friendship with and concern for the marginalized of society, his fidelity to the prophetic vocation that was his, his view of God as irrevocably compassionate, the unassuming dignity that was his because of his radical honesty, the passionate commitment to bettering the lives of people, that is, establishing God's new community — these are aspects of Jesus that are fundamental to one's understanding of what it seems to be Christian. (Cooke, "Christian Understandings" 84)

It is not only the Jesus of history about whom we speak in our retreats and other ministries. From the earliest days of his followers, attention has been directed, likewise, to him as the Christ, the one raised by God from death, a Lord of glory. How did those, whose stories, thoughts, and actions which led to New Testament tradition, perceive the Christ? Basic beliefs became foundational, normative, to their shared Christian existence. These remain essential to us now:

> ... Jesus is alive; Jesus is humanly alive, though in some different situation of human existing; Jesus remains in relationship with those who accept Christ in faith — as a matter of fact, there is a life bond that unites Christians with Jesus; in his new fulfilled situation, Jesus enters into the definitive stage of his ministry, because he can now share with others the full power of his Spirit which is God's Spirit also. (Cooke, "Christian Understandings" 85)

Rahner referred to Jesus as an "absolute savior," (Rahner 206-212), in and through his words and deeds, we can hope for "everything." Put another way, in Jesus of Nazareth, God has once and for all, in a specific individual, communicated to us, and that communication is to be absolutely, unequivocally, accepted, as the Creator has accepted it. (Dych 10-12) Jesus understood himself. . .

> ... however incompletely and gradually, to be this savior, and his resurrection established and manifested that he is such. He did not regard himself as simply another prophet, but he made our reaction to him decisive for our entrance into the kingdom... Indeed, Jesus himself is the kingdom. (McBrien 476-478)

THE PEOPLE OF GOD: THE CHURCH

The typical person's grasp of Christianity and the "consequent self-identification as Christian is often a mixture of piecemeal information, folk tradition, civil religion, and authentic openness to the gospel" all mixed in with doubts, questions, searchings. (Cooke, "Christian Understandings" 81) Like the family, religion in American life (still largely a privatized phenomenon, that is, segmented from our political and secular circles) often has provided simply a "haven in a heartless world," loving fellowship, and support to individuals. Thus, religion remains ineffective to "challenge the dominance of utilitarian values in the society at large." (Bellah 224) Not surprisingly, many Americans see religion as an individualistic thing more than a larger, organizational commitment. If any organizational loyalty is involved, the foremost setting remains the local congregation. George Gallup's research has indicated that many Americans think an "individual should arrive at his or her own religious beliefs independent of any churches or synagogues." (Bellah 226) Religion is a topic, frequently enough, readily handed over, by many of us, to the so-called specialists, and the representatives of our local churches. (Gallup and Castelli 253f)

A contemporary emphasis in Roman Catholicism, moving away from the strict, institutionally-centered views of "the Church," as the one and only, toward views of ourselves as community and people of God, signals a shift in theological insight, a reclaiming of gospel-authentic tradition, a change in Christian self-identity, and a broadening of power and responsibility in the ranks of the Christian body. What is the purpose or mission of this church? How should it, the people of God, pursue the goal?

Christianity without structure, in a sense amorphous and institution-free, would be an illusion and a mistake. Minimal, once-a-week, Sunday Catholicism remains a stumbling block to some, but a way of religious life for others. Well-intentioned Christians, here and there, want to strive, idealistically, with much work, for the fulfillment of the Church as community and, ultimately, for the realization, existentially, of the reign of God proclaimed through the Scriptures. Through it all,

> Devoted Christians must be helped to live with the human inadequacies of church structures; but something more fundamental is at stake. The experience of being Christian should be the experience of being a disciple of Christ and, along with one's fellow Christians, the body of Christ. Clearly, people cannot have such an experience if they do not understand what these terms mean. They need not be given a complicated technical explanation... [they] do need to have some grasp of the mystery dimension of Christianity and some grasp of the way in which they as disciples of Christ form part of that mystery. (Cooke, "Christian Understandings" 82-83)

To be sure, a Catholic Christian perspective on Church will teach that human beings are dwelling, already, in God's presence. People need not pass through, absolutely, a church, or "the Church," in order to be in relationship with the Creator. The kingdom or reign of God is in our midst, somehow, in some way, but not yet fully realized. Catholic Christianity, as a corporate expression of faith in the God-for-us, as a faith tradition in harmony with the gospel, is a unique way by which we can identify with and respond to the God who loves and saves, and by which we can stretch, in mission, toward that Horizon we call hope and fulfillment in creation.

CALLED TO BE FOLLOWERS: CHRISTIAN LIFE DISCIPLESHIP

So, what does it mean to be a follower of Christ, a good Christian, a disciple of the Lord? This question is yet another expression of the fundamental, human question: Why be a Christian?, or even Why be a Catholic Christian? Donald Senior has cautioned:

Obviously "following" or "imitating" Jesus does not mean simply copying the surface details of his life, such as wearing first century garb or becoming an itinerant preacher. Imitating Jesus... means that Christians are to shape their own lives in the pattern of Jesus. This is no simple process nor is there only one way of expressing the pattern of Christ's life in our own. Here is where the authentic disciple becomes a true learner by constantly reflecting on the teaching and example of Jesus and trying to see their meaning in our everyday lives. (Senior 31)

Quite clearly, sin and evil, and oppressions and injustices, are much in evidence in human activities, personal human choices, and human (social) institutions, including "the Church." Sinfulness, therefore, must be our human way of saying no to God's graciously-given, free offer of life and relationship. Christian conversion, as we have described it, is the choice(s) we make against alienation and the decision for love of God, one-self, and others. The path ongoing toward such a Christian love-lifestyle is, frequently, difficult, circuitous, full of pitfalls, search, and doubt, and — to true believers — indispensable. Current thinkers try to stress certain things about this lifelong journey....

....should not truly Christian behavior go beyond avoidance of sin, beyond the correct social behavior expected of any person? One clear way of responding to this question is in terms of discipleship. A Christian should translate in his or her life the example of Jesus into actions needed in our world. However, it would be a mistake to understand "disciple of Christ" as one who succeeds Jesus in the ministry he carried on two millennia ago. Rather, since Christians in community are truly the body of Christ, discipleship is a matter of co-working with the risen Christ who is still present in Spirit to the human history that Christ seeks to transform. To be a disciple of Christ, to be truly Christian, a person must allow the direction of the Spirit to be the norm for his or her choices and actions; one must be faithful to Christ's Spirit. (Cooke, "Christian Understandings" 94-95)

These demands of discipleship in Jesus should be made known to those who live and work and grow up in the hectic, real world today, made known on an ongoing basis, throughout the human life cycle, through various faith-formation processes, including the spiritually intensive experiences we call youth retreats. Accurate knowledge (rather than vague, diverse, half-truth opinions) about grace, revelation, the Creator, faith, Jesus the Christ, and the Church remains important. How could this not be so? Yet, knowledge and understanding about God and about how we are hearers of the Word, ultimately, won't cut it alone. A genuinely lived faith life, a lifelong conversion, a lifelong initiation, if you will, must be coupled with accurate insight into the good news and faith.

WORKS CITED

Bellah, Robert N. et al. *Habits Of The Heart: Individualism And Commitment in American Life*. San Francisco: Harper & Row, 1985.

Buckley, Michael J. "Within The Holy Mystery." *A World Of Grace*. Ed. Leo J. O'Donovan. New York: Seabury Press, 1980.

Carr, Anne E. "Starting With The Human." *A World Of Grace*. Ed Leo J. O'Donovan. New York: Seabury Press, 1980.

The Challenge of Adolescent Catechesis. Washington DC: National Federation for Catholic Youth Ministry, 1986.

Cooke, Bernard. *Sacraments and Sacramentality*. Mystic CT: Twenty-Third Publications, 1983,

_____. "Basic Christian Understandings." *Education for Citizenship and Discipleship*. Ed. Mary C. Boys. New York: Pilgrim Press, 1989.

DiGiacomo, James J. "The New Illiteracy: Catechetics And Youth." *Readings In Youth Ministry, Volume II*. Ed. John Roberto. Washington DC: National Federation for Catholic Youth Ministry, 1989.

_____ and John Walsh. *Meet The Lord*. Minneapolis: Winston Press, 1977.

Dych, William V. "Theology In A New Key." *A World Of Grace* Ed. Leo J. O'Donovan. New York: Seabury Press, 1980.

Ekstrom, Reynolds R. "Youth Culture and Teen Spirituality: Signs of the Times." *Readings In Youth Ministry, Volume I*. Ed. John Roberto. Washington D.C.: National Federation for Catholic Youth Ministry, 1986.

Flannery, O.P, Austin. *Vatican Council II: The Conciliar and Post Conciliar Documents*. Collegeville MN: Liturgical Press, 1975.

Gager, John G. *Kingdom and Community: The Social World of Early Christianity*. Englewood NJ: Prentice Hall, 1975.

Gallup, George and Jim Castelli. *The People's Religion: American Faith in the '90s*. New York: Macmillan Company, 1990.

Groome, Thomas H. *Christian Religious Education*. San Francisco: Harper & Row, 1980.

Haight, Roger. *An Alternate Vision: An Interpretation of Liberation Theology*. Mahwah NJ: Paulist Press, 1985. (See especially chapters 6, 7)

_____. *The Experience and Language of Grace*. New York: Paulist Press, 1979.

Kimball, Don. *Power and Presence: A Theology of Relationships*. San Francisco: Harper & Row, 1987.

McBrien, Richard P. *Catholicism*. Minneapolis: Winston Press, 1980.

National Conference of Catholic Bishops. *To Teach As Jesus Did*. Washington DC: United States Catholic Conference, 1972.

National Conference of Catholic Bishops. *Sharing The Light of Faith: National Catechetical Directory.* Washington DC: United States Catholic Conference, 1979.

Nelson, John S. "Faith and Adolescents: Insights from Psychology and Sociology." *Faith Maturing: A Personal And Communal Task.* Ed. John Roberto. Washington DC: National Federation for Catholic Youth Ministry, 1985.

Nolan, O.P., Albert. *Jesus Before Christianity.* Maryknoll NY: Orbis Books, 1978.

Rahner, S.J., Karl. *Foundations of Christian Faith: An Introduction to the Idea of Christianity.* New York: Seabury Press, 1978. (See also, Rahner's volume, *Hearers of the Word.* New York: Herder & Herder, 1969.)

Rite of Christian Initiation of Adults, Study Edition. Chicago: Liturgical Training Publications, 1988.

Roberto, John. *Adolescent Catechesis Resource Manual.* New York: Sadlier, 1988 .

Senior, Donald. "Called To Be Disciples." *New Catholic World* Jan/Feb 1982: 4-9.

Shelton, S.J., Charles. *Adolescent Spirituality.* Chicago: Loyola University Press, 1983.

Theissen, Gerd. *Sociology of Early Palestinian Christianity.* Philadelphia: Fortress Press, 1978.

A Vision Of Youth Ministry. Washington DC: United States Catholic Conference, 1976.

Walsh, John. *Evangelization and Justice: New Insights for Christian Ministry.* Maryknoll NY: Orbis, 1982.

VATICAN II DOCUMENTS CITED:

Ad Gentes Divinitus, Decree On The Church's Missionary Activity, 7 December 1965.

Dei Verbum, Dogmatic Constitution On Divine Revelation, 18 November 1965.

Sacrosanctum Concilium, The Constitution On The Sacred Liturgy, 4 December 1963.

Chapter 3

Moral and Psychological Foundations of Retreats

Charles Shelton, S.J.

Recently, I shared with a friend my interest in adolescent morality. I informed him I was writing on this topic. In an off-handed way, my friend replied, "It must be an awful short dissertation!" We both had a good laugh. Over the past few weeks, however, I have pondered my friend's reaction. In reality, his response made sense. As adults, we all too often fail to realize the challenges that adolescence presents to the construction of the moral self. Yet, it is in adolescence that moral responsibility becomes possible; in other words, it is only in adolescence that the requisite human capacities and experiences are present which allow for authentic moral choice and commitment.

I do not mean to claim that the adolescent's growth in moral responsibility (the capacity to engage with integrity in life-actions) is an "all or once affair." On the contrary, acquiring moral maturity is a long, and at times, unpredictable venture in which the adolescent, erratically, at first, comes to experience himself or herself as a moral person. Such a developmentally-based view of moral maturity has significant consequences for youth ministry, religious education, and retreat ministries.

WHAT IS ADOLESCENCE?

A definition of adolescence is in order. Although the definitions are numerous, I find the defining features of this age to be:

a chronological period beginning with the physical and emotional processes leading to sexual and psychosocial maturity and ending at an ill-defined time when the individual achieves independence and social productivity. This period is associated with rapid physical, psychological, and social changes. (Nicholi 519) [1]

This definition has several advantages. It stipulates a developmental perspective. Consequently, the adolescent years are viewed as a significant time-frame, incorporating junior and senior high, as well as the undergraduate college years. Secondly, this definition points out the multi-dimensional factors that define adolescence. In other words, economic, emotional, physical, and social factors must be given consideration. Finally, it sets forth intervening realities which impact on the adolescent's experience. These include the family and society, as well as competing factors, which shape the adolescent.

To further clarify this issue, I would define adolescent morality as:

the adolescent's personal striving, in the midst of his or her own developmental struggles, to internalize and commit the self to prescriptive ideals within a situational context that incorporates the interplay of developmental levels, the concrete situation, and environmental factors, and which in turn lead to self-maintaining and consistent thoughts, attitudes, and actions. (Shelton 194, 195)

MATURITY IN ADOLESCENCE: EBB AND FLOW

When asked, most adults will give a somewhat ambivalent summary of their own adolescence. This, most likely, reflects the acutely-felt vicissitudes so characteristic of these developmental years. Rare is the adult who can think of his or her adolescence without recalling feelings of interior joy, moments of guilt or dread, and periodic confusion. Why is this so? I suggest that no other stage of life offers such intensely-felt uncertainty.

For the adolescent, the security of childhood yields to a time of searching and questioning, without the stability and experience typified by the adult's grounding. In other words, at least initially, there is little of what I term morally-felt foundations — those experiences which integrate psychic stability and value choices.

On a cognitive level, the adolescent is aware of moral rules and maxims, yet he or she often lacks a more deeply experienced understanding of these moral utterances. Thus, the lonely adolescent, all too often, falls prey to the influences of not so well-intentioned peers. The troubled young person seeks solace in stereotypic attitudes. The insecure youth retreats to the world of self-destructive behavior (for example, alcohol and drug abuse). As a consequence, on a general level, moral rules are known, but, on an experiential level, uncertainties, fears, and insecurities coalesce to lead the adolescent to engage in non-growthful and deviant behaviors.

The emotional world of the adolescent is often in various levels of disarray. Youth thrive on felt experience. Unfortunately, lacking a foundation for their affections (for example, stable and secure relation-ships), they resort to moodiness and, often, volatile outbursts of feelings. Emotions exercise a salient role in the adolescent's moral experience. Often, the defining criterion for morality during this period is how one feels. Unfortunately, emotions are all too often at the mercy of developmen-tal needs, and become a license for self-absorption, rather than moral clar-ity.

FACTORS IMPEDING MORAL MATURITY IN ADOLESCENTS

When the Christian speaks of moral growth, there is the explicit recognition of what we might term sin. Moral theologian Timothy O'Connell captures, I think, the most perceptive understanding of sin's meaning. Fr. O'Connell says sin only makes sense in the presence of a rela-tionship with God. "Apart from God, in the absence of God, sin is literally meaningless." (O'Connell 278) Sin is a fact. It is also a personal act which, over time, leads in a direction. In sum, sin portrays one's very existence. It speaks of an inner alienation both from God and from one's brothers and sisters. It points to the ongoing false paradigms and viewpoints which cloud (and disorient) one's journey.

I have often been asked about stressing sinfulness with adolescents. Some object that youth, overwhelmed by developmental insecurities and inner doubts, should not be addressed in language such as sin. I think such objections confuse content and process. It is essential that the adult in min-istry convey the meaning of sinfulness to adolescents (the process), in ways filled with compassionate sensitivity and loving guidance. Yet, the very fact of sin (the content) needs clear articulation. In short, if religious educators, retreat ministers, and others downplay a young person's capacity for sin, they run the risk of depriving the young person experiences of personal for-giveness, the central reality of Jesus' redemptive message. A tremendous disservice is done if an adolescent neglects the empowering richness of the Christian mystery of forgiveness.

LACK OF LIFE EXPERIENCE

The absence of experience predisposes the adolescent to moral vul-nerability. Identity typifies the adolescent's life experience. Few develop-mental issues underscore the adolescent's developmental age as the search for identity. On one hand, it is identity-acquisition which allows the adoles-cent to own moral responsibility. On the other hand, the development of a moral self necessitates experimentation, the trying on of various behaviors in order to experience, literally, what psychically fits. The consequences of these haphazard and, at times, impulsively chosen commitments lead to erratic, foolish, and even destructive experiences which harm the adolescent and others. The adolescent who follows, blindly, the peer group or who acts out, sexually, is often attempting to discover "who I am." With time, as well as adult sensitivity and challenge, the vast majority of adolescents are able to form a moral identity, although the questions and issues which forge this identity linger long into the young adult years.

INSUFFICIENT REFLECTION

Related is the limited nature of reflective thought, so integral for making an ethical decision. I have found this to be true for both secondary school youth, as well as college undergraduates. Unfortunately, we fail to appreciate the limited depth of adolescent reflection. Often, we dialogue with youth as if they reason and reflect as we do. We fail to recognize the chasm in their moral thinking which arises from lack of life experience and reflection. Lacking a personal history of thought-out moral choices, which allow him or her to respond to a variety of dilemmas, the adolescent is all too prone to succumb to situational stresses often acutely felt.

PEER APPROVAL

A splendid example of situational stress is the adolescent's vulnerability to adopt the peer group's standards when encountering a moral question. One of the most convenient ways to separate from parents and define self as independent, is to embrace the lifestyle and behavior of one's peers. This adoption of peer standards gives the adolescent the best of all possible worlds. On the one hand, he or she is able to say no to the adult world (thus proclaiming a psychological sense of independence). At the same time, one can be absorbed in the security of the peer group. Stereotypic characterizations of youth as different from adults have been exaggerated by the media. Adolescents and their parents are not dissimilar on many issues. When an issue is of great import (for example, college choice), the adolescent is likely to seek parental advice and forsake the opinions of peers. (Coleman 408-431)

Given a particular issue or a specific situation, almost any adolescent, at one time or another, is apt to question and challenge adult rules and values. A certain level of questioning and challenge of adult rules is psychologically healthy. The overly-controlled adolescent, acquiescing to every adult command, portends a future developmental arrest. The presence of a peer group is yet an ever-present reality.

I vividly recall an adolescent who told me that she was so thankful that her parents insisted that she be home by midnight from a party. She told me that, on her own, she would never have been able to withstand the pressure of her peers and leave the party. Psychologically, this adolescent, unable to assert her moral self, reached for external structures to shield her from peer demands. In sum, the tyranny of the peer group is a double-edged sword. On the one hand, it offers an avenue for the adolescent to establish a healthy sense of independence. On the other, it proves a tempting invitation to escape responsibility and the challenging demands of moral maturity.

INCONSISTENCY

Adolescent behaviors are often played out in developmental inconsistencies. James Fowler describes this as compartmentalizing. (Fowler 61) With parents, the adolescent is prone to act one way. When he or she is with peers, the young person's actions are apt to be dissimilar. I categorize this phenomenon as a group of roles which the adolescent adopts. Son or daughter, student, athlete, friend, club member, brother or sister, worker, etc. A listing of these roles highlights the potential for role conflicts and the all too commonplace discrepant behaviors which accompany these diverse roles.

Many adolescents, continually, engage in these contradictory behaviors, without really attending to the contradictions which exist. These discrepancies in role behaviors are a direct result of the adolescent's inability to develop a cohesive sense of self-identity. A retreat minister, a parish youth minister, or a catechist can be a valuable resource in helping adolescents reflect on their inconsistencies.

MODELING

Intellectual development in adolescence allows the young person to think, critically, about adult standards and behaviors. With the shedding of simplistic, childhood notions, the adolescent, oftentimes, resorts to a critical examination of adults. The adolescent discovers, often, that adults fail to live up to their professed standards. Some adolescents view this as hypocritical. This engenders disillusionment and negativity. For some youth, adult failures, as good Christian role models, become justification for their own less than ideal behaviors. The adolescent's predicament seems like a tightrope. A walk between youthful idealism and ever-present cynicism. The former nurtured by optimism, focused on an adult world yet-to-be experienced, the latter sustained by their disappointments.

RELATIVITY

The foremost shift in adolescent thinking, an ethical standpoint, is the alteration of beliefs of childhood resulting from the newly-discovered experience of questioning and reevaluation. This shift from certainty to ambiguity can create a period of moral crises.

Some adolescents regress from serious examination. They retreat to an uncritical and rigid acceptance of parental standards. Other adolescents adopt a philosophical view of life to extinguish the insecurities which go with questioning and doubt. Still, other adolescents negotiate a variety of beliefs, as they attempt to come to some type of life meaning. Finally, other youth avoid altogether any serious confrontation with moral concerns. In other words, these call a time out from moral examination and are satisfied with other pursuits. For most adolescents, however, some type of moral evaluation takes place.

This engenders relativity, uncertainty, and questioning. In the midst of his or her own life changes, and in newly experienced intellectual prowess, the youth flexes a cognitive muscle. Adolescents discover that relativity is the "true" world perspective. Indeed, this insight blends nicely with the moral pluralism so dominant today. [2] In effect, the combination of relativity and pluralism leads many adolescents to identify truth solely in terms of subjective experience. What is right is decided by the individual. The adolescent comes to believe that what is moral depends upon a person's own life pursuits (with situational components).

The adolescent's assumption is: Who is to decide what is right? This moral relativity leads to a moral subjectivism, which is manipulated by developmental needs. All in all, the ever-present reality of relativity is one of the major challenges for adolescents as they negotiate the construction of a mature moral self.

CULTURE

Recently, one area receiving attention, in moral education, is the imposing presence of cultural factors which influence the adolescent. Psychic numbing, occasioned by nuclear war threats, alienation fostered by competition, and insidious lures in our consumer culture are hard to combat. Facing an uncertain economic future, today's youth are vulnerable to the trappings of society. (Kavanaugh 1981 and Ekstrom 1989) Adults now realize that they cannot simply encourage youth to be moral. Needed are environments in which young people can discuss, dialogue, and share their common concerns and doubts. It is unrealistic for adults to expect youth to develop a mature, moral self if they are not provided the forums and opportunities in which questions can be discussed and shared. Such opportunities arise on youth retreats, in follow-up sessions, in catechetical classes, with youth support groups, and elsewhere.

I have become uneasy with the simplistic notions evident in much of social justice education. All too often, such literature simply talks about violence-peace or justice-injustice, without giving adequate attention to the complex realities which are threaded through questions of national or international importance (the economy, international relations). Youth have the right to hear that there are many sides to these issues. Men and women of goodwill might legitimately disagree what particular end best achieves the goals of the gospel. Simplistic portrayals of issues disregard very basic developmental experiences. Having a more complex view of the world, through cognitive maturation, the labeling of complicated political issues in simplistic terms does youth a true disservice.

Who is to say that one position is just or unjust? Clearly, ideals must be articulated. Yet, the various, and sometimes contradictory, means for achieving these ends must be given a fair hearing by religious educators, retreat team members, and other pastoral ministers today.

DIALOGUING WITH YOUR YOUTH

Taken together, these factors point to the competing influences in the adolescent's life. I would like to offer several practical reflections which might prove helpful for religious educators, retreat ministers, and other youth ministers. Use these as a basis for fruitful dialogue with adolescents. For the most part, these questions are best used with older adolescents.

Lack of life experience: For you, what does it mean to be a moral person? How has your view of being moral changed over the last few years? In what ways? What have been the experiences that have shaped your views on morality?

Insufficient reflection: Who influences you? Are you sometimes more impulsive than reflective in your actions? When is this impulsiveness more apt to be present? Do you have particular times and places in which you reflect?

Peer influences: How do you define friendship? What makes someone your friend? Who are your friends? What values do you share? How are you unlike them? How are you different? Do you have to feel yourself part of the group? Are you comfortable disagreeing with friends?

Inconsistency: What roles do you have in your life? What is important to you in each of these roles? Can you be consistent in these roles? How do you handle conflict (when it occurs)? Do your values differ in various roles? Why? When do you find it hard to be yourself? How does each life role help you be Christian?

Modeling: Who are your heroes? Who do you value most? Why do you value these people? Who would you want to be like? Who wouldn't you be like? Why? What are these people's values?

Relativity: What are the deepest truths by which you try to live? What principles and guidelines guide your life? Are these valid in every situation? Are there any dilemmas that you are not sure how to solve? Give an example. How do you respect individuals who differ from you?

Culture: What are the goals of our culture (in your view)? Are these like or not like your goals? What do you value about American culture?

What things might you change, if you could? When you encounter a very complex problem, how do you make a moral decision? Describe the steps. Can you respect people who differ from you?

HELPING ADOLESCENTS DEVELOP MORALLY AND SOCIALLY:
PSYCHOLOGICAL INSIGHTS FOR RETREAT MINISTERS

What processes or components are necessary to a truly Christian morality for adolescents? Earlier, we spoke of an adolescent morality sensitive to the development of the adolescent. Such a morality must pay particular attention, also, to the entire adolescent experience, and pay attention to situations and environments which influence the adolescent's perceptions and sensitivities. (Shelton, *Morality and the Adolescent* 135ff)

I would like to offer several dimensions needed to discuss morality as it pertains to the adolescent's experience. I will first present the dimension itself, I will then elaborate on the consequences of this dimension for Christian morality today.

EMPATHY

Empathy provides a basis for a theory of morality that is fundamentally distinct from Lawrence Kohlberg's perspective. (Shelton, "Christian Empathy" 209-222; Kohlberg) Empathy can be defined as an awareness of the pain and hurts of another, and a corresponding emotional arousal to another's suffering. In turn, this arousal to another's plight leads one to actively engage in behaviors which alleviate the other's distress. Psychologist Martin Hoffman has provided the most complex and sophisticated theory of empathy's development. (Hoffman 958-966)

Hoffman sees empathy as a naturally-occurring phenomenon. It orients the human person to behave altruistically towards others. Empathy is a human mechanism which fosters social bondedness and human community-building. This universal experience of empathy blends nicely with the Lord's call for universal good towards one's brothers and sisters (for example, the Good Samaritan). Moreover, empathy forms the impetus for making real the Gospel's command to love (John 15:17). It is the human capacity to empathize which allows us to feel, to understand the needs, the concerns, and the cares of another. In a sense, empathy is the constitutive, human element that grace builds upon. It allows the person to reach out, compassionately, towards others.

Our Lord vividly portrays this empathic experience. "For we do not have a high priest who is unable to sympathize with our weakness, but one who was tempted in every way that we are, yet never sinned" (Heb 4:15) and "He is able to deal patiently with erring sinners, for he himself is beset by weakness" (Heb 5:2). Jesus' own experience of impoverishment allowed him to be a source of care and support for every person. Empathy is a profoundly human experience, enabling one's gifts to build up the Christian community.

Paul's struggles with the Corinthian community displays the empathic experience which underscores Christian community-building. Given in the Lord (1 Co 12), gifts are to be used to bring about unity. In a dispute over speaking in tongues, and in the dissent caused by eating the food of idols, Paul speaks eloquently on behaviors and gifts that build up and bring unity to the community. These very concrete and human experiences of early Church community-building demonstrate the critical importance of empathy. Without this, Paul's urgings would be exercises in futility.

Empathy is suited, ideally, to the developmental needs of adolescents. They desire intimacy. They need relational encounters. They place value on community. Point to the pivotal role that empathy can exercise in bringing about a deeper understanding of a moral self.

Implications: When dialoguing with adolescents, adults should see how the adolescent empathizes with others. Time needs to be spent processing feelings the adolescent might have toward those who are hurting, or those to whom he or she is emotionally bonded.

Situations that cause adolescents to be emotionally aroused (the distress of others) must be given special attention. A time and place must be provided for adolescents to talk and explore their aroused feelings towards those who are in distress (for example, the adolescent who works in a social service project needs a forum which allows him or her to process [sort out] various feelings which arise from exposure to victims of social injustice). The empathic arousal which results, on a retreat or in other group experiences, from youth's sensitivity towards others needs to be channeled into constructive outlets. Adults can provide suggestions on activities and reading which can direct, in a productive fashion, the adolescent's arousal. Scripture texts (for example, Mt 25) can prove very helpful. They will aid youth — showing how their own sensitivities are similar to Gospel concerns.

IDENTITY

In understanding the moral maturity of the adolescent, the most important psychological construct is identity. There is no precise, unanimously accepted definition of identity in developmental literature. There are several noteworthy characteristics which need to be discussed. Identity is concerned with the self in a continuous life history. Identity represents the person's capacity to discern some life-directions which speak of a past, and a present, with its numerous possibilities.

Identity is concerned, also, with the future — the capacity to invest in the present, yet not seek life options which preclude possibilities for growth in self-knowledge. Identity represents the person-in-relation-to the world. Whereas the self refers to internal psychic experience (I know that I am), identity is concerned with relationships, that is, how one is invested in relational commitments. This becomes a critical issue since relationships are pivotal in gaining self-knowledge in adolescence. Identity speaks of one's values. It represents a basic integrity of self. The person states, "I value this," or "I believe this." Identity allows the individual to invest the self in life actions which speak of these values.

Implications: With adolescents, discuss various roles (for example, son/daughter, friend) which the adolescent experiences. Two areas are of particular importance. First, spend time in reflecting on the various role conflicts which can arise. How the adolescent resolves these conflicts can say much about the adolescent's coping capacity and maturity level.

Secondly, the discrepancies experienced in these various roles can also be explored. The adolescent can be challenged to reflect on why he or she might act differently in his or her roles. Such reflection can be a valued source of insight for the adolescent. Reflection questions, such as, "What do you value most?" and "What do you really want out of life?" allow the adolescent to really own his or her moral identity. They encourage the young person to focus on what is important, truly, and to reflect upon the direction that his or her life is taking.

COMMITMENT

Commitment best expresses the realization of values in everyday life. Pluralism and relativism, so dominant in American culture, make this a fragile experience for many youth. Commitment represents the fidelity of one's self to Gospel values, lived out in relationships and self-consistent behaviors. Commitment is best viewed in the Jesus-question: "But who do you say that I am?" (Mt 16:15), or in the challenge, "Come follow me" (Mk 10:21). These invitations are highly personal. They call one to give oneself to the Lord, through a commitment to Jesus and his saving message.

This commitment, of course, is not perfectly lived. It is subject to vagaries and human limitations which plague life. But, the invitation is always present. It beckons us, further, to deeper commitment.

Implications: Youth's relational style makes commitment a crucial variable. Adolescents are constantly summoned to understand the meaning of commitment, through friendships and peer relationships. These relationships encourage the adolescent to reflect on various life values, to explore deeper levels of self-knowledge, and to comprehend, at a meaning level, their actions and behaviors. Adolescents can profit from adults who dialogue about values. Posing Jesus as friend, the meaning of friendship, and how the adolescent lives out the commitment of friendship, with Jesus, are fruitful avenues to explore.

Discussion on how relationships with friends mirror relationship with Jesus is helpful. This last point is noteworthy, especially when issues of honesty, openness, forgiveness, and acceptance are experienced, as struggles in the adolescent's relationships.

Dimensions of Morality

I have always been struck how children apply moral rules in a variety of situations. In other words, one might be highly consistent with various moral principles in one situation, but in another setting, these rules might not seem to apply. A classic case is the adolescent or adult who thinks one way in more personal concerns, while interpersonal relations dictate a different set of moral priorities. My own belief is that morality is best conceived not as a uniform measure such as a moral IQ. Rather, morality must be qualified by its dimensions.

There exist three spheres of morality: the personal, the interpersonal, and the social. Although these domains are not mutually exclusive, they do set forth three fairly distinctive areas for a person to address his or her moral commitments. Accordingly, personal morality is concerned with self-consistent moral principles which one adheres to regardless of whether others are present. One follows the dictates of these principles because demands arise from being human. Thus, honesty and fidelity are qualities one embraces, regardless. Conscience is often seen as the moral foundation for this morality.

On the other hand, interpersonal morality is concerned with the moral quality of behaviors which affect others. Personal friendships, family relations, and peer interactions fall here. Finally, social morality is focused on the application of social justice principles. As already noted, adolescents are quite likely to differ among themselves on these three dimensions. It is highly unlikely that many adolescents will show a highly developed moral sense on all three dimensions.[3]

Implications: We should clarify what dimension is being specified whenever conversing with an adolescent. Movement from personal to social morality involves levels of complexity and discourse that often take a variety of forms. Often, adolescents are aware of the demands of personal morality. But, they are unduly influenced by situational factors and lack of emotional maturity.

Interpersonal morality often falls victim to the fragility of identity and acutely-felt intimacy needs. As noted above, a social morality is subject to competing ideologies, complexity of issues, and lack of developmental abilities (for example, inability to deal conceptually with abstract issues). Adults who minister to youth must be aware of these varying dimensions of morality. We should not expect a level of moral maturity that is unrealistic.

There exists no overall, conceptual understanding of how adolescents develop a moral self. Psychology teaches us that issues of justice and compassion must be balanced by an adequate understanding of the adolescent's experience and capacities necessary for authentic moral commitments. Retreat ministers, youth ministry leaders, and religious education personnel must provide a challenging presence, an optimum environment for attending to the various dimensions of adolescent growth, in order that Jesus' call might be meaningfully experienced by youth.[4]

HOW WE SPARK CONVERSION IN ADOLESCENTS

Several days ago I took a short break from my writing and wandered through the Jesuit community library. I took a few moments and browsed through the books on religious education and pastoral ministry, paying particular attention to those published several decades ago, in the 1950s and '60s. What struck me was the sense of certainty these books conveyed to the reader. In working with youth, there seemed in these books to be readily available answers — it was all right there.

Indeed, pastoral ministry to youth in the 1980s and beyond is anything but certain! At the same time, however, I would hope that the reader will realize the significance of his or her own actions when working with youth, as well as the excitement and challenge that such work entails. Your presence is of vital significance for the adolescent's moral growth. There can be no greater priority for a faith community than the development of the moral consciousness of its young people. Without this thrust, as a central mission of its work, the community's very viability as a community of disciples and prophetic witness is compromised.

I would like to conclude with several points. First, the cultural climate in which we live these waning years of the twentieth century is anything but conducive to the development of moral sensitivity. As Robert Coles notes, "for some young people, much of our culture is a bad second home." (Coles 18) The poisoning climate of drug abuse, the tenuous nature of family life, the allures of materialism, and the constant battle for impulse control in the midst of ready sex and the never-ending stream of consumerism makes the role of the adult minister all the more significant in the lives of youth today. Viewed another way, the adult's presence can provide a ready point of reference for the adolescent who is facing all too many obstacles along the road to adulthood and true Christian conversion.

In addition, in my clinical and pastoral work, I have increasingly experienced (and have grown increasingly concerned) about a phenomenon I have noticed in some parents. For lack of a better term I will label it "parental paralysis." All too often, many parents are bewildered by the stresses and strains of parenting, are unsure of the moral values they should be articulating to their children, or if they are clear as to what values they wish to convey, they are unclear as to just how this might be done. This feeling of paralysis has led them to question their own roles as parents and, in some cases, led them to adopt an almost laissez-faire approach to parenting. In such instances, the role of the adult minister is all the more vital in filling the void left by parental uncertainty. To be sure, the vast majority of parents strive to exert a moral presence in their child's life. Yet the growing sense of self-doubt that I have witnessed is a concern.

In addition to this self-doubt, I believe there exists a "personal" reason why many parents find it difficult to be sharers of moral values with their children. Stated simply, in addition to the stress and insecurity that many adolescents experience, there are a great number of parents who are under a considerable if not overwhelming degree of stress, too. That includes the stress of modern life, the pressures of dual-career or one-parent families, financial issues, personal life issues, or the combination of some if not all of these. Parents often lack enough energy to provide adequate parenting without extraordinary if not heroic sacrifice.

Finally, and most tragically, there are some homes that are so dysfunctional — homes where the psychological hurt is so deep and parents as adult human beings are so wounded — that parents simply do not have the psychological resources to offer their children adequate role models. In these homes, parents often are inevitably invested in their own selves and do not have the adequate psychological capacities to provide for their children, even though they often desire to be present to them.

For all these reasons, the role of the adult who ministers to youth — whether as retreat minister, teacher, counselor, youth minister, or some other — takes on more and more significance. Moreover, I have no doubt that the role of adult witness, in the faith community, will grow. In this regard, there will be greater and greater need for the adult to be readily available to youth, as a witness to Gospel values. Given this reality, increasingly, adult ministers will need to have a wide degree of self-knowledge in order that their relationship with adolescents will be an encounter of openness and trust rather than a perceived or imagined threat or fear.

Likewise, there will be the need for the adult minister to be knowledgeable about the faith community's understanding of a wide variety of issues, and be willing to dialogue with the adolescent regarding endless questioning of sexual matters or the ongoing debate of the Christian's role in the modern world, and to carry on such dialogue in an informative as well as receptive way.

To journey with the adolescent on the road to moral maturity is no doubt a trip that will have many twists and turns. Along this journey, the adult's compassionate sensitivity and loving challenge can be a steady guide. More than anything, it is the Church's offer of help to her young people that will be the best guarantee for the future that, to a searching and troubled world, "Christ is being proclaimed!" (Phil 1:18).

ENDNOTES

[1] American Psychiatric Association, *A Psychiatric Glossary* (Washington, DC: 1975) 48. Quoted in Armand M. Nicholi, Jr., "The Adolescent," in *The Harvard Guide to Modern Psychiatry*, Armand M. Nicholi, Jr., ed. (Cambridge: Harvard University Press, 1978) 519.

[2] For a discussion of this issue, see W. M. Kurtines and J. L. Gewirtz, eds., "Certainty and Morality: Objectivistic Versus Relativistic Approaches," in *Morality, Moral Behavior, and Moral Development* (New York: John Wiley) 3-23.

[3] I argue for a three dimensional view of morality in other writings.

For a deeper look at and reflections on adolescent moral and spiritual growth, refer to: Charles M. Shelton, S.J., *Morality and the Adolescent: A Pastoral Psychology Approach* (New York: Crossroad Publishing, 1989).

WORKS CITED

Coleman, John C. "Friendship And The Peer Group In Adolescence." *Handbook of Adolescent Psychology*. Ed. Joseph Adelson. New York: John Wiley, 1980.

Coles, Robert. "Adolescence; Listening to the Youth of the '80s." *Sojourners* April 1988: 18-19.

Ekstrom, Reynolds R. *Access Guides to Youth Ministry: Pop Culture*. New Rochelle: Don Bosco Multimedia, 1989.

Fowler, James and Keen, Sam. *Life Maps*. Waco: Word Books, 1978.

Hoffman, Martin L. "Development of Moral Thought, Feeling, and Behavior." *American Psychologist* 34 (October 1979): 1958-66.

Kavanaugh, John F. *Following Christ in a Consumer Society*. Maryknoll, NY: Orbis, 1981.

Kohlberg, Lawrence. *The Psychology of Moral Development*. San Francisco: Harper and Row, 1984.

Nicholi, Armand M., editor. *The Harvard Guide to Modern Psychiatry*. Cambridge: Harvard University Press, 1978.

O'Connell, Timothy E. "A Theology of Sin." *Chicago Studies* 21 (Fall 1982).

Shelton,S.J., Charles. "Adolescent Morality: A Revised Paradigm." *Religious Education* 79 (Spring 1984): 195.

_____. "Christian Empathy: The Psychological Foundation Of Pastoral Ministry." *Chicago Studies* 23 (August 1984): 209-222.

_____. *Morality and the Adolescent: A Pastoral Psychology Approach*. New York: Crossroad Publishing, 1989.

Chapter 4

Types of Youth Retreats

(A) Evangelization through Youth Retreats

James C. Kolar

Once I received a telephone call from a rather disgruntled pastor. During the course of our conversation, he posed a question, born of more than a little frustration and exasperation, "What do you do with young people today?" I sensed from the tone of the question that he had some definite things in mind that he wanted to do "to" them, but that his better judgment and pastoral concern prohibited such a course of action.

As I have traveled around various parts of the country during the last ten years, I have heard that question, and ones like it, raised again and again. It has been raised most often by people who were working with youth in some kind of church context and who wanted to do something for them. The motivation for the question is at least twofold. The first is an awareness that the church, or some people from the church, have a responsibility to do something for young people. Oftentimes, that something is not very clear.

The most pressing occasion for that "something" is to get young people to attend youth groups or youth group activities, or to attend religious education classes or events of one kind or another, especially confirmation-preparation. At other times, the "something" is to get young people more involved in parish life by working on a service project or being on the parish council.

The second motivating factor is the awareness or knowledge that a lot of things do not seem to be working all that well in the lives of many young people. Growing up through adolescence in the best of times was not that easy to do. And today, for many reasons, that process seems to have become more difficult and problematic for many young people. Identity problems, loneliness, rejection, relationships at home, decision making, relating to the opposite sex, school, facing the future, handling the ups and downs of emotions, drugs, and alcohol present some real difficulties for young people. The results are evident in the lives of young people through the use of drugs and alcohol, boredom, depression, and in general, overall anxiety and frustration. It is often these things that motivate people from the churches to want to do something for youth.

The crux of the matter is "something" should be done. Regarding this "something," those active in youth ministry have available to them a variety of options, offered as the keys to opening doors to the "something." For some the key is self-image, helping young people to feel better about themselves. For others, it is communication skills, learning how to identify their needs, wants, and desires so that they can more effectively communicate them to others. For others, it is relationship building, meeting young people where they're at, and developing warm, positive relationships with them. For others, the key is liberating young people from oppressive structures that adults have placed them in — school, advertising, certain civil laws. For others, it is education that has based on the latest psychological and developmental theories. For still others, it is values clarification, helping young people to recognize and choose their own values and lifestyles.

The problem, then, is not in finding keys to open up the world of "something," but in determining which, if any, is the real key.

I was once in a discussion with the staff of the St. Paul Catholic Youth Center (St. Paul, MN) on the topic of what "something" was to be done with young people, and what the key to that "something" was. The occasion for the discussion was the retreat program for young people at the Center. More particularly, the discussion was focused on how the retreat program could more effectively work with young people. In the year prior to this meeting, we had tried a number of the keys, mentioned previously, with varying degrees of success. The retreat program was growing. Some of the keys we had used were producing some change and growth. Yet, there was a vague sense of something important missing.

It was that vague sense, rumbling around in the corners of the discussion, that prompted us to continue the discussion. We were not quite sure where it would lead, or how we could grab hold of that elusive "something" important. One member of the discussion, during a momentary lull, recalled a comment that he had recently heard. "For too long people in the Church have been giving good advice rather than good news." At the time, it seemed a provocative one-liner. But, we were not quite sure how to understand it or how to apply it to the matter at hand. We soon began to find more clarity, in both understanding and applying it.

During the next few months, that same year, a number of people in the Center's retreat program got involved in the charismatic renewal. For one, it was through a conference on healing, in a neighboring state. For another, it was a chance visit at a local prayer meeting. For another, it was simply to observe this questionable new "thing." For each of us, it was, I believe, a search for that elusive "something" that prompted our inquiries into the charismatic renewal. What we found in the renewal was much more than we expected. Yet, it began to clarify for us the nature of the "something" that we were looking for — both for the retreat program and our work with young people, generally, and for ourselves.

What we found, initially, were people who were enlivened with the presence of the Holy Spirit. Their praise and worship of God was joyful and enthusiastic. Their stories about how God was active in their lives made it sound as if God were really doing something. Their appreciation and use of Scripture to guide, direct, and shape their lives, their trust in the care and love of God, their amazement at the mercy and greatness of the Lord, made a great impression upon us.

Those of us on the staff at the Center attended these prayer meetings for a short time. Then, we began meeting on our own to pray and sing, to worship God, and to share Scripture with one another. Soon, others who were involved, on a volunteer basis, with the Center's ministries began to join us.

Looking back now, the "something" more we had been looking for was the person and work of Jesus Christ. We had begun to see what God had done in him and how the way to life was through him. We also had begun to see that the key to "something" more was conversion.

We quite quickly began to see that this "something," and the key to it, was the absolutely irreplaceable foundation upon which our lives and the lives of young people we worked with had to be built. We were, in a word, being evangelized. Since that time we have learned, again and again, in some situations that were painful and others that were joyful, that the real power to live the Christian life comes from that one foundation, the foundation of what God has done for us in Jesus.

There is a current saying that has wisdom and experience behind it. It says, "Anyone who has a conversion experience should be locked up for at least six months." Many of us have stories about being overcome by those who have found the truth. In our zeal to communicate the importance of what we have found, it is more than possible to overwhelm someone else with our discovery. And so it was with us. We redesigned the focus for the whole retreat program, then unleashed it on our volunteer staff, those who work with the young people on retreats.

We tried to do too much, with too many, too quickly. To move from the focus of feeling better about yourself, to communication skills and values clarification, to conversion and commitment, to Jesus Christ, in one weekend, is a formidable undertaking! Relationships that had been built on one foundation were now being moved and deepened to another. Understandings of what the goals of retreats should be were being changed in substantial and significant ways. There were discussions, testimonies, new songs, tears, hurt feelings, and laughter, all at the same time. All in all, it was an important beginning. The foundation was being laid.

The focus, from that time on, was the person and work of Jesus. Scripture and the life of the Church became the reference points for the design and the content of the retreats. Many of the topics that had previously been part of the retreat program remained, but the focus was different. For example, presentations on self-image focused on what God has done for us, and how the basis for our value is found in our relationship with the Lord. Peer pressure became focused on how we were to live our lives, and how we were to determine the standards to live by.

The overall thrust was to help young people see more clearly their great need to respond to what God has done for them in Jesus. As a result, overcoming obstacles to receiving what God has done for us became a major element in the retreat design.

Much of the difficulty young people have in receiving the Lord has to do with basic areas of disorder in their lives. Whether that disorder is in how they perceive themselves, their family, their school, or their future, they need to respond more to the Lord's initiative, drawing them to his life, than respond to the area of confusion or disorder in their lives.

Early on, in the redesigned retreat program, we discovered some very significant things. These are, in one sense, most obvious, given the teachings of the Scriptures and the Church, but they were not obvious to us, nor were they obvious to many of those searching for that elusive "something."

One discovery was the power of God's Word in Scripture. We found that we had tended to replace the Word of God, as it is revealed in Scripture, with the words of contemporary writing, especially psychology and human development. We tended, for example, to develop a process on the findings of a current theory, throwing in a Scripture verse here and there (if we could find one that had some similarity with the point a secular theorist was making). The real authority behind our approach had been current thinking. Replacing that authority with the authority of the Word of God was a significant change. It brought much more effectiveness to our work with young people on retreats.

Catholic young people tend to be uninformed as to what the Scriptures teach about who God is, what our real condition is without knowledge of God, what God has done in Jesus, the purpose that he has for our lives, and how we can give our lives to him. These basic themes of redemption provide the basis and the power for the Christian life. There is nothing which can replace these saving acts of God. Scripture, as it comes to us, through the life of the Church, authentically presents and interprets these mighty words of God on our behalf.

Scripture, then, passed on to us through the life of the Church, is the standard by which we are to understand and live out our lives. This is true for young people, as well as for those not so young. Hearing and responding to basic gospel realities initiates the process of evangelization. It is these basic gospel realities which provide the foundation for or entry way into Christian life. It is no accident that the central elements in Christian life, such as liturgy, ecclesiology, and moral teaching, are accessible only through the basic gospel message. This may seem a bit abstract, especially with regard to the evangelization of youth, but it does have applicability. Its applicability is something that we learned as we began to redesign our retreat program, then as we implemented our redesigned models.

Many of the requests that we receive from parishes, schools, and special groups are for retreats, with themes such as liturgy, Confirmation, Eucharist, Reconciliation, or a particular area of personal or social morality, dating, sexuality, drugs and alcohol, family relationships, world hunger, or a specific personal concern such as self-image, peer pressure, or friendships. These are certainly significant issues, ones worthy of considerable discussion and reflection. A large number of resources make discussion and reflection possible.

The context for these issues and the perspective one would take, as well as the principles one would use, are rooted in basic realities of the gospel. For example, if a person does not understand the meaning of redemption, of our need for a Savior to overcome the impossible situation we are in, and of how God has given us in Christ the way to a new life, in which we can be what we were truly intended to be, then the Church's sacramental life will be essentially unintelligible and opaque. If a person does not understand the unique and irreplaceable role of the person of Jesus in our redemption, and how that is mediated through Scripture, and the teaching and life of the Church, then, following the teachings of Jesus will be subject to other factors, such as personal preferences, cultural pressures, and the opinions of the latest experts.

The underlying focus of our retreats reflects the significance of the basic gospel, covering topics such as, "Who did Jesus say he was?"; "What did he say about our condition?"; "What did he say sin was?"; "Freedom?"; "Truth?"; "Life?"; "Who is the Holy Spirit?"; "What do Jesus' passion, death, and resurrection mean?" The wonderful thing about topics such as these is that they form the backdrop for the whole Christian life, and provide the power to live it.

This reflects a fundamental principle of catechetics: didache (catechesis) is rooted in the kerygma (basic gospel message). Some time ago, Archbishop Patrick Flores of San Antonio remarked that many Catholics have been catechized without ever being evangelized. We have certainly found that to be accurate in our work with young people on retreats. I believe the real power of Christian life lies in the basic truths of Christianity. As we move more and more deeply into those truths, we will find more clarity, also more power to live their meaning in our lives.

I find it most interesting that when the gospel is presented, it often has an effect on the way young people experience the sacraments, particularly Eucharist and Reconciliation. At the end of our weekend retreats, we ask young people to share one or two things that have had the greatest impact on them, things that made the most difference for them. The part of the weekend mentioned most often is the sacrament of Reconciliation. For many, it is a time for encountering the person of Jesus, finding in that encounter forgiveness, grace, healing, and life.

Sacrament finds it power and its source in the gospel. The gospel teaches who Jesus is and our proper response to him. Young people, older ones as well, are not noted for their frequent reception of the sacrament of Reconciliation. The experience of young people on weekend retreats gives clear indication of this sacrament's effectiveness when it is situated within the context of the basic gospel. We have found the same to be true for Eucharist.

This is not intended to imply that the situation in which the sacraments are celebrated creates the conditions for the grace of the sacrament. It is said simply to point out a major factor to fruitful reception of the sacrament. I do not mean to imply that all young people respond in the same way. The simple fact is that they do not. The major point that I want to make, however, is that the central truths of Christian life are found in Scripture. These truths are given to us so that we might know and have the power to live out the truth.

I want to make two more comments about the focus of our retreat program. The first has to do with some tendencies present in youth ministries today. Many today, who are active in youth ministry, either in a full-time or volunteer capacity, are searching for the "something" that will enable them to be more effective in their work with youth. Oftentimes, most often in desperation, the tendency is to grab hold of the latest idea or approach to helping young people deepen their understanding of and commitment to the person of Christ. The difficulty is when someone takes the latest approach, seeing in it the whole thing.

More to the point, the danger is replacement of Scripture and the basic truths of the gospel with the latest approach. I have seen people like ourselves who have replaced the gospel with transactional analysis, or assertiveness training, or becoming your own person, or nondirective approaches to working with young people, or values clarification. The list can go on. None of these approaches can replace the gospel. They can be helpful once they have been measured against the gospel.

The second comment is related to the first. In our desire to work effectively with youth, we run into frustration because, oftentimes, the young people are not, or do not seem to be, responding in a good way. This frustration can lead to the search for the "latest thing," which accounts for the tricks-and-gimmicks market in youth ministry. Young people can be difficult to work with. They can be unresponsive, or worse yet, responsive in the wrong ways. I do not want to convey, in my reflections on our retreat work, the impression that we have found a model that is guaranteed to reach, effectively, every young person and to help deepen relationships with Christ. We share in the frustrations and difficulties that go along with youth evangelism. We do believe that power to change young people comes through the person and work of Christ. Where Christ is preached and his Word taught, his life is released and the invitation is sent forth.

The primary thrust of our work continues to be evangelistic. The talks, music, drama, small groups, relationship-building, and liturgies are directed toward that one, basic end. There is a variety of ways that one basic end is approached, but the underlying direction is the same. A primary task is the development of ways to follow-up on the work that the retreat teams do. In our local area, we have weekly prayer meetings, monthly open-house liturgies, and a week-long leadership training session at our camp to offer some follow-up. We are seriously considering other means of follow-up. We hope to have begun use of more print and video follow-up resources, and to provide more training for leadership within the local area.

Our own movement in this area, and our growth in it, was not undertaken at our initiative. It was something that we happened into. We recognized the need, to be more deliberate and intentional in our future planning. We also do not want to plan ourselves out of God's leading and initiative. It is a delicate balance. And it is a balance we are praying to keep.

Chapter 4

Types of Youth Retreats

(B) Catechesis through Retreats

John Roberto

Most of the retreat programs offered for young people today are primarily evangelization experiences, focusing on developing a personal relationship with Jesus Christ in the context of supportive relationships and experiential activities. Evangelization retreats proclaim the Good News of Jesus Christ and invite young people to make the Good News their own by becoming disciples. They provide an excellent foundation for catechetical retreats, second-level retreats which would deepen and expand the young person's growth in discipleship. Without catechetical retreats the initial evangelization experience can wither and die.

The *Challenge of Adolescent Catechesis* provides guidance in differentiating the aims of evangelization retreats from catechetical retreats. Catechetical retreats seek "to sponsor youth toward maturity in Catholic Christian faith as a living reality" (*Challenge* 5). Catechetical retreats should aim "to foster in youth a communal identity as Catholic Christians and to help them develop their own personal faith identity" (*Challenge* 8). This first task calls us to "present the faith convictions and values of the Catholic Christian tradition and invite adolescents to adopt and own these values and convictions" (*Challenge* 8). The second task involves us in helping "adolescents respond to God in faith, in prayer, in values, and behavior" (*Challenge* 8).

Retreats offer an excellent format for adolescent catechesis. They combine all the essential ingredients needed for effective catechesis in a conducive environment and concentrated time period: experiential learning, community building and social activities, small group learning, worship, sharing of religious experiences, one-on-one discussion, and sacramental celebration.

HOLISTIC APPROACH TO CHRISTIAN FAITH

Catechetical retreats need to embrace and promote a holistic understanding of the Christian faith. One of the foundational principles in the
Challenge states that adolescent catechesis "fosters Catholic Christian faith
in three dimensions: trusting, believing, and doing." Too often retreats
emphasize only the trusting or affective dimension of faith, neglecting the
believing (cognitive) and doing (lifestyle, action) dimensions. The trusting
or relational dimension of faith is very important. However, an overempha-
sis on the affect can easily lead to over-emotionalism on retreats thereby
inhibiting critical thinking on the part of the adolescents. Young people
need to be able to express what they believe and what they have learned
through the retreat experience. They need to be able to envision concrete
ways that can lead lives as disciples of Jesus Christ. Retreats that do not
promote these outcomes are not serving young people or the Catholic faith
very well.

DEVELOPMENTALLY, SOCIALLY, AND CULTURALLY APPROPRIATE

Catechetical retreats need to be planned around the developmental,
social, and cultural needs of adolescence, respecting the changing developmental and social characteristics of the various stages of adolescence. This
means providing a significantly different content and approach for younger
and older adolescents. Too often retreats are not grounded in a solid developmental, social, and cultural foundation. This can lead to poor selection of
appropriate themes or inadequate design parameters. Programs need to be
designed and conducted in light of the ability and readiness of young people. This effects topic selection as well as learning activities, schedules,
meals/snacks, community building and social activities, program intensity,
amount of sleep, etc. Planners must ask the question, "What is developmentally, socially, and culturally appropriate for these particular young people?"

A THEMATIC APPROACH

The *Challenge* provides a menu of faith themes which can be used in
designing catechetical retreats. As an essential part of comprehensive youth
ministry programming, catechetical retreats should be offered each season
or year as both an alternative scheduling format for young people and as a
way to deepen evangelization retreats. Consider offering the following faith
themes from the *Challenge* on overnight or weekend formats at least once
over several years of youth ministry programming. This will provide young
people with attractive options for their catechetical involvement in youth
ministry.

Faith Themes for Young Adolescents

Church — understanding and experiencing the Catholic Christian story and mission and becoming involved in the Christian community.

Jesus and the Gospel Message — helping younger adolescents follow Jesus, develop a more personal relationship with him, concentrate on the person and teaching of Jesus, discover what a relationship with Jesus means, and respond to Jesus from a growing inner sense of self.

Morality and Moral Decision-Making — applying Catholic Christian moral values as maturing persons who are becoming increasingly capable of using decision-making skills to make free and responsible choices.

Personal Growth — helping younger adolescents develop a stronger and more realistic concept of self by exploring who they are and who they can become.

Relationships — developing more mutual, trusting, and loyal relationships with peers, parents, and other adults by emphasizing skills that enhance and maintain relationships.

Service — exploring Jesus' call to live a life of loving service, discovering that such a life is integral to discipleship, developing a foundation for a social justice consciousness, and participating in service that involves relationships and concrete action.

Sexuality — learning about sexual development, understanding the dynamics of maturing as a sexual person within a Catholic Christian's value context, and discussing sexuality with their parents using a Catholic Christian value-based approach.

Faith Themes for Older Adolescent Catechesis

Faith and Identity — exploring what being a Christian, a Catholic, and a person of faith means and developing a personally-held Catholic faith.

The Gospels — understanding the historical and literary development, structure, and major themes of the four Gospels; and learning how to interpret the Gospels.

Hebrew Scriptures — understanding the historical and literary development, structure, and major themes of the Hebrew Scriptures and learning how to interpret the Hebrew Scriptures.

Jesus — exploring who Jesus Christ is in the Gospels and history; discovering the meaning of Jesus for the adolescent's life.

Justice and Peace — developing a global social consciousness and compassion grounded in the Catholic social vision and being attentive to the needs of those who are hurting and who are oppressed.

Love and Lifestyles — exploring maturing sexual identity; developing intimate, trusting, enduring relationships; and discovering how spirituality can be lived out through a variety of lifestyles.

Morality — developing an interiorized, principled moral value system and understanding the role of Christian conscience and moral decision-making in the development of this interiorized moral value system.

Paul and his Letters — understanding the historical context, literary style, and major themes of Paul's Letters; learning to interpret his writings; and discovering Paul as apostle, preacher, theologian, and man of faith.

Prayer and Worship — developing a personally-held spirituality and a rich personal and communal prayer life.

CATECHETICAL METHODOLOGY

Catechetical retreats needs to utilize an effective catechetical process which operationalizes the aim, tasks, and principles of effective catechesis. All too often retreats embody a deductive methodology. Recall the retreat programs that begin with a talk given by an adult or peer leader, followed by a discussion of the main points of the talk, followed by a creative activity to express what had been learned through the talk and discussion. Such a methodology begins with the scriptural-theological teachings that need to be impressed upon the retreat participants and then continues to reinforce these teachings through discussion and activity. This deductive methodology does little to draw out the lived experience of young people. It also runs the risk of suppressing the freedom of the young people by channeling their responses to agree with or adopt the teachings presented. Catechetical retreats need to use a different methodology.

The Challenge of Adolescent Catechesis offers another approach. "The fundamental process of adolescent catechesis involves discovering the relationship among the Catholic Christian tradition; God's present activity in the life of the adolescent, family, community, and world; and the contemporary life experience of the adolescent" (*Challenge* 8). This process is a dialogue between the life-world of the adolescent, with its joys, struggles, questions, concerns, and hopes; and the wisdom of the Catholic Christian tradition. Effective catechesis is in tune with the life situations of youth — their language, lifestyles, family realities, culture, and global realities. But effective catechesis does not stop here. It creatively and imaginatively presents the Christian message so that young people can understand it and interpret their life situation in light of it. This means that catechesis will challenge young people with the demands of Christian discipleship.

The process described above can be translated into all of our catechet-ical efforts. We can design catechetical retreat experiences which embody the central dynamic of engaging the life of the adolescent with the Christian tradition and fostering the kind of interaction that helps young people reflect on the wisdom of the tradition. Thomas Groome, in *Christian Religious Education,* has described a learning process which embodies a contemporary approach to catechesis. This learning process begins with the life experience of the young person, engaging him or her in critical reflec-tion on that experience, and then relating that experience to the Scriptures and Tradition. The process concludes by engaging the young person in reflecting on the meaning of the Scriptures/Tradition for his or her life and what the implications of these meanings are for his or her belief and lifestyle. The entire learning process can span one session, several sessions, or an entire course.

FOCUSING ACTIVITY

The purpose of the *focusing activity* is to bring the attention of the group to bear on the theme of the lesson or session so that the young people can begin to identify it in their own life, their family, culture, society, and church. The focusing activity is meant to grab the attention of the young people through an experiential learning activity. We are trying to help the young people look at their own activity (beliefs, values, attitudes, under-standing, feelings, and doing) around the theme for the session. Some learn-ing experiences need very short focusing activities because the topic is easy to draw out from their life experience and concerns (sexuality, personal growth, relationships, moral dilemmas). Other times we will need to be very creative to draw them into the topic because it may, on the surface, seem removed from their current life experience and concerns (Scripture, prayer and worship, justice and peace).

The focusing activity can be programmed in a number of ways. For example: group activity, story, poem, rock music and videos, a project, Scripture reading, role playing, field trip, movie/video, simulation game, creative art, case study, demonstration, reflection or questionnaire.

Movement One: Experiencing Life

Having focused young people on the topic/concept of the learning experience as it is already present in their own life experience, Movement One invites them to express themselves concerning this life experience. Movement One enables the young people to express their own life activity (knowing, action, feeling) or that of their community, ethnic culture, youth culture, dominant culture or society on the topic or concept of the learning experience. Young people are encouraged to express what they already know about the topic/concept, or how they feel about it, or how they understand it, or how they now live it, or what they believe about it.

Inviting the young people to express their life experience on the topic of the learning experience can be accomplished in a variety of ways: presentations, reflection questionnaires, drama/role playing, making and describing something, symbolizing or miming. Helping young people express their present action needs to done in a non-threatening way. Always make it clear that the young people should feel free to share or simply to participate by listening. Be sure to leave time for silence.

Movement Two: Reflecting Together

The purpose of Movement Two is to allow the young people an opportunity to reflect together on what they have expressed in Movement One about their own experience/activity. This will sometimes be intuitive as well as analytical. Movement Two engages reason, memory, and imagination. This is often done by sharing an actual story of their experience or an action they have taken. Young people are invited to reflect critically on the meaning of their own experience — share the consequences of their present experience/action and implications for the future.

An important element of Movement Two is engaging the young people in interpreting their life experience in the broader picture of their families, ethnic culture, youth culture, dominant culture and society. Each of these contexts influences the shape of their life. We need to engage young people in a critical reflection on the impact that society and culture has on their values and lifestyles. Young people are influenced by the media (through TV, commercials, music and videos) and the values of the dominant culture in the United States. Through critical reflection, young people are able to name the impact on their life. On many subjects, like sexuality and morality, we must deal with the messages young people receive from media and the dominant culture or the Christian message will not be heard. We cannot name these impacts for young people, but we can guide them to reflect critically on these influences, name it for themselves, open them to the Christian vision of life, and help them make decisions about values, attitudes and lifestyles.

Movement Three: Discovering the Faith Story

Movement Three presents the *Story* and *Vision* of the Catholic Christian community in response to the topic or concept of the learning experience. The *Story* is a metaphor for the whole faith identity of the Christian community. Here the young people encounter the *Story* of faith that comes to us from Scripture, Tradition, the teachings of the Church, and the faith-life of Christian people throughout the ages and in our present time. The *Vision* is a metaphor for what the *Story* promises to and demands of our lives. It is God's Vision of God's Reign (the Kingdom of God). We engage young people in exploring how we are called to faithfully live God's Vision, individually and as a community — at the personal, interpersonal, and social/political levels of human existence.

From a Christian faith perspective, it is within the *Story* and *Vision* that we interpret, make sense out of and respond to our own stories and vision. In Christian faith, our own stories must be interpreted within the Christian Story — in dialogue with it. Own own visions must be critiqued and lived within the Christian Vision — in dialogue with that Vision.

Sharing the *Story* is accomplished through a variety of means: presentations, guided study (of the Scriptures), media (film, filmstrip, music), reading, discussion, research, field trip, group project, demonstration, or panel presentation. We seek to involve both the teacher and the learner in sharing the *Story* and exploring the *Vision*. Young people need to be actively involved in Movement Three. We should not encourage passive reception of the *Story* and *Vision*.

It is important to keep in mind the following points as you prepare Movement Three: 1) The *Story* shared reflects the most informed understanding the community (magisterium, scholars, faithful) knows at this time; 2) The *Vision* proposed and the *Story* shared promotes the values of God's Reign in people's lives — peace, justice, love, freedom, life, and wholeness; and 3) The *Story* and *Vision* engages the participants: touching the focus, stories, visions of their lives as expressed in the Focusing Activity and Movements One and Two.

Movement Four: Owning the Faith

Movement Four provides the young people with an opportunity to compare their own life experience and faith with the *Story* and *Vision* of the Catholic Christian community. Through this dialogue young people can test out their experience and their experience can be informed by the Christian Story and Vision. The *Story* will confront, challenge, affirm, and/or expand the faith of young people. The purpose of Movement Four is to enable the participants to take the *Story* and *Vision* back to their own life situations, to appropriate its meaning for their lives, to make it their own. It attempts to promote a moment of "aha" when the participants come to know the *Story* as their own, in the context of their lives.

There will be as many responses to this dialogue as there are young people. It is vitally important at this step to allow young people the freedom to come to their own answers and conclusions. With this freedom young people can be guided to see the "why" of the Christian Story and Vision.

Movement Four can be accomplished in a variety of ways: reflection questionnaire comparing Movement One and Two responses with the Movement Three story; creative expression of one's learning by writing, creating a role play or a dramatization or a case study, creating an audio-visual presentation (video, slide show), creating a symbol or poster; group activity/discussion; imagination activities where young people envision how they can live the learnings from the session.

Movement Five: Responding in Faith

The purpose of Movement Five is to help bring young people to a lived faith response. By inviting young people to decision, the fifth movement aims to help them translate their learning into a lived faith response. Once again, applying the learning from the learning experience must be a free response. Some young people will be changed by the learning experience and motivated to concrete action, while others will need time to ponder its meanings and implications, and still others will not be affected by the learning experience. We must provide an environment which invites a faith response, a decision for living more faithfully as a Christian, but respects the right of young people to choose their own response, even if it is not the response we had hoped for.

Responding in faith will affect the three levels of human existence: the personal, the interpersonal/communal, and the social. To help young people respond in faith, we need to probe the implications of their learning for all three of these levels of life. We can engage them in developing concrete plans for the coming week (personally, interpersonally, socially); in individual or group action projects which involve them in living their faith (action in the faith community, school, family, community/society); in prayer experiences which celebrate or draw young people into reflection on their response; and in journaling activities where they can reflect on how they are living their faith.

DESIGNING CATECHETICAL RETREATS

Structuring catechetical retreats needs to be conducted differently than is the case in evangelization retreats. In structuring catechetical retreats, work with longer blocks of time. For example, on a weekend retreat there are a total of six 2-2 1/2 hour sessions available for conducting learning experiences. The overnight model makes available three or four 2-2 1/2 hour learning sessions. In effect, a weekend or overnight catechetical retreat offers a new and enriched context for conducting a mini-course.

Using Shared Christian Praxis, you can structure a catechetical retreat in at least two different ways. The two approaches outlined below work with a weekend format (Friday evening - Sunday afternoon).

Approach 1 — One Theme, One Shared Praxis Cycle

The first approach organizes the five movements of Shared Christian Praxis around the six sessions of the weekend, exploring one particular faith theme. Schematically it might look like this:

Friday Evening: Session 1 — Focusing Activity

Saturday Morning: Session 2 — Movement One

Saturday Afternoon: Session 3 — Movement Two

Saturday Evening: Session 4 — Movement Three

Sunday Morning: Session 5 — Movement Four

Sunday Afternoon: Session 6 — Movement Five

In addition to the learning sessions, time for community building, social and recreational activities, prayer experiences, one-on-one discussion, and sacramental celebrations would be added.

Approach 2 — One Theme, Six Topics, Each with a Complete Shared Praxis Cycle

The second approach takes an overall theme and identifies six topics which explore the theme (similar to a mini-course with six sessions and six topics). Planners need to organize the topics into a six-session sequence, selecting one topic as the focus for each retreat session. Using Shared Christian Praxis, planners would design each individual topic/session using all five movements of praxis. In effect, each session becomes a self-contained learning experience. The six topics/sessions together form a sequential catechetical retreat, systematically exploring one faith theme.

Schematically it might look like this with each session encompassing all five movements of praxis:

Theme: Gospels

Friday Evening: Session 1 — How the Gospels Were Written

Saturday Morning: Session 2 — Gospel of Mark

Saturday Afternoon: Session 3 — Gospel of Matthew

Saturday Evening: Session 4 — Gospel of Luke

Sunday Morning: Session 5 — Gospel of John

Sunday Afternoon: Session 6 — The Gospels in My Life

In addition to the learning sessions, time for community building, social and recreational activities, prayer experiences, one-on-one discussion, and sacramental celebrations would be added.

WORKS CITED

The Challenge of Adolescent Catechesis. Washington DC: NFCYM Publications, 1986.

Groome, Thomas. *Christian Religious Education*. San Francisco: Harper and Row, 1980.

Roberto, John. *Adolescent Catechesis Resource Manual*. New York: Sadlier, 1988.

Chapter 4

Types of Youth Retreats

(C) Spiritual Direction in Youth Retreats

Dennis Kurtz

NOTES ON ADOLESCENT SPIRITUALITY

Recent studies on the social, psychological, cognitive, and moral development of the adolescent give us the basis from which we gain better insight on adolescent spiritual development. Adolescence is the time for searching — for the meaning of life, for self, and for religion beyond the superficial. There is a transformation, a conversion happening to the adolescent. Conversion from the vague, pietistic faith of childhood to a committed faith in Jesus Christ, for example. This transformation is a movement "from a voluntaristic attraction toward an ideal, to the fidelity of response to . . . personal calling" (Babin 54).

Even though the adolescent is only a "novice at spirituality, adolescents begin to experience life in transrational, paradoxical and mysterious ways" (Kraft 14).

William Kraft, in "Spiritual Growth in Adolescence and Adulthood," identifies three interrelated processes within any stage of spiritual growth, "transition, crisis and implementation" (Kraft 15). Transition is the threshold experience of leaving one stage and moving into the next stage. Crisis is a housecleaning period. One throws away no longer useful things to make room for new things. The greatest dilemma is deciding what is no longer useful. The process of incorporating new found understandings about the meaning of life is implementation. This is a less tumultuous phase. One can now fully integrate the resolutions made from the crisis phase into one's everyday living.

James Fowler clarifies this in view of adolescent faith. Fowler sees transition within various faith stages in the human life-cycle. When one sees serious contradictions within a given stage of faith-development, one is enabled to pass onto the next stage. According to Fowler's schema, Stage 3, Synthetic-Conventional Faith, is appropriate to the adolescent. The transition which the typical young adolescent experiences is departure from Stage 2, Mythic-Literal Faith, which is characterized by beliefs that are "appropriated with literal interpretations, as are moral rules and attitudes. Symbols are taken as one-dimensional and literal in meaning" (Fowler 149). Crisis is then experienced. The typical adolescent worldview extends beyond family to school (and work) groups, peer groups, religious groups, and influence by media. Such influences can conflict with one another, thus forcing the adolescent to choose one group over others. At such points, the adolescent calls upon faith to provide a coherent orientation in the midst of that more complex and diverse range of involvements. Faith must synthesize values and information; it must provide a basis for identity and outlook. (Fowler 172)

Implementation by adolescents, usually between ages 16 to 18 according to Kraft, includes initial experiences of living out one's discovered spirituality. Fowler would see this as the beginning of transition into the next stage of faith-development, Stage 4, Individuative-Reflective Faith.

Let us look closely at several other areas of adolescent spiritual development: morality, value systems, and prayer life.

Adolescent morality is often described as conventional morality. Lawrence Kohlberg has pointed out that first evidence of postconventional morality is found in adolescence in youth's push for autonomous moral principles. But the key to understanding Kohlberg here is to see that postconventional morality is only first possible in adolescence. Adolescence, however, is not usually characterized by the moral conduct of a postconventional agent. Thus, in reality, the adolescent lives on an edge, in the transformation between conventional and post-conventional moral thinking. Charles Shelton has pointed out that Kohlberg, in recent writing, notes that the realistic reasoning process employed by the adolescent is conventional reasoning. According to Lawrence Kohlberg, then, adolescents predominantly operate in two conventional stages of morality: 3 — "approved good behavior," and 4 — "the law and order" orientation. (Kohlberg 1981)

The classic view of Kohlberg's conventional morality, Stage 3, is the Golden Rule. The next development in conventional moral thinking is characterized by adherence to institutional law and order. Adolescents in this stage become very self-righteous and see things in absolutes. Compare this adolescent attitude with the Pharisees. Pharisees used law and order to underscore their self-righteousness.

Youth workers are challenged to use the adolescent's ongoing process of self-discovery to make him more aware of this particular attitude, and to temper youth's idealism with reality and acceptance of their humanness. A counterpart to the Pharisees, the Publican, can perhaps lend us an image that will give adolescents insight into what it means to be truly righteous.

Adolescents also compartmentalize behaviors. Individuals act one way around home, other ways at school, and still other ways when with particular friends. This occurs for two reasons. Acceptance by all significant others is important. Second, because sense of self is still developing, an adolescent cannot have a personally owned morality; rather he or she holds a group morality. At best, adolescent morality is chameleon-like, changing to blend with adolescents' particular groups or life situations. An adolescent advanced in his or her cognitive development may be able to recognize this and move beyond this conventional behavior, as Kohlberg has noted.

Adolescent value systems are likewise characterized by conformity, "that is to say, the ideas, expectations, and views of others are internalized in order to foster a growing identity." (Shelton 70) An adolescent constructs his value system by questioning and by relying on significant others to help him arrive at answers.

As the world becomes more complex, the adolescent realizes there are many roles to play given the many social groups in which he or she participates. Also, "mutual expectations of self and others emerge along with deepening relationships with significant others." (Shelton 70) There are two dangers to consider. It is very important for the individual to have a significant other or others with whom one can articulate and explore values. A "truncated value system in which the adolescent simply buys into the values" (Shelton 72) held by significant others must be avoided. One working with adolescents, as a significant other, must pay particular attention to this. Some adolescents fail to develop good interpersonal relationships. An adolescent who fails to develop interpersonal relationships does not have the all-important significant other. Thus, when a crisis arises, or when contradictions within life are experienced, there is no one to whom the youth can turn. Despair may result. The youth may opt to forego human relationships and turn to God and religion. This kind of relationship with God is one of compensation, therefore unhealthy.

The role of significant others (including God) in adolescent life is paramount to the development of adolescent moral values. One experiences those virtues lived out by significant people and adopts them. In imitating significant others, adolescents discover that what I was when I did it is more important that simply what I did.

Within adolescence, there is great sensitivity to the sacred. A true sense of sacredness, in addition to the search for significant others, makes adolescence a prime time to introduce, or reintroduce, individuals to prayer.

Prayer is a particular, personal relationship with Jesus Christ. As an adolescent develops solid, "significant other" relationships, the individual experiences the joy of faithfulness, through these relationships, and insecurity in the disappointments of these relationships. Introducing adolescents to Jesus as "significant other" enables them to "realize the joy and richness of Jesus' love (Shelton 129), and helps them experience the faithfulness (*hesed*) of Christ. It is easier to move adolescents into prayer when they have established personal relationship with Jesus.

How do we move adolescents toward a personal encounter with Jesus? Most important in meeting Jesus is having someone introduce him to you. Prayer maintains the relationship and sets time for solitude. Given the busy adolescent life, in which there is seemingly no time for quiet, how can one help an adolescent turn to the somewhat threatening experience of solitude? Charles Shelton suggests "for younger adolescents it is often helpful to work within a group setting. Group experiences can take place during a retreat, in a classroom, or in a group discussion" (Shelton 123). With older adolescents, facilitate experiences that are one-on-one or in small groups. For example, have older youths reflect on a significant relationship they presently have. Help them to clarify for themselves the importance of that relationship. How much time is spent together developing this relationship? How much energy is spent in keeping the relationship fresh and new? What role does communication play in this relationship? Then, ask them how much time they spend in relationship to Jesus.

It is important to challenge the individual to begin to spend time in developing a relationship with Jesus. If the challenge is given in a warm and encouraging manner, adolescents will be willing to give it a try. Facilitators of such experiences only set up a "blind date," introducing the adolescent to Jesus, but cannot be in control of whatever happens in the ensuing relationship.

Adolescents may be novices at spirituality. But there is a genuine hunger within them to know God in a personal way, a "God who knows, accepts and confirms the self deeply, and who serves as an infinite guarantor of the self with its forming myth of personal identity and faith" (Fowler 153).

SPIRITUAL DIRECTION AND THE ADOLESCENT

When the child grows up, he stumbles onto his true heritage at a particularly graced time, through sudden revelation with someone who knows the truth. Scales fall from the newly discovered one's eyes; a new dignity and purpose are born (Edwards 90).

In recent years, there has been a movement to reestablish spiritual direction. Based on classical models, for example, the Spiritual Exercises of St. Ignatius, the directee is brought to deeper relationship with Jesus through active prayer life and the reading of Scripture. I would like to define spiritual direction and, in light of adolescent development, explore how spiritual direction can be used to enhance adolescent spiritual growth.

Spiritual direction is a process entered into freely by director and directee to enable the directee to develop more fully his or her own relationship with God. Spiritual directors do not try to "create relationships between God and directee; they try to foster such relationships" (Barry and Connolly 31). William Barry and William Connolly indicate two fundamental tasks of the spiritual director: 1) help the directee pay attention to God as he reveals himself; 2) help the directee recognize his or her reactions and decide on responses to this God (Barry and Connolly 46).

A spiritual director does not need elaborate techniques, nor does he or she have to be from another world. Because of his or her own religious faith, the spiritual director is one open to and cognizant of the gentle movement of the Spirit within the directee. The real spiritual director is the Holy Spirit. There is a key difference between counseling and spiritual direction. Spiritual direction involves directees meeting Jesus in faith, through the guidance of the Holy Spirit. A talented spiritual director helps the directee work through personal religious experiences and see how they are connected to Scripture and the individual's faith tradition. It is sometimes necessary, as adolescents enter spiritual direction, to help them acquire a vocabulary to speak about religious experiences, old and new. Different authors use different imagery for the spiritual director: soul friend, guarantor, mentor, and spiritual friend. The purpose always remains the same: to strengthen the directee's relationship with Jesus, not with the director.

In his article, "Models of Spiritual Direction," David L. Fleming, gives us five different models of spiritual direction: 1) institutionalized; 2) interpersonal relationship; 3) charismatic; 4) sacramental; and 5) incarnational. I would like to describe briefly the fifth model, since it is referred to often today. Fleming explains:

Direction is seen in its ordinariness of one man helping another to clarify and objectify God's will in his life . . . This model of direction is also properly identified as incarnational in that no aspect of a person's life is left apart from the direction context, since man as a whole — physically, psychologically and spiritually — must grow in his response to God's unique call to him. (Fleming 355)

This holistic model can be most helpful in giving spiritual direction to youths. It deals with the whole person when it seems that everything that the directee has known for sure is suddenly changing. The adolescent experiences physical change, thus there is the search for self-identity. There arises a need to know a personal God. If in this crisis-centered time there is an individual available, such as a spiritual guide, to walk with the young person, not as someone who has it all together, but as a fellow sojourner, the young person will be able to have a place to go, not inhibited by any group pressures, to ask questions and deal with feelings about the whole tumultuous process.

A place of peace and quiet is needed in spiritual direction processes in which there is another, a spiritual friend, to help one to get in touch with God in times of transition.

Introducing adolescents to prayer and encouraging them to reflect always on life through prayer can create in adolescents a sense of sacred time, time to be with "my" God, time to speak to God from the heart. Spiritual directors help directees speak to God from their feelings. They encourage directees to "speak it as it is" with their God. Through such relationships, the adolescents will be better able to deal with faith crises; for they will have a sounding board, in prayer, a significant other, God. Granted, periods of deep questioning and struggles with organized religion will continue, yet a spiritual director can be a loving and caring person to go to honestly in such times.

Whenever one part of a person is enhanced, all the other parts of that person are given the opportunity to flourish. Spiritual direction can be a strong catalyst that helps directees continue the process of becoming whole. Human growth gives rise to cognitive skills that enable one to reflect and rationalize. These are skills needed in spiritual development, in discernment of one's personal relationship with God. Spiritual growth leads to greater self-understanding, enabling one to feel better about oneself and more able to relate to others. In relating to others, one discovers more about personal potential, about the world around us, and about the nature of God.

Spiritual training through spiritual direction can help adolescents take life's situations to God in prayer, good and bad experiences alike. It will help them take time to reflect on life and try to discern God's will. "As life affects us, God affects us, and as we react to life we react to Him" (Barry and Connolly 68).

Jesus' meeting with the woman at the well left her life changed forever. Christ enabled her to see the gift within herself; thus she was no longer thirsty. A spiritual director can guide adolescents to similar relationship with Jesus. Spiritual direction can enable the individual to recognize those gifts from God within himself or herself.

A question that stands at the horizon: can spiritual direction really be done with adolescents? The only conclusion is that spiritual direction is vitally necessary at this very pivotal time of life called adolescence.

Adaptations of existing models are needed. Adolescence is the time when the "raw material" is available. What a rich vein it is! The challenge is to develop and adapt models of spiritual direction that will perceptively meet the particular needs of adolescents — early, middle, and later adolescents. We should be compelled to accept the challenge. Tap the rich vein of spirituality found within adolescents.

IMPLICATIONS FOR YOUTH RETREATS

A vignette: On a recent retreat, I observed a boy sitting by himself, isolated from the group. When I drew near to share some words with him, I heard him ask, "Who will lead me into the heart of God?" I was stopped in my tracks. Who would lead him into the heart of God? I sat down in front of him. I took his hands. I said, "Together we'll go into the heart of God." (Theophane 54)

Retreats bring alive a faith tradition for youth, a vibrant, alive faith tradition, lived out by the people with whom they come into contact through retreat experiences. Retreats offer them opportunities to develop significant relationships with others, creating companions on the journey to the heart of God. Adolescents may be novices at spirituality but there is a genuine hunger within them to know God, in a personal way, a "God who knows, accepts and confirms the self deeply, and who serves as an infinite guarantor of the self with its forming myth of personal identity and faith." (Fowler 153)

Retreats assist in the holistic development of young persons. Even though retreats are varied in format and objectives, all can be significant opportunities for the spiritual direction of adolescents. Scripturally, the perfect model of spiritual direction is given to us in the story of the disciples on the way to Emmaus (Lk 24:13-35). As a spiritual guide, Jesus joins the disciples and listens to their story, listens to their fears, and their hopes, allows them to give meaning to the events in their life. Then, ever so gently, Jesus assists the disciples in taking their lived experiences and placing them, side-by-side, with the stories of Scripture. He helps them see the connection between life and Scripture, bringing scripture alive, showing its relevancy, and revealing God in their midst.

Spiritual direction for adolescents, usually, does not happen in the formal sense, with them calling you to set up appointments. Most times, it is very informal. Retreats often create environments in which youth experience the freedom to explore the God question as well as life questions. The journey into the heart of God is best accomplished with a spiritual companion who is freely chosen. When individuals conducting retreats understand adolescent development (physical, emotional, and spiritual), they can serve as significant spiritual companions.

There are various ways by which informed spiritual direction can occur through youth retreat experiences. Consider these as components in the larger schedule of a day or weekend retreat. For instance:

(1) Guided meditation, in which youth can encounter Christ. Provide structured experiences of guided meditation that have clear direction, and a facilitator who understands the objective of the exercise and steps to process the experience with youth afterwards.

(2) Use of music, both liturgical and contemporary. This should address faith themes as life issues that can serve as a basis for reflection. Often, it is very helpful to have questions to guide youth during music reflection time. Process the experience in small-group discussion, in large-group activity, in a prayer service, or some type of para-liturgical experience.

(3) Emmaus walks. In these, youth, two-by-two, can explore their life experiences — the joys, the hurts, the challenges — and draw meaning from them. Team members, then, can assist youth in sharing appropriate Scripture passages. Have youth discuss the parallels between their life experiences and Scripture.

(4) When prepared well, the sacrament of Reconciliation can be a powerful experience of spiritual direction. The sacrament must be placed in a context that is appropriate to the nature of the sacrament, as well as the flow of the retreat. Liturgical directives should, also, be observed. When a quality prayer service precedes the opportunity for confession, youth usually are open to the sacrament. Time should be planned so individual youth can feel free to spend time with a confessor they choose. Having other adults available, so youth can talk with them, if they wish, can also be a quality experience for youth.

(5) Quality prayer and liturgical celebrations. Youth are spiritually aware, and search for ways to connect with their God and the community around them. Ritual is a way to connect with both. Youth respond well to well-done, appropriate ritual. If we reflect, as adults, on the lives of youth today, we can see many rituals, e.g., homecoming week at school, football games. These are not sacred rituals, but they are significant rituals in their lives. As a Church, we have wonderful rituals which, when done well, allow youth to participate in significant ways. Music also is significant. Youth often write me after a retreat experience and ask for a copy of the music I used. When I ask why, usually they respond, "So I can listen to it at night before I go to bed, or while I am doing homework." I have come to the conclusion that songs touch their lives significantly. Music continues to do so long after retreat experiences. Young persons move to reflective, even meditative levels in such moments.

(6) The use of Scripture. This can be a way to assist in the spiritual journey to the heart of God. Scripture is folded into the fabric of retreat experiences and retreat team members exemplify Scripture values in their conduct. Scripture can be used, very effectively, on retreats when speakers demonstrate its connectedness to human life, rather than only using Scripture to preach from. In using Scripture effectively on retreat experiences, we set up time capsules. Triggered by life experiences, they open up after retreats, enhancing the spiritual journey of the participant.

There are many ways that spiritual direction can occur within retreat experiences. We are challenged to integrate such spiritual encounters into the fabric of our retreats. We must have adults trained to direct and process these experiences so that, in all things, youth are directed to God and not human gurus. Above all, we must always remember that the Holy Spirit is the true spiritual director. The adult in retreat ministry is but a mere instrument of our loving God bringing, in this case, youth to a deeper relationship with the divine.

WORKS CITED

Babin, Pierre. *Crisis of Faith: The Religious Psychology of Adolescence.* New York: Herder & Herder, 1963.

Barry, William and Connolly, William. *The Practice of Spiritual Direction.* New York: Seabury, 1983.

Edwards, Tilden H. *Spiritual Friend.* New York: Paulist, 1980.

Fleming, S.J., David L. "Models of Spiritual Direction." *Review for Religious* 34 (1975): 355.

Fowler, James W. *Stages of Faith: The Psychology of Human Development and the Quest for Meaning.* San Francisco: Harper & Row: 1981.

Kohlberg, Lawrence. *The Philosophy of Moral Development: Essays on Moral Development, Volume 1.* San Francisco: Harper & Row: 1981.

Kraft, William. "Spiritual Growth in Adolescence and Adulthood." *Human Development* 4:4 (Winter 1983).

Shelton, S.J., Charles M. *Adolescent Spirituality.* Chicago: Loyola University, 1983.

Theophane the Monk. *Tales of A Monastery.* New York: Crossroad, 1987.

Chapter 5

Conversion:
The Underlying Dynamic

Robert Duggan

(**Editor's Note**: The issues of conversion and faith-development patterns in human life, particularly how these relate to adolescent experience, were introduced in Chapter 2 and to a degree in Chapter 3. In this essay Robert Duggan examines the process of conversion at some length. The importance of his reflections should be readily apparent to those engaged in retreat ministries with and for young people. Faith-growth activities, such as retreats, call youth, in search of identity, hope, and answers about the future, to relationship with Jesus, to relationship with the church, and to lifestyle changes that motivate them to work for full realization of God's reign. Those who work with adolescents know youth's questions and their need to search and discover, in the caring company of others. They know that religious growth and change, for adolescents, often, is realized slowly, painfully, sometimes long after direct ministry with them has ceased.

In this piece, Fr. Duggan draws carefully from recent theological developments and Church documents to discuss the phenomenon of conversion, as it impacts adolescents, as well as persons at other stages of the lifecycle. Sensitively, he proposes a notion of conversion consistent with what has been said earlier in this volume. He proposes that conversion is process, gradually-evolving, of profound change for the whole person, by which one begins to consider, judge, and arrange one's life according to the love and revelation of God. This change occurs because true conversion means a personal change from within through which one becomes progressively more like Christ.

This essay emphasizes that conversion's arena is "ordinary life," that it grows through immersion in the world, its joys, hopes, sorrows, and in one's caring efforts to work for justice and social transformation. Fr. Duggan also identifies numerous, conversion-related themes which appear many times in this volume on retreat ministry to adolescents. He reminds us that every faith-development ministry seeks the conversion of others, conversion which is experienced, at its heart, as relationship with Christ; as a sacramental encounter; as a transforming reality; as a comprehensive, rhythmic, reconciling phenomenon which affects the whole person, cognitively, behaviorally, and affectively. This essay will provide you, likewise, with rich food for thought about the prayer and reconciliation experiences provided through adolescent retreats. As you read Fr. Duggan's words on the nature of the conversion process, keep in mind how each point can be applied to the specific retreat ministry activities in which we engage as we accompany young people on their spiritual journeys.)

In this essay we wish to consider the rich understanding of conversion which our tradition affords us, with the conviction that a better grasp of that elusive, mysterious reality will result in a more fruitful praxis of evangelization as well. The issue is an important one because we are exposed regularly to ideas about conversion which are defective, incomplete, or even erroneous. The issue is also a complex one, and its consequences are significant. If one misperceives the nature of the conversion experience, pastoral agendas can be off target, ecclesial structures deformed, and God's children led astray rather than in the paths of the Gospel. No more graphic illustration of this can be offered than the horrible events of November 18, 1978. On that day, 912 members of the People's Temple, a religious sect whose adherents had undergone a "conversion experience," gathered at the community's main pavilion and one-by-one consumed a strawberry flavored drink mixed with heavy doses of cyanide, tranquilizers, and pain-killers. "It is time to die with dignity," James Jones told his followers. And the converts came forward in orderly procession — infants first, followed by entire families — to play out the last bizarre act in a conversion journey that had gone from trust to madness.

Jonestown was admittedly a unique situation. But conversion, even healthy and authentic conversion, has always operated at the limits of "common sense." The early Christians sang joyful songs as they entered the amphitheater to die; Francis of Assisi's conversion led him to strip naked before the bishop in the town square; Martin Luther's conversion led him out of the Church of his birth; Spanish conquistadores "converted" the natives of the New World under the threat of death. The examples could be multiplied many times over, but the point should be obvious. In dealing with conversion we treat a volatile reality with explosive potential. Lest it destroy the very faith it is meant to evoke, the ministry of conversion which we exercise must be based on sound understandings and solid tradition.

AN AMERICAN IMAGE OF CONVERSION

The reflection on conversion which this essay suggests is particularly appropriate in this volume. Christian people of every time and place have had their unique ways of understanding conversion and evangelizing. The American people, however, are second to none in the cultural importance they attach to a religious conversion experience. Ours is a nation whose founders sought a place of freedom to live out the consequences of their religious faith, and our cultural mythology is inextricably linked to many of the great biblical conversion motifs. The New England Puritans nurtured on John Bunyan's *Grace Abounding to the Chief of Sinners*, his spiritual autobiography, developed a deep sensitivity to religious experience through their constant preoccupation with the inner workings of grace. Under the psychological sophistication and theological acumen of Jonathan Edwards, a refined image of the conversion experience received a distinctively American stamp. It was this image which the Great Awakening of 200 years ago saw translated into revivalism, an evangelization strategy which flows directly from a particular vision of conversion.

That characteristically American approach to conversion and evangelization is deeply imbedded in the national consciousness, thanks to a series of powerful preachers from Billy Sunday to Billy Graham. This approach, which can be aptly described as a "fundamentalist understanding of conversion," is constantly reinforced in the media, with stories of dramatic conversions to exotic religious cults and with intense personal witnessing from prominent "born-again" personalities, eager to share their conversion experience with others.

Our reflection from the American perspective cannot ignore this fundamentalist understanding of conversion, since traces of its influence are to be found within our Catholic communities as well. But the breadth of the theological and ascetical traditions to which we as, Roman Catholics, are heirs allows us to critique its adequacy, noting its shortcomings and offering richer alternatives.

The image of conversion operative in the fundamentalist perspective is powerfully evocative, charged as it is with religious story and symbol that resonate with the high drama of great figures from the pages of Scripture and heroes of the Christian faith throughout the centuries. Who could fail to admire the example of a St. Paul or a St. Francis of Assisi?

But fundamentalist conversion is also a two-edged sword: its very drama is its own undoing. Because it stereotypes the "born-again" experience in such powerful terms, it sets up an unattainable ideal as the norm for every believer. Like every stereotype, it betrays the very reality it purports to describe. Because it reduces the conversion experience, in a sense, to its "essentials," great clarity is achieved. The fundamentalist expects one who is born again to be able to pinpoint and describe the moment of transformation. But its description is so rigidly enforced that the variety of religious experience is suppressed and narrowed excessively. Whatever does not fit the classic pattern — a time of suffering which leads to a moment of crisis, an awakening in that moment both to sin and to personal salvation from Jesus, and a transformed consciousness characterized by joy and peace of soul — is disqualified and excluded from consideration as authentic spiritual conversion.

The emphasis is on the event, to the detriment of the process. The experiential base is exaggerated to the point of demanding a focused, explicit awareness and a charged emotional tonality. The hidden, quiet workings of the Spirit are ignored or minimized, and the gradual awakening as faith develops seems discounted entirely. Such is the classic American image of conversion within the fundamentalist context.

A ROMAN CATHOLIC IMAGE OF CONVERSION

We call attention to this stream of our American heritage, not only that it might serve as a counterpoint to our rich and, we believe, more nuanced Catholic understanding, but also because it has not failed to have an impact on the shape which Catholic evangelization has sometimes taken in our country. While the fundamentalist perspective is not without its merits, as we have indicated, our remarks would like to suggest the advantages of rooting our praxis more thoroughly in the best of contemporary Catholic theological reflection on conversion.

A BIBLICAL THEOLOGY OF CONVERSION

One of the great strengths of Catholic theology today is that it has recovered its scriptural roots. Reflection on conversion, too, has profited from this return to the sources of faith, especially in the pages of Sacred Scripture. Unlike the fundamentalist reading of Scripture, however, Catholic theology has incorporated the critical approaches of contemporary scholarship in its retrieval of the biblical data. This means that a Catholic biblical theology of conversion recognizes that there is no single understanding of conversion normative for all of Scripture. Rather, there are many understandings operative, some complementary and others that seem to compete.

The Hebrew Scriptures contain classic prophetic notions of conversion that reflect an evolving personal sense of sin, together with a progressive interiorization of the idea of return to covenant fidelity. Also present in the Hebrew Scriptures are the Deuteronomic writings whose theology of conversion stresses more the repetitive cycle of grace-apostasy-punishment-repentance, as well as later, more legalistic notions of conversion as obedience to the Torah or the performance of cultic ritual.

It is in the Christian Scriptures, however, that a contemporary biblical theology of conversion has been most richly nourished. There, too, scholarship has recognized various strata in an evolving understanding which stretches from John the Baptizer's cry for metanoia to the Johannine corpus' developed reflection on the dynamics of faith. The conversion preached by John the Baptist was a reviviscence of the prophetic demand for purity of heart. But his linkage with a once-and-for-all water rite and his strong eschatological focus on the One who comes was a distinctive break with all that preceded him.

By his own baptism in the Jordan, Jesus affirmed the rightness of John's message, but he thereby also enacted prophetically Israel's repentance and acceptance of salvation — its conversion. This "source experience" for Jesus became the raison d'etre for his joyful proclamation of the good news, which sets off his call for metanoia (Mk 1:15) from the grim warnings of the Baptist.

The call for conversion on the lips of Jesus, in fact, took the form of a proclamation of God's reign and an invitation to enter into its reality. By word and deed, in the parables he told and in the lived parable of his ministry, Jesus made present the human possibility of an entirely different kind of existence, which he termed the kingdom or reign of God. By embodying the gracious love of a God whose unconditional offer of salvation was available to all, Jesus made conversion a matter of relationship and discipleship with him in that kingdom.

A biblical theology of conversion moves from this level of the first disciples' following of the earthly Jesus, to the decisive shift which occurred in the Easter event. Henceforth, conversion was to Jesus as the Christ, the risen One. He who proclaimed the kingdom becomes himself the object of proclamation, and conversion assumes new meanings in the experience of the post-resurrection apostolic community.

From there, one can trace the developing theologies of conversion within the different communities responsible for the formation of various Gospel and epistolary traditions. The Matthean community's preoccupation with Church order resulted in different emphases than those found in a Lucan community, with its universalist perspective and its more developed pneumatalogy. Pauline and Johannine theologies of conversion similarly show different concerns and emphasis.

The result of all this contemporary scholarship has been a tremendously invigorating stimulus to those concerned with the mission of

Christ's followers in the modern world. A much more nuanced scriptural vision allows a kind of reflection which is open to a variety of pastoral options. By showing how different understandings of conversion, even within the New Testament era, resulted in different pastoral emphases and ministerial initiatives, we are encouraged to greater flexibility and creativity in our own efforts. By highlighting the interrelationships between these factors, we are encouraged to a more critical reflection on our own praxis and the vision which underlies it.

A LITURGICAL THEOLOGY OF CONVERSION

We move now to a second contribution which Catholicism brings to reflection on conversion. From earliest times our tradition has looked upon liturgy as the primary embodiment of the faith of the Church. Creed, dogma, and teaching are all derivative in the sense that they attempt to articulate an experience of faith which is first lived at worship. *Lex orandi, lex credendi,* the Latin adage which attempts to capture this insight, means that a reliable guide to the belief of the Church can be found in the lived faith of the Church at prayer.

For our purposes, we turn to two primary liturgical sources in our effort to derive a thoroughly Catholic understanding of conversion. The rites of Baptism and Penance are the Church's two major rituals of conversion which promise to yield important data for those who wish to minister more effectively to the conversion experience. A careful reading of the Rite of Christian Initiation of Adults (RCIA) should be a primary source for Catholic evangelizers and retreat ministers, inasmuch as its whole focus is the Church's care for the conversion journey of those to whom she reaches out. Secondly, but also importantly, the Rite of Penance (RP) which deals with continuing conversion should be allowed to focus our understandings of conversion and shape our ministry of pastoral care.

We cannot explore in detail the richness of the RCIA's vision of conversion and evangelization any more than we were able to exhaust the contributions of biblical theology. But a schematic overview of what the RCIA can teach us about conversion will hopefully be suggestive of the possibilities in a more careful review.[1] Analysis of the Introduction and prayers of the RCIA reveals that a Catholic liturgical theology of conversion is summarized in the following six points:

1) *Conversion is understood as entrance into a covenantal relationship.* At root, the conversion experience is a matter of human response to divine initiative. This implies the priority of the divine call, but it also underlines the element of human freedom in accepting or rejecting that call. In addition, using the metaphor of covenant highlights the fact that

conversion deals with an interpersonal relationship in which there has been a mutual commitment by both parties. The polarities of this image help to contextualize the tensions of growth, as well as reinforce the need for constant renewal of fidelity amidst the developments of a changing relationship.

2) *Conversion is radically Christocentric.* This affirmation, which is repeatedly made in the prayers and rites of the RCIA, reminds us both of the foundation and of the direction in every authentically Christian experience of conversion. It is to Jesus Christ that one turns, none other. The transformation called for is a "putting on" of the Lord Jesus Christ, so that ultimately one may proclaim with St. Paul that "I no longer live . . . Christ lives in me" (Gal 2:20). By proposing the paschal mystery of Jesus as the heart of conversion, the RCIA speaks to a fundamental pattern of experience which must be assimilated in the process of spiritual growth. In fact, the closest the Rite comes to an actual definition of conversion is found in the Introduction (#8) where it refers to a person's "sacramental sharing in the death and rising of Christ."

3) *Conversion is a thoroughly sacramental experience.* This is to be understood in two senses. First, the interior spiritual reality of transformation into Christ must of necessity be embodied. Ours is a profoundly incarnational faith, and we instinctively insist that spiritual experience be enfleshed in the lived reality of daily existence. There is no room for Gnostic dualism in this vision. Conversion, we are told, is sacramentalized in the converted life.

Second, conversion is sacramental in the sense that participation in liturgical ritual is integral to the experience. The celebrations of the conversion journey provided in the RCIA are not mere window dressing. They express and effect what they signify. By giving voice to the awakening of the Spirit's life in an individual, the rites celebrated become constitutive ingredients of the developing conversion, not only articulating that experience but supporting and building it as well.

4) *Conversion is an essentially ecclesial event.* The RCIA reminds us that conversion occurs "step by step in the midst of the community" (#4). Any conversion experience that remains individualistic and leads to religious privatism is defective in this view. The Christ to whom we turn is found in his body, the Church, and to escape from God's people is to flee from God. Our evangelization, then, is a call not just to an experience of Jesus as personal Lord and Savior. It is to an encounter with the living Christ incarnate in the Church of every age. Conversion, according to the RCIA, involves developing more and more ties to a particular community of believers and making that foundational commitment to God via a whole network of interpersonal relationships. Conversion is also ecclesial in the

sense that the entire community is undergoing change, not just the new-comer. The Rite stresses that the faithful must accompany and support the new members by sharing their own conversion journey.

5) *Conversion is understood as a spiritual journey.* This insight of the RCIA uses the image of journey to convey the developmental nature of the transformation involved. Conversion is a process, not just an event. Unlike the fundamentalist stress on the decisive moment of encounter with Christ, the RCIA recognizes the gradual nature of growth in faith, without denying the importance of marker events as well. A journey has a beginning, middle, end.

Similarly, conversion unfolds sequentially in an individual's life. There are seasons and rhythms, and it is in the nature of things that this unfolding experience should ebb and flow. One should not harbor the expectation of a "spiritual high" indefinitely. Prolongation of such a state would more likely be the result of pathology than healthy growth. In fact, the "down" times are as much a part of conversion as the periods of exhilaration. Evangelization strategies aimed at artificially sustaining only one dimension of the conversion journey miss seasons of growth that are equally important. The journey theme also reminds us that conversion is a lifelong process, not something that ends with formal membership in the Church.

6) *Conversion is a comprehensive reality involving transformation of the whole person.* One of the most helpful insights of the RCIA is this reminder that every dimension of the human person is affected by the conversion experience. The social sciences speak of holistic growth as involving cognitive, affective, and behavioral components. This same balanced perspective can be verified in the RCIA's approach to conversion. Cognitive development is a constant concern of the Rite.

What is at issue here is not mere indoctrination, however. Conversion is about acquiring "know-how" as much as it is about the acquisition of new knowledge. New learnings must include the appropriation of a specific tradition, but this entails an intuitive feel for the "Catholic thing" as well as mastery of Church teachings. Affective growth is expressed in the Rite in a variety of ways, but ultimately is a reminder that conversion is about falling in love — with God and with God's people.

As part of conversion one begins to speak the language of love and prayer both in the intimacy of solitude and in the exuberance of communal ritual. Conversion also means behavioral change, a break with sin, adoption of a specifically Christian ethic, and recognizable fruits embodied in the life of charity. Apostolic zeal, the witness of personal values, action for justice, responsive love, these are the ways in which conversion is lived out in the holistic understanding of the RCIA.

The constraints of a brief essay prevent us from a more detailed analysis of the RCIA's understanding of conversion and its implications for our retreat ministry praxis. We will now focus on another primary liturgical source for reflection on the topic of conversion, the Rite of Penance. Like the RCIA, this ritual was one of the last and most mature fruits of Vatican II's liturgical renewal. Its pastoral-theological Introduction is quite developed, its prayers and ritual forms are richly elaborated, and its lectionary is extensive.

While the RCIA focuses on the conversion experience of those entering the Church for the first time, the RP is focused on the conversion experience of the already baptized. Thus it nicely complements the RCIA and offers help with another group of persons who are the beneficiaries of evangelization, Catholics themselves. The insights of this document should be particularly valuable to those who minister to inactive Catholics and who are currently exploring pastoral structures for a more effective outreach and retreat ministry effort on their behalf.

What, then, does the RP tell us about ongoing conversion in the life of the believer? One of the most striking features of the renewed ritual mandated by Vatican II is the use of a new name to describe the sacrament: the Rite of Reconciliation.

This choice was not a casual one, as is evident from the fact that the Introduction devotes its opening paragraphs to an extensive reflection on the mystery of reconciliation in the history of salvation and in the life of the Church. By this change in terminology we are invited to a deeper awareness of how conversion involves the restoration of a reciprocal relationship between the penitent and God. The former terminology of "penance" or "confession" (which are only parts of the total sacramental experience) emphasized the human component alone. To speak of the effect of the sacrament only in terms of forgiveness of sins also exaggerates this focus on individualistic purification.

Reconciliation, however, evokes a balanced understanding of conversion as a response to the divine gift. The new ritual further redresses the imbalance by highlighting this divine initiative in yet another way. Each form of the Rite now includes a Liturgy of the Word which precedes the sacramental action. Christian conversion, it seems, is at root our response to the Word which invites us to salvation.

As with so many other areas of the Church's life in the post-Vatican II era, this restoration of the Word of Scripture to a place of preeminence in the RP has called attention to its crucial role in the dynamic of ongoing conversion. A significant relationship is only possible between those who come to know one another deeply, and the restructured RP constantly signals how crucial is the Word proclaimed in leading a penitent to know the Lord more clearly, to follow him more nearly, to love him more dearly.

Another feature of the renewed RP worth considering is the prominence it gives to the ecclesial/social dimension of both sin and reconciliation. Something important is being said in this about conversion as more than just an interior reality. It also involves reshaped relationships with the community and the larger world. In countless ways the Rite stresses that reconciliation to God happens through reconciliation to the Church.

Conversion to God is mediated by a communal experience, one in which both the penitent and the Church discover the Spirit at work as they reach out to one another. But lest conversion lead the Church and her members only to turn in on themselves, the Rite also stresses that authentic reconciliation leads to heightened awareness of the broader social needs. Conversion, we are reminded, enables one to "work with all men of good will for justice and peace in the world" (#5).

The Introduction to the RP contains its own descriptive definition of conversion. Using the traditional Scholastic framework of the "parts" of the sacrament (contrition, confession, penance/satisfaction, absolution), the Rite nonetheless reveals a thoroughly contemporary understanding of the process of conversion. Here conversion is described as "a profound change of the whole person by which one begins to consider, judge, and arrange his life according to the holiness and love of God . . . For conversion should affect a person from within so that it may progressively enlighten him and render him more like Christ" (#6a).

The focus here, in this section on contrition, is not on an introspective preoccupation with sin and guilt. Rather, healthy conversion has the sinner look to the Lord, where sin is seen as a betrayal of covenant love rather than narrowly perceived as a personal defeat.

The perspective is religious, not merely psychological, and offers a strong reminder that conversion is more than feelings. The essence of conversion, in this view, is an experience of God which transforms, one that lifts us out of our sinful self-preoccupation and "turns us around" by a taste of God's unconditional offer of love.

The second "part" of the sacrament, confession, further specifies an essential element in the conversion process. Historically, this component of the ritual was more an act of praise ("confessio laudis") than a self-accusatory recitation of personal faults. But even with this latter emphasis in which the RP still preserves, there is evidence of a recovery of the earlier tradition. The "Proclamation of Praise," though separate now from the time for self-accusation, has been made integral to the Rite. This element of confession (whether of praise or of sin) makes some important contributions to our understanding of conversion.

Interior contrition alone results in a truncated experience of conversion. As embodied creatures in the world, our inner states cry out for expression in human terms. Our ecclesial identity likewise requires ecclesial recognition — both by us and by the community — of our conversion experience. Regardless of what form it takes, our "confessio" is a way of allowing our conversion to enter the world in a decisive way and become "real" in a more full manner.

Cultural and liturgical factors will continue to shape the sacrament's particular expression of this dimension of conversion, but the underlying necessity is unmistakable. In fact, in a retreat- and evangelization-focused ministry directed toward ongoing conversion, it seems important to provide opportunities for "confessio" both of human evil and of divine goodness. The pastoral structures of this "confessio" likewise would need to be both individual and communal if we are ministering to a balanced experience of conversion.

The third "part" of the sacrament, penance/satisfaction, further unfolds this imperative that interior conversion be given outward expression. The "penance" referred to here is a way of manifesting the transforming power of the Spirit in one's life, not a punishment for misdeeds. To be complete, conversion must issue forth in the fruits of a Spirit-led life.

Focus on this element in the process reminds us that "ordinary life" is the locus of all true conversion. Authentic conversion leads us not just to longer hours of prayer in the Church, but to a deeper immersion into this world, its joys and hopes, its griefs and sorrows. The Rite of Penance offers a perfect example here of the wedding of liturgy and life, reflecting how the conversion experience leads to a reconciled Christian existence in the world, an "ordinary life" that is a "holy sacrifice, truly pleasing to God" (Rom 12:1).

After focusing on these three "acts of the penitent," the Rite describes the final "part" of the sacrament, absolution. Here, too, something significant is being said about conversion. For the Christian, conversion is not complete unless it finds a responsive embrace in the bosom of the Church.

The priest's absolution is the present liturgical form to express this. Like all the parts of the sacrament, however, this ritual element is indicative of a much broader reality involved in the conversion process. *Pax cum Ecclesia*, peace with the Church, was one ancient way of describing the final resolution of the conversion experience. Understood merely in a juridical sense of receiving absolution, the expression trivializes conversion. But for one imbued with a deep appreciation for all that the Church is meant to be in the life of the believer, the expression is a fitting culmination to the Rite's overview of conversion. Peace with the Church, in this view, is peace with self, others, all creation, and God. It is final and complete conversion, an evocative symbol of that total reconciliation which awaits us on the final day.

AN INVITATION

Much, much more could be drawn from the Catholic tradition to enrich our understanding of conversion, and numerous implications for retreat ministries, and other forms of ministry, could be elaborated. But this essay is meant to be suggestive rather than exhaustive. We have tried to show how conversion, the underlying dynamic of faith-growth ministries, can be approached from a variety of perspectives. We began by describing the American fundamentalist notion of conversion, which we found wanting. We then turned to the Scriptures and the lived faith of the Church at worship as two sources from which to gain enlightenment.

We have left untouched the extensive reflection on conversion available today in teachings of the magisterium, in contemporary systematic theology, and in the social sciences. Those, too, merit careful attention and study. What we have done, hopefully, is to frame the issue of conversion as crucial to the tasks we are about in our ministries, and to introduce the reader to a process of reflection that will lead to an improved praxis. It is for the reader, now, to continue what has been begun here. [2]

ENDNOTES

[1] See the author's extended analysis of conversion in the RCIA in *Emphemerides Liturgicae* 96 (1982) 57-83, 209-252; 97 (1983) 141-223.

[2] Those interested in a deeper look at these issues might consider the following: (1) From a theological perspective: Robert Doran, *Psychic Conversion and Theological Foundations* (Chico, CA: Scholars Press, 1981); Donald Gelpi, *Charism and Sacrament: A Theology of Christian Conversion* (New York: Paulist Press, 1976); (2) From a social-scientific perspective: James W. Fowler, *Stages of Faith* (New York: Harper and Row, 1981).

Chapter 6

Spiritual Growth
and the Retreat Minister

Joanne Cahoon

(**Editor's Note:** During 1987, Joanne Cahoon, the author of this chapter, developed a questionnaire to assess attitudes and practices regarding personal spirituality among Catholic youth ministers. Approximately 250 copies of this questionnaire were disseminated, and results were incorporated into this essay. During the course of this essay, she will allude to findings drawn from her survey on youth ministers' spirituality.)

THE SPIRITUAL CHALLENGE OF THE MINISTER

Ministry means the ongoing attempt to put one's own search for God, with all the moments of pain and joy, despair and hope, at the disposal of those who want to join this search but do not know how. (Nouwen, *Creative Ministry* 114)

As Henri Nouwen describes, it is essential that we ministers have an ongoing search for God to put at the service of others. Our authenticity as ministers becomes clear when we effectively proclaim a reality beyond us. Genuine ministry flows from an openness in one's approach to life and to God — the openness the writer, artist, or musician knows in performing and creating. Creative vulnerability keeps us humble. It challenges us to remember that even though we spend every day communicating the symbols and riches of our faith; even though we have all the skills necessary to facilitate, to train, to invite, even to create community; even though we provide an atmosphere, many times, in which others are disposed to seek their God; we must seek and risk daily contact, in love, with the One Who Is.

The emphasis on ministry as a profession that has dominated our thinking during the past several decades may have led us to put too much confidence in our abilities, skills, techniques, projects, and programs. In so

doing, we have lost touch with that reality with which we are called to connect, not so much by what we do, but by who we are. (Nouwen, *Living
Reminder* 29)

The minister's spirituality is central to his or her ministerial formation. Persons doing ministry, who have wished to do ministry about God
but without God, have inhabited the Christian Church more often than we
like to acknowledge or imagine. (Finn 14) Young people are most adept at
recognizing when our words and ministry become hollow, not rooted in
balance and challenge, nor in prayer and searching. A parish youth minister
in West Virginia, has addressed this.

> "Working with youth challenges me spiritually because I can't pre-
> tend to be what I'm not — I have to live the values and faith I try to
> pass on to youth."

Of course, we youth ministers don't have to live up to what we say.
But if we don't, the young people for whom and with whom we work will
surely be able to identify it.

Tim Fallon claims that youth ministry "becomes a priority when the
Church is losing its ability to help youth grow up in faith." (Fallon 87)
Many adults (parents, educators, pastors) have become concerned with
youth's seeming lack of connectedness with church or lack of ownership in
faith. However,

> Youth do not grow up in isolation, and for the most part they reflect
> — although often with more intensity — the struggles of the entire
> Christian community.... One of the major reasons why the adult com-
> munity is having problems passing its faith on to youth is because we
> are not in touch with our own spirituality. (Fallon 87)

Retreat ministers and others engaged in youth outreach, at parish,
school, and diocesan levels, often become the chief means of connection
and communication between youth and the Church. True, youth ministry is
the responsibility of the front-line persons whom youth meet. Such ministers must be in touch with their own spirituality in order to share it. Many
have said for years, "What the young need today are not adults who will
hand over information, but adults who will hand over themselves and the
secret of their own faith." (*Vision* 10)

Young people engage, with intensity, in the struggle for personal
identity. Often, they do so without the benefit of strong systems of support
(for example, immediate and extended family, neighborhood, church).
Youth ministers create supportive, Christian contexts for young people. We
try to develop such contexts and communities, at least for the short-term, in
retreats for adolescents. As individuals, we should be signs of spiritual help
and assurance, not spiritual confusion.

If we are out of touch with ourselves, we will have difficulty listening to other people and understanding their experience. We too easily project our own needs and struggles onto them or we react out of our own unresolved conflicts, so miscommunication becomes the name of the game. (Seelaus 396)

We are called to be part of the divine movement which is ministry. Those who take on specific ministerial roles will discover particular opportunities and hazards. Such hazards make it clear that the ongoing, authentic spiritual and human development of the minister is necessary. Youth ministers, particularly, are challenged to authenticity. As one youth minister, working on a vicariate level in a Catholic diocese, puts it, "I am constantly forced to deal with how God relates to the lives of people I work with and therefore I have to struggle with naming how God is acting in my life. I am frequently challenged to live out that which I believe."

The Emmaus journey (Lk 24:13-35), as described in the landmark document, *A Vision of Youth Ministry*, clearly shows us the essential dynamics of youth outreach, within retreats and many other settings. (*Vision* 3) The story tells of Jesus traveling with two troubled disciples on a road, offering them his presence, enabling their questions, offering them a place and time to discover God in their lives, and then celebrating with them. The account is rich with ministerial parallels. Recently, while revising a senior retreat model for the high school in which I worked, the retreat director and I pulled together a retreat model based on this journey theme. As I have worked with this model through nine retreats, I have had a chance to play and pray with its implications. One of the riches of this theme is inherent in the term journey, implying movement.

Young people exhibit a certain passion for the journey. This draws me to them. It is one of the things I like most about them. Unlike some of their adult counterparts, they have not opted to stop moving, to merely watch others go by. They struggle and question. They wonder and re-articulate and search. This is due to where they are developmentally. Youth ministry should nurture this passion for the journey. It should enable youth to courageously engage in the search and struggle for deeper faith and greater authenticity. With retreats and other spiritual-growth endeavors, we offer adolescents nourishment as they travel. We offer hope, a community of pilgrims to travel with, and places to sit and refresh and renew awhile. Youth don't need youth ministers who have decided not to undertake the spiritual journey. Youth ministers cannot successfully help others to grow unless they themselves are involved in the growth process. Effective youth ministers, actively involved in growing, are prepared to take the next step into their own spiritual journey, unsettling though it may be. (Costello 41)

SPIRITUAL DEVELOPMENT OF THE RETREAT MINISTER: AN INTRODUCTION

Those who find themselves in ministry soon recognize that there are occupational gifts and hazards. I am reminded of the Chinese word for crisis, written as the combination of two individual characters, representing, separately, danger and opportunity. With respect to healthy human and spiritual development, there are specific dangers and opportunities which persons in ministry encounter because of the work they do.

In recognition of this dynamic, I asked some youth ministers to respond to several questions. I present and explore some of their comments and responses here. Before doing so, however, a few important preface statements are in order. First, some of the responses are specific to youth ministry contexts. Some, however, also apply to broader ministry contexts. Others approach what is at issue in being part of our Church today. Still others seem to wrestle with dynamics that are primarily part and parcel of living in contemporary culture. Responses, therefore, were quite broad in range with multiple interpretations possible. Therefore, I cannot pretend to specifically speak of occupational gifts and hazards to spirituality that only youth ministers or retreat ministers experience. It is the total church-and-societal context wherein ministers experience dangers to and opportunities for growth, in wholeness and holiness, today.

HAZARDS TO THE MINISTER'S SPIRITUAL WELL-BEING

"Spirituality is the most important aspect of my life; however, I don't find it easy to be nourished in this job. Funny, isn't it? It's what we're all about." This compelling comment, from a parish youth minister in Michigan, challenges each of us to look at what we're all about. Does our work make spirituality difficult to nurture? There seem to be three particular blocks to spirituality connected with an active ministry. These were often commented on by youth ministers participating in my recent survey. The first is familiarity with the sacred. The second: absence of sufficient relationships of support, both social and spiritual. The last, time, could itself be the sole subject of a chapter such as this. It was mentioned by almost every survey respondent.

FAMILIARITY

Familiarity breeds contempt. One minister quoted this old cliche in his survey. A different phrasing of this could read, "familiarity breeds absence of wonder." The vicariate-level youth minister, quoted earlier, also commented, "At times there is a tendency to say I am always working with the things of God and therefore don't need . . . quiet reflecting on his presence in my life." Another survey participant, a diocesan-level youth ministry leader, noted, "If I am working with God all day, busting my butt, he'll understand if I'm too tired to pray."

Amidst the tasks of ministry, ministers are inundated with the language, symbols, activities, and things that are "of God." These are our everyday tools, our professional languages, our work atmospheres. This is especially true for those involved, frequently, in leading and giving retreats. There can be an everydayness to our experience of the holy. Joanmarie Smith says,

> Work in the innards of organized religion can be disenchanting. That is, like Dorothy seeing how the Wizard constructed his production numbers in Oz, one may feel the magic is gone. Even as being abandoned on an island teeming with fruit one can lose the taste for fruit. (Smith 102)

There is a real need to constantly revitalize our experience of these "things of God." Otherwise our familiarity may become boredom and may tempt us to turn off the messages, or challenges, they bear for us. For those of us in ministry, the sacred must be a daily experience, but that need not profane it.

For years, I usually coordinated eight three-day retreats and four one-day retreats during the months of October through May. I have worked with more Lenten and Advent themes than I can even itemize; also liturgy themes, songs, program covers, creative processions, prayers, and Christmas services. These things have been part of my work. They could likewise be part of my prayer and holistic development when I allowed them to be. Similar themes, oft-used symbols, favorite Scripture passages, one more retreat. Consistent exposure to the sacred can make revered symbols or certain words find a home in us. As we come across these relatives of our heart, dwelling with us and in us, as we go about our duties, we find that continual exposure is enlivening. Not a source of boredom. A source of special nourishment.

If we strive to allow the sacred to find a home in us and teach us its mystery, we will find our daily exposure with the things of God to be gift rather than hazard. Our familiarity with the sacred will foster wonder. Boredom presumes we know all and have experienced all. Wonder opens us to new understanding, new experiences, and new depth to life.

ABSENCE OF SUFFICIENT RELATIONSHIPS OF SUPPORT

"The problem [for me] is that I don't feel close to other ministers. The ones I know are just not my friends. And the people to whom I am spiritually close have 'normal' schedules and so I lose touch with them often. It's a struggle, and is probably why I won't stay in the field."

The parish youth minister who wrote this quietly speaks for many. They express concerns about maintaining a sound relational network. Ministry scheduling can be erratic. One's primary energies and relational investments get directed into ministry. Weekends and evenings are often devoted to ministry activities, particularly if one is engaged in retreat-oriented work. Little is left for peer relationships, social friendships, or intimacy. Many dedicated ministers speak of having sacrificed potential relationships for their work. Others comment on the difficulties in simply remaining in touch with friends not in ministry. Yet, if our ministries are to be most effective, we need our own nourishing relationships to draw from. We need the support of friends we can depend on. Lacking sound relationships, our lives and work may simply become expressions of work addiction, "detached from life, distanced from others and terribly alone." (Helldorfer 200)

Relationships with others engaged in ministry may be collegial, but these are not always friendships, nor are they always supportive to a degree which could nourish spirituality. An area in which many of us could work is nurturing friendships within our field. I speak here of friendships that are personal, not merely professional. Times together in which youth ministers and retreat team members don't talk shop but simply socialize. Ministers' sharing of their relationships with and understandings about God will be more revitalizing than any professional discussion. I do not believe that a mature and healthy ministry is possible unless ministers minister first of all to each other. (Nouwen, *Living Reminder* 10) Many of us are accustomed to depending on each other for help with various projects, for fresh ideas, for retreat themes and models, for retreat activities and process, and for committee tasks. We identify each other's talents pretty well. We try to fill each other's calendars with "could you help out with . . ." But we could better fill each other's lives with productive, sincere, caring friendships, and with spiritual challenges.

All ministers must learn that time for themselves and for relationships is quality time, something that must be protected. One youth minister has said, "There is an importance in being good to yourself, e.g., rest, prayer, spiritual direction, play, and adult support groups." Time devoted to primary relationships makes us more whole — perhaps more holy, certainly more able to minister, particularly to adolescents and their families.

TIME

A question I asked on my recent survey read: What are some obstacles/traps/issues in your own spiritual journey that you have encountered due to work? "Time" was the (nearly) unanimous response. "There is always more work to do than hours in the day," one diocesan minister noted. We will always have young people among us. And, there will always be needs we would like to address. Effective management of time and energy will remain an issue for those in ministry to youth, as with most other human services personnel.

One danger, in working in situations in which there is always much to do, is that one can come to believe he or she must do it all. One begins to feel indispensable. I have been struck by a concept in the book, *Emerging Laity*. The Spirit honors absence. (Whitehead 25-33) Recently, as I was approaching my own final year of work in a high school, for which I had initiated a campus youth ministry and a student leadership model, this concept became especially important to me. James and Evelyn Whitehead speak of the Spirit's coming once Jesus had left, of new leadership and new talents which emerged once the old leadership had departed. Nouwen, likewise, cautions about ministers becoming almost too available at times.

We ministers may become so available that there is too much presence and too little absence, too much staying with people and too little leaving them, too much of us and too little of God and his spirit. It is clear that much of this is connected with a certain illusion of indispensability. (Nouwen, *Living Reminder* 48)

I focus here on an excess of presence and an unwillingness to be less than indispensable. We need to learn the art of creative withdrawal . . . "without this withdrawal we are in danger of no longer being the way, but in the way" of God's action in peoples' lives. We have time. We must decide maturely how to handle it. (Nouwen, *Living Reminder* 49) Almost any one of us involved with youth retreats, or some other form of ministry with adolescents, could agree, at times, with a diocesan youth minister from Pennsylvania, "The work is so intense and time consuming that often I do not have time for my own spiritual life."

Many participants responding to my survey spoke of difficulties in balancing time needed for one's own spiritual development and the demands of ministry.

"I have to be aware of burnout and lack of quality time for nourishing my inner self."
"It is often hard to balance time for ministry with time for reflective contemplation."

"I don't take time out to nourish myself and I lose my personal contact with Jesus."

"I think the biggest difficulty . . . is that we define our worth by the amount of stuff we're involved in, and that the staggering load of stuff pushes out the time and energy for spiritual renewal and development. The really terrible thing is that we all know this is the wrong way to be, but that we — I, anyway — feel powerless to change it. This is a source of great frustration to me. I guess what I'd like to find out . . . is how people fight this, and how they over come it. Because it's clear to me that a great deal of youth ministry is coming out of a solid spiritual core, so somebody must have licked the problem. And I'd like to lick it myself."

We ministers should know the value of prayer. We know people need time for reflection, and for relationship with God. We know persons are more than what they do, or what they produce. We know, too, that we are human. We know all these things, but do we believe? Tim Fallon believes that there is "no ministry that we can ever engage in which gives us the right to neglect our own spiritual growth and our own prayer. Apart from prayer, ministry makes no sense." (Fallon, *Nurturing Nourishers*) Still, we ministers have no lack of excuses, and often concoct very sophisticated ones, for staying away from prayer. (Nouwen, *Way of the Heart* 70) Our work is normally time-consuming, and full of erratic scheduling. Yet, each of us has the power to choose. We can tame our schedules, finding time and spaces we need and want for prayer. Certain seasons, months, or weeks may make this hard for retreat ministers, but, as a friend of mine said not long ago, ministry will eat up any time I allow for it. On some days, I'd still be busy if there were three of me.

Personally, I must define my limits, schedule my priorities, and make choices. As John Shea reminds us, "Humans need a space beyond hassle to hang a sanctuary lamp and consult all there is about who they are." (Shea 54) Once we recognize this power to choose, our time issues will get reconsidered. Do we want (or choose) the time for quiet, for reflection, for prayer? Or, are we more comfortable in our busy-ness, in justifying our worth by numbers and projects? Does the American work ethic (my work is my worth) motivate you? When creativity is replaced with compulsiveness (working to escape some other area of life or to prove personal worth), life is in disharmony. Are we afraid of leisure and of what God might reveal to us in quiet?

Prayer could lead us to radical availability, to a newly attentive stance toward life, toward new challenge, toward richer retreat moments with others. Perhaps adolescents' ministers generally are good at challenging and loving, but not so good at being challenged and loved. Perhaps ministry gives us an excuse to remain aloof or distant, because we say we must care for others and thereby avoid concern for ourselves. Notice these honest, incisive reflections from youth ministers.

"I realize the importance of prayer and sometimes it is so easy to justify 'business' as a substitute for quality prayer time."
"I often use lack of time [due to the demands of ministry] as an excuse not to pray and reflect."

Perhaps we are afraid to step out in the open, before God, life, and ministry, to let them all profoundly affect us. Perhaps, in fact, we are like much of humanity — afraid of letting go, of being loved, of being in profound relationships with others, yet needing these so. "Solitude contains its own share of danger precisely because it inevitably leads to God." (Wiesel 25) Taming our time is difficult enough. Taking time to enter a new level of danger can prove even more difficult.

For ministers, there typically is guilt associated both with taking necessary personal time and with saying no. One survey participant said, "The main obstacle seems to be time and not feeling guilty about taking the time. We feel guilty spending time on ourselves. We see personal retreats, personal time, personal direction, as a luxury." We should turn this around. We should challenge one another if we don't take such personal, spiritual time. Thomas Merton makes sense on this theme.

To allow one's self to be carried away by a multitude of conflicting concerns, to surrender to too many demands, to commit one's self to too many projects, to want to help everyone in everything is to succumb to violence. Frenzy destroys our inner capacity for peace. It destroys the fruitfulness of our work, because it kills the root of inner wisdom which makes work fruitful. (Merton 73)

True, we live in a world full of conflicting concerns. Retreat ministers, typically, experience varied demands on their time and energies. We must alter the pace, avoid such frenzy, and make wiser choices about schedules. Still, we are ever called to live within the world. Jesus in no way wants us to turn from our complicated world. Rather, he wants us to live in it, but firmly rooted in the center of all things. Jesus does not speak about a change of activities, a change in contacts, or even a change of pace. He speaks about a change of heart. (Nouwen, *Way of the Heart* 42)

This change of heart, like a new sight or new vision, can give us back the precious gift of time, even in the midst of much activity. This is what it means to bring real presence to the youth for whom and with whom we labor, in retreat programs or elsewhere. With it, we will not run from reflective moments. No, we will find a most-powerful renewal in the midst of all our activities.

OPPORTUNITIES FOR THE RETREAT MINISTER'S SPIRITUAL GROWTH

The hazards to one's spiritual development can become, paradoxically, rich opportunities for growth. Three opportunities for spiritual growth were identified by youth ministers who took part in my recent survey. These include 1) experiencing God in ministry; 2) learning from relationships with young people; and 3) increased trust in and surrender to God. These three are not easily separated. Thus, they will be woven here. A pertinent comment comes from a deanery-level youth minister from New Jersey. "Time and again I have experienced God through young people, through the goodness of our volunteers, in working together, in the miracles of God's presence coming through in various experiences."

Youth ministry is relational. It is centered on an openness to finding God present in people, to incarnation. Youth ministers recognize God in youth, in their struggles and joys. They find themselves reflected therein. One from Saginaw says, "It's so easy to see the Divine in teenagers who are striving to make sense out of life — their struggles are my struggles — the struggles of all time — the struggles of the Bible."

A diocesan-level youth ministry leader has noted, "My work has continually caused me to be in situations, to meet people in whom the Spirit of God was so present that 'it made my heart sing'."

Youth struggle and grow. It is often we ministers who first see God's presence within them. Adolescents' search and crises often surface during times of prayer, or at worship, or during retreats. Such opportunities prompt a more conscious vision and articulation of their life experience, its meaning, and their beliefs. Often, in the midst of this vision, we see God's love for them, before they can name it for themselves. We gain a privileged view on the ongoing work of the Divine. Such a view has implications for our faith lives and spirituality. Ten years ago, I worked part-time in a day care center. There was a little girl named Missy there. She was a five-year-old terror, much disliked by staff because of her behavior. I was nineteen. I fell in love with her. I plotted ways to tame her. I'd return her craziness and acting out with tenderness. In her efforts to make the whole world mad, she made me laugh. We became friends, sort of. One day, I thought that the relationship Missy and I had was similar to the one God and I had. If I could tenderly care for this little, hurting, struggling girl, how much more must I be loved and cared for tenderly.

In witnessing the struggle and growth of young people, I see God present. I can be objective enough, as an adult, to see God's action in their struggles. It reminds me of God's presence in my own life and struggles. There are special moments with youth — retreat experiences, counseling sessions, preparation of witness talks, sharing of stories, during which God's presence and love for them is almost palpable. How much these moments can teach us! They are sacramental, surely. We see and understand how our own struggles and joys are filled too with God's touch.

In ministry to youth and with youth, there is likewise a call to surrender, to trust in God. A friend of mine, Cynthia, a DRE and youth minister in West Virginia, has noted,

> "I'd say the biggest lesson that I've learned from youth ministry [as opposed to my other ministries] is that of surrender to God — that first of all, I have to look on my work as seed-planting, and I have to be willing not to see measurable results, because the seeds may take years to flower. Secondly, that my single-handed determination to accomplish a particular task does not mean that the task will be accomplished — that God, in fact, is in charge. Big lesson, for me."

We each have memories of those who deeply affected us in our adolescent years. We may not have been able to tell them, in our youthfulness, about their help to us, but they were important. Faith development is such a delicate thing. We can never measure, accurately, our success, as ministers, in fostering personal and communal faith in young Catholics. Thus, our work requires trust, that it's worth it, that we're doing something right. We suffer with our limitations. We worry over uncertainties about adolescents' readiness for our message. We try to respond to pressures for quantity-results by those who give us our jobs and our funding. Sometimes we encounter, in certain youth, a reassurance that what we do does make a difference. Most often though, I believe we are called, moment by moment, simply to trust we are, indeed, spiritually nurturing our young people. We are truly seed-planters. The seeds are not our own. Thank God that God's in charge.

Youth offer us an added gift. It is a "willingness to live with life's unexplainable issues," as that diocesan youth ministry leader, from Pennsylvania, has put it. Youth constantly live with mystery. They identify issues. They investigate that mystery which is life. Intimacy needs and relationships are new mysteries explored. The future remains a question mark. Some learn to live, and laugh, in the midst of these tensions, respectful of the mysteries they uncover. Youth ministers can learn from young persons a courage and grace before that which is inexplicable. This is yet another way to trust in God, in life, in time, and in ourselves.

Faith-formation ministry dedicated to adolescents, as it continues to define its focus, goals, components, and means for operation, is still new territory. The number of adults moving into this new territory grows nationwide. Such pioneering is fraught with hazards and graced with opportunities. These can change us, shape our spiritualities, offer us growth moments. This reflection on the spiritual challenges and opportunities that are part of working creatively within retreat ministries, and in other youth ministry contexts, is, necessarily, limited. Still, I hope it provides you some glimpses of the richness such ministry can offer to all those who would become servants of youth and church community. It is up to each of us to choose to share in the spiritual feast our ministry sets before us.

SOME HELPS FOR THE SPIRITUAL JOURNEY

Ongoing spiritual growth is essential for the minister. Thus, it becomes relevant to speak about what can be done to enable such growth and development. We can readily identify several nourishers of ministers' spirituality: contact with a spiritual director, consistent (daily) quiet, prayer, small group sharing, escapes into nature, personal retreats, exposure to Scripture, parish and sacrament focus, reading, journaling, music, and contact with the poor. Although these can be identified, a number of respondents in our survey clearly said that they lacked consistent touch with even those spiritual nourishments they claimed as practiced priorities. For example: "I used to journal and write poetry, but haven't lately. I also used to play my guitar and pray on my own."

There is poignancy in this statement. Here is a heart longing for spiritual connectedness and personal renewal, nearly certain that these will not be uncovered amidst the usual, daily busy-ness of ministry. For me, the most critical help in the process of spiritual growth is a foundational conviction, at heart and gut level, that we are called individually to wholeness, and to holiness, as well as to ministry. There need not be a disconnectedness and yearning, ". . . if I only had time." Spiritual harmony is possible. It's right there, awaiting our acceptance.

> Spirituality does not deal with the question of whether or not my God is in the moment that I am now living, but whether I recognize the Presence of God in that moment . . . There are two separate levels of relationship involved in this awareness. The first level is recognition: I know that you are there. The second level of awareness is: I know you are there — with love. Spirituality involves the second level of the awareness of presence. I know that my God is there with love. (McCloskey, *Contemplation* 269)

The most basic gift a contemporary minister, or any person, can give to himself or herself is acknowledgement of the presence of God, One who already is in a personal relationship of love with each of us. This is fundamental to all spiritual development.

Of course, there are many times in almost every individual's journey that call for an objective person (or persons) to provide support and direction. Many retreat ministers readily address this, saying that they often need some direction, but are not sure what kind or how to find it. One of the most repeated refrains, in today's ministry, echoes the value of sharing about spirituality with trusted friends. "I have a best friend with whom I often share insights and reflections. I find that extraverting my innermost feelings provides me an opportunity to pray aloud my new found knowledge of God," says one person.

Retreats for youth ministers have become vogue in a number of dioceses. They are spoken of with high regard. Youth ministers, from dioceses without them, request them. Still, the central question remains, how can we foster spirituality in some ongoing manner with consistent direction, input, and sharing?

"Make spiritual directors available to all professional lay ministers — and I mean really available. And provide them at diocesan or parish expense."

"Have programs of directed reading or monthly mornings of prayer."

"Provide spiritual direction and/or counseling services."

"I wish dioceses would offer group spiritual direction meetings monthly and provide a spiritual director for such groups and/or offer opportunities for personal spiritual direction with recommended spiritual directors."

"I wonder about setting up a 'spiritual monitoring' or ' spiritual pairing' availability in the diocese."

This is a hopeful sign. Individuals in ministry seem to recognize a need for ongoing spiritual growth, not simply periodic check-ins. This is not to minimize the worth of annual retreats for those in ministry. Such opportunities are rich and promising. But periodic programs, regardless of their worth and merit, can never replace that which can truly foster an individual's ability to grow daily. There remains a crucial difference between attending a banquet, full of rich fare, and taking daily-provided, simple means. I enjoy and I grow through attending the occasional banquet, but I survive nicely on my daily meals. Insofar as a yearly retreat for ministers enables connections with others, which may then develop into ongoing support-and-sharing, or which offers strategies for daily living, or which encourages further development through spiritual direction, or which provides quality moments for prayer — it is a service which most dioceses should offer. Spiritual development for local-level ministers, retreat teams included, should not simply be left at that, however.

Retreat ministers need active Christian communities (just as young people do) which enrich their spiritualities. Small group meetings, support groups, and basic Christian community models are sprouting up everywhere. We all benefit from a continuing sharing of prayer, Eucharist, instructions in the Spirit, and community life, in order to experience the wonders of God's daily action. In community we recognize God in one another. We more fully express the God within us too. Such contexts need to be creatively built. Coming together as a community of Christians is not merely a skills-sharing nor professional development of a team in the normal sense of these terms. It is a sharing of God's words and deeds among us. Such community building becomes a fertile soil from which one's ministry is effectively nourished.

The finest gifts a diocese can give its ministers, especially those who will be engaged in coordinating or facilitating youth retreats, in enabling them toward spiritual growth, include the following. In each training program, there should be an emphasis on and challenge to the individual's spiritual formation. All skills-training should be tied to the ultimate reason why we learn skills, why we minister, and why we pray. This will further emphasize that ministry flows from spiritual sources rather than simply the tasks we acquire. There should also be a visible spirituality, a practiced priority, among those who would minister unto ministers. Specific spirituality programming — monthly meetings, annual retreats, afternoons of reflection — should be offered. Viable resources for ministers' spiritual growth ought to be made available or made known to the field.

Whenever possible, parishes should help support, through funding, their youth ministers' spiritual formation, in addition to their professional updating. A budget line and time-allotted for a minister's personal retreat will communicate about spiritual priorities. Education of pastors, of administrators, and of ministers themselves must be offered so that the need for ministers' spiritual formation is better recognized and acted on. Initiation and support of community-building efforts among ministers and ministry teams should be considered a priority, too.

A number of the religious and priests who participated in the youth ministry survey saw their own communities or order settings as sufficient for their own spiritual formation. These folks have a great gift to offer to the ever-increasing number of their lay colleagues in retreat ministry, those who hunger for some of this richness. Lay ministers, in turn, have a richness of social context and perception to offer their ordained and religious community counterparts. As lay ministry and lay leadership become more and more evident, the need for spiritual formation among lay ministers becomes more critical. We are called to be contemplatives in action. We "... become so, either by going through the front door of a prayer life which demands expression, or by going through the back door of an active life which needs prayer to see Christ in what [we] are doing." (McCloskey, *Discipleship* 204)

Regardless of the door we enter, we can be of support to one another in the process of becoming who we are — ministers, contemplatives in action, persons loved by God, who in freedom choose to convey that love by communicating God's touch to others, particularly to youth.

WORKS CITED

Costello, Richard. "Adult Training Program for Youth Ministry." *Resources for Youth Ministry.* Ed. Michael Warren. New York: Paulist Press, 1978.

Fallon, Timothy. "Reflections on Spirituality and Ministry." *Resources for Youth Ministry.* Ed. Michael Warren. New York: Paulist Press, 1978.

_____. *Nurturing Nourishers.* Kansas City: National Catholic Reporter, Credence Cassettes, 1987.

Finn, Virginia. *Pilgrim in The Parish: A Spirituality for Lay Ministers.* Ramsey NJ: Paulist Press, 1986.

Helldorfer, Martin C. "Church Professionals and Work Addiction." *Studies in Formative Spirituality* VIII:2 (May 1987).

McCloskey, Joseph M. "The Contemplation to Attain Divine Love: Another Approach. *Review For Religious* 44:2 (March/April 1985).

_____. "Discipleship: Has the Cost Gone Up?" *Sisters Today* 58:4 (December 1986).

Merton, O.S.C.O., Thomas. *Conjectures of a Guilty Bystander.* New York: Doubleday, 1976.

Nouwen, Henri J.M. *Creative Ministry.* New York: Image Books, 1971.

_____. *The Living Reminder.* New York: Seabury Press, 1977.

_____. "The Monk And The Cripple: Toward a Spirituality of Ministry." Growing Together: A Conference on Shared Ministry (Washington DC: Boys Town Center, Catholic University, 1980).

_____. *The Way of The Heart.* New York: Seabury Press, 1981.

_____. *Making All Things New.* San Francisco: Harper and Row, 1981.

Seelaus, V. "Effective Ministry Through Contemplative Self-Knowledge." *Review for Religious* 3 (1982).

Shea, John. *The God Who Fell from Heaven.* Niles IL: Argus, 1979.

Smith, Joanmarie. "Ecumenical Spirituality and The Religious Educator." *The Spirituality of the Religious Educator.* Ed. James M. Lee. Birmingham: Religious Education Press, 1985.

A Vision of Youth Ministry. Washington DC: USCC, Department of Education, 1976.

Whitehead, James D. and Evelyn E. *The Emerging Laity*. Garden City NY: Doubleday, 1986.

Wiesel, Elie. *Messengers of God*. New York: Summit Books, 1976.

Part Two

Overview

Youth Retreats: Models And Strategies

The tone and the spirit of Part Two are set by its very first words and assertions. While Part One is designed to examine some of the foundations and some of the why's to doing retreat ministries with and for adolescents, Part Two is presented to introduce and examine a number of the practical guidelines, models, approaches, and emerging possibilities for retreat work today.

The staff of the **Office of Youth and Young Adult Ministry** from the Diocese of Sacramento summarizes its key convictions and best practical insights in Chapter 7, "Retreats For Adolescents: Practical Guidelines." This is followed, closely, by second contributions by **Butch Ekstrom** and **John Roberto**. In Chapter 8, John Roberto details the steps to be taken in planning effective retreat experiences for adolescents. These practical directions should assist many local retreat teams, in their deliberations, as they prepare their events. In Chapter 9, Butch Ekstrom refers to some principles for the selection of appropriate retreat models and, then, identifies a number of models (of various durations) for retreat ministers' consideration.

The remaining chapters look at other aspects to presenting effective, faith-filled retreats and at key, emerging concerns about which those who implement youth retreats ought to be familiar. In Chapter 10, **Pam Heil** details concrete ways to involve adolescents as peer ministers and peer witnesses in various kinds of retreats for youth . The first of two contributions by **Rebecca Davis** to this volume explores the impact of family systems and family and intergenerational issues on our retreat ministries. Becky provides, also, several models for involving family members in outreach ministries to youth. **Robert McCarty** draws upon his experience in Chapter 12 to discuss important, sometimes delicate issues that can arise for retreat ministry directors and staff members. **Jeff Kaster** describes some approaches to team development, retreat evaluation, and implications of evaluating adolescent retreats in Chapter 13. Finally, Becky Davis returns with a concluding Chapter 14 to investigate the all-important issue of doing adolescent retreat follow-ups in our ministries. She describes for us a selection of practical models for doing so.

A final aspect to be considered in planning and implementing retreats is the area of retreat liturgies. In the *Access Guides to Youth Ministry* series, the third volume, *Liturgy and Worship*, is dedicated to questions of praying with young people. We call your attention especially to **Thomas N. Tomaszek's** article, "Preparing and Evaluating Worship for Youth" (73-96) for a full presentation of this important component of youth retreats.

We hope this *Access Guide* helps you to document some of the foundations of the youth retreats renewal and to discover many of the better, practical developments which have helped make this form of ministry activity so vital today. We want this book to challenge you, to cause you to reflect on various, new approaches within retreat work, and, perhaps, to adopt some new techniques and methods. Yet, as you read and use this book, we hope you will keep in mind that all techniques, all strategies, all good ideas, and all developments in ministry must serve well the goal of helping people, young and old alike, to get to know the Lord. A brief story, originally told by Brennan Manning, an evangelist and retreat director (who lives not far from me in New Orleans), as recounted by writer Anthony Campolo, will illustrate the point as we conclude these introduction:

> He had conducted a variety of [retreat] sessions with these nuns and had found them responsive, except for one particular nun. She remained stone faced and unmovable, contributing nothing toward any of the sessions. At the closing gathering, Brennan asked the group, "Would any of you like to share something special that has happened to you this weekend?"
>
> It was then that this withdrawn nun spoke. "Something wonderful happened to me last night," she said. "When I went to bed, I had a dream. And in that dream, I was in a beautiful dance hall. The women were all wearing lovely gowns, and the men were dressed in formal attire. This rather interesting and intense man came and asked me to dance with him, and, as we danced together, I realized that he was Jesus. Halfway through the dance, Jesus leaned over and whispered in my ear. Do you want to know what he said to me?"
>
> The rest of the group sat at the edge of their seats and could hardly wait.
>
> "He said, 'Catherine, I'm crazy about you.' Then he hugged me, and the dream was over." (Campolo 24-25)

As writer Campolo interprets this, "If there's anything that every struggling teenager needs to hear, it's the good news of how special he or she is to the Lord. If there's anything that a good youth leader should try to communicate to the average kids. . . it's that Jesus is crazy about them." (Campolo 25) We genuinely hope this *Access Guide* assists you in doing so, as it simultaneously points you in some new directions for retreat ministry efforts with your adolescents.

WORKS CITED

Campolo, Anthony. *Growing Up In America*. Grand Rapids: Zondervan, 1989.

Retreat practicum

Chapter 7

Practical Guidelines for Retreats with Adolescents

Diocese of Sacramento

The youth retreat is a component of the Church's pastoral ministry to adolescents. Retreats are part of a total ministry to youth. They complement efforts to meet the spiritual, intellectual, emotional, and relational needs of adolescents. The purpose of the time-apart on retreats is to allow youth to reflect upon the movement of God in their lives, to provide a climate in which young persons might encounter Christ alive among us, to experience community, and to formulate their personal responses to the call to discipleship, received in baptism.

The word "retreat" has many meanings within contemporary society. It is important to define its meaning within pastoral settings. A youth retreat is a time when adolescents withdraw from their normal activities, to reflect upon their lives and on their identity in Christ Jesus. This withdrawal, alone, or with a community of youth, provides the young person with an opportunity to deepen his or her knowledge of self, God, and others; to experience community in Christ; and to explore the shape of his or her response to Christ, lived out in daily life.

Sacred time apart is apparent in Scripture. The Old Testament prophets were often led to desert solitude to prepare for their prophetic tasks. Jesus invited his disciples to come away for a time, for refreshment and renewal. Jesus himself withdrew, for prayer and solitude, before beginning his public ministry. Throughout the Gospels, we find reference to his going apart, for prayer, then returning to his ministry of teaching and healing. Scripture portrays retreats as a time of preparation for renewed ministry. Rest and revitalization energized the retreatant to return and continue a given mission. Today's youth retreats are not solely for providing rest and sense of community. They should empower youth to live discipleship and should enable them to more fully own their identity in Christ. Retreats

..rengthen young people for the continuing task of witnessing to
.vithin their schools, parishes, and families. Youth retreats are most
.c_ .ve when participants freely choose to take part.

Retreats form a vital part of any well-rounded, faith-development
ministry. They directly address the adolescent's need for reflection time, a
sense of belonging, and communal bonding. Retreat benefits can prove
counterproductive, though, if they are not complemented by programs
which continue the process of attending to youth's needs after retreat experiences end. Youth who participate in programs which provide intense
bonding and sharing, which present an idealized vision of Christian life,
can become disillusioned, easily, when they return to their parishes and fail
to find faith-nurturing ministry. They feel disillusioned if the parish faith
community, in its reality and weakness, does not match the idealized vision
presented on an adolescent retreat.

Retreats must be recognized as one tool in the faith-growth process.
They are means of evangelization and catechesis. Many young Catholics
have been prompted to conversion through retreat experiences. Retreats
cannot be the only approach used by a parish or movement. Retreats are
most effective when they become part of an integrated ministry program
which addresses the multiple needs of youth.

GUIDING PRINCIPLES FOR YOUTH RETREATS
THEOLOGICAL PRINCIPLES

1. Youth retreats should be designed to foster a personal relationship
with Jesus. They should lead to discipleship within the community of the
Church.

2. Through retreats, the Church exercises pastoral ministry to youth:
by proclaiming the Good News of Jesus Christ, by fostering the formation
of Christian community, by providing opportunities for participants to
reflect upon their life-questions, in light of the Gospel, and the traditions of
the Church, and by challenging retreatants to a personal, active Christian
response.

3. The doctrinal content of youth retreats should be theologically
consistent with the official teaching of the Catholic Church.

4. Prayer, in its liturgical, communal, and private forms, is an essential aspect of every youth retreat experience. Prayer opens participants to
ongoing conversion and deepens faith.

5. Retreats for youth should provide enlivening liturgical experiences, celebrated according to the liturgical norms of the diocese, appropriate for the occasion, and offered with sufficient time, to allow full
participation by the assembly.

DEVELOPMENTAL PRINCIPLES

1. Retreats should help participants reflect on their experiences and, thereby, deepen their sense of belonging and meaning.

2. Retreat environments must be characterized by acceptance, growth, and freedom, avoiding emotional manipulation.

3. Retreatants should be given opportunities to participate in diverse experiences of self-experience and self-expression.

4. The psychological well-being of participants is safeguarded by maintaining a good balance of recreation, reflection, structured activity, rest, and sound diet.

5. Peer ministry is a valuable aspect of sharing the Christian experience with youth. It allows them to exercise their baptismal call, to give witness, and to lead others to Christ.

6. Retreat experiences are one aspect of the entire personal formation process. Therefore, parish-based preparation and follow-up, after retreats, are essential to retreat ministry.

PRINCIPLES FOR CONTENT AND PROCESS

1. Human experience is the starting point for youth catechesis. The personal stories of youth must be joined to and seen in light of the Christ story.

2. Retreat designs and components should be based upon the developmental stages of participants:

a) in psychological growth;

b) in social growth;

c) in intellectual growth;

d) in moral growth;

e) in faith-growth.

3. The content of youth retreats should be suitable for various age groups. Content should reflect appropriate faith-themes, as recommended by the document, *The Challenge of Adolescent Catechesis* (National Federation For Catholic Youth Ministry, 1986).

4. Interactive processes and total group activities, such as small-group sharing, games, and non-verbal exercises, should use only group dynamics appropriate for youth groups, content, and goals of adolescent retreats.

5. Storytelling, faith-sharing, and personal witness should be respected as valuable elements in communicating the Gospel message.

6. The process in catechetical proclamation within adolescent retreats involves a four-fold movement: experience, message, reflection, and action.

RECOMMENDED RETREAT COMPONENTS

PHYSICAL
Adequate sleep
Adequate recreation time
Balanced diet
Access to outdoors and nature, if possible

SPIRITUAL
Liturgical celebration: priority on Eucharistic celebrations for two-day retreats; reconciliation service, if in keeping with retreat design
Prayer: communal; private; reflection time
Scripture

PSYCHOLOGICAL/SOCIAL/CATECHETICAL
Balance of private time and group time
Opportunity for guidance and counsel
Reflection on human experience
Community building
Opportunities for participation and involvement
Creative activity and expression
Input and presentations
Discussion and sharing opportunities

SUPPORTIVE COMPONENTS
Orientation or preparation of participants, pre-retreat
Follow-up process
Evaluation by team and participants
Team-training, plus sound planning and program-design

Chapter 8

Planning Adolescent Retreats

John Roberto

The following guide is meant to integrate many of the insights and elements of effective retreats into a series of steps that a leader or team can use in their work. We will examine the specific ingredients in effective retreat planning. Providing an effective retreat experience for young people requires, like any other worthwhile venture, a great deal of time and effort in both planning and executing. There are many practical considerations that must be taken into account in such planning. It is well worth the time and effort.

Prior to using this guide, it would be helpful if you reviewed the foundational chapters in this book, especially Chapters 2, 3, and 4; and the guidelines presented in Chapter 7. Material in these chapters will not be re-presented in this planning guide.

Despite bibliographies, resources, and sample models of retreats, there is no such thing as a ready-made retreat that will meet your needs right out of the "box." Developing your own tailor-made retreat program to meet your specific purposes is a lot of work, but it is also filled with fun, excitement, and challenge. Planning is a "process" that takes time and the involvement of many persons. The first thing to keep in mind regarding any specific retreat is that you must begin well in advance of the actual event so that each step of the planning process will have adequate time to be accomplished. The planning process should begin at least six months in advance of the retreat. Facilities may not be available if your planning begins too late; the leadership you want may not be available at short notice; the finances you need may not be available without some prior fund raising efforts.

STEP ONE: SELECT A RETREAT PLANNING TEAM

Your most important resources are the adults and teens who will serve in preparing and conducting the program. Begin your planning process by carefully selecting a retreat planning team. Include youth and adults in this group. Keep the group small so it can function well. It is not essential that every member of the planning group also conduct the retreat. The number and variety of your retreat team for a given retreat experience is determined by the objectives of the program and the number of participants. You may find that you will have to broaden your planning team in order to conduct the retreat experience.

STEP TWO: ESTABLISH PURPOSE AND OBJECTIVES

The planning process for a specific retreat begins with the development of a general purpose statement and a list of retreat objectives. If that purpose statement and the various objectives are in place, then the planning for a specific retreat can begin. First, be sure to identify the type of retreat experience you are planning: evangelization, catechetical, or spiritual development; and how the retreat will be integrated within the overall youth ministry or campus ministry. This will shape your purposes.

In planning the objectives and determining the type of experience to be provided, be sure to integrate the retreat into the overall youth ministry for the year. If the participants have been working with a particular theme(s), perhaps that could well serve as a springboard for planning the retreat and selecting appropriate activities. If this is intended as a catechetical retreat, what faith theme will you explore?

The retreat team develops the overall purpose statement, brainstorms potential objectives to carry out the overall purpose, and then selects realistic objectives based on their young people's needs. You may want to test these out with more youth and adults before making a final decision.

Consider the following questions in your planning:

Why have a retreat? The task here is to explore some basic questions concerning the rationale and purpose for having such an event.

Who will be involved? Spend some time examining the characteristics of the participants: their religious and social background, their ages and maturity levels, their familiarity with one another. Ask: "What are the current concerns of the young people who will be attending this retreat?" What are the interests of those who will attend? What are the faith needs of those who will attend?

What are realistic objectives? This is a very important part of planning, and it revolves around determining specific objectives and weighing realistic potential for achieving these objectives, given the nature of the participants and the resources available. Determine here what the group needs, what the group is ready for, and how far you can realistically expect them to come within the limitations of the program.

STEP THREE: PROGRAM CONTENT AND FORMAT

Once the purpose and goals are developed, the planning team develops the program design: program content and format. Once again the type of retreat (evangelization, catechetical, spiritual development) will shape the theme, program content, and style. The task is draw up a schedule of events and activities that follow a logical progression and that flesh out through specific activities those objectives determined earlier in the planning process. Your team can easily adapt the two retreat formats in Chapter 4B and the variety of models in Chapter 9 to construct the flow of events and activities on the retreat.

Be sure to vary the activities in your retreat: community building and social activities, small group interaction, staff presentations, audio-visual presentations, individual reflection or journaling, physical activity, liturgical (Eucharist, Reconciliation) and prayer experiences. Remember that the best learning happens when the young people are taking part in the learning process.

Determining the program's content and format leads to a set of logistical questions:

When should you have the retreat? Some of the things to be considered here are the length of time the retreat will last, the length of time needed to achieve the objectives, the "attention span" of the participants in a retreat setting, and the best time of the year to conduct the retreat. Coordination of the retreat with overall church or youth ministry programming is important so that it is compatible both in program and in timing with other major events.

Where should you have it? Investigate various facilities that might be available for retreat purposes. You do not have to be limited to those places listed under retreat houses in the yellow pages. However, wherever it will be, consider both your physical requirements (sleeping quarters, kitchen facilities, recreational opportunities, meeting rooms) and the administrative detail of securing, through some kind of a written contract, the facility that is to be used on the specified dates. In brief the retreat team should review available sites, select the site, determine budget needs, and visit the site.

What do we bring? Depending on the type of experience to be provided, there could be a considerable list of materials that will be required ranging from markers to portable altars, from food to name tags.

What rules do we need? Establishing rules is an important element of program design. The retreat team should review parish/school policies, review retreat center policies, establish guidelines, and then communicate the guidelines to participants and their parents. (See Chapter 13 for additional suggestions.)

STEP FOUR: LEADERSHIP RECRUITMENT

After the planning team develops the content and format, it is time to consider the retreat's leadership needs. Three roles are suggested: the Retreat Coordinator, the Program Leaders, and the Logistical Leaders. Every retreat needs a *Retreat Coordinator* who supervises the overall preparation and implementation of the retreat. This person is usually the retreat director as well. *Program Leaders* prepare and conduct the retreat with the Retreat Coordinator. They lead small groups, present talks, lead activities, etc. *Logistical Leaders* handle facilities, transportation, cooking, etc.

For some retreats the same people must manage all three areas of need; for others, you'll have different people working in the three areas. It is a good idea to have one youth and one adult on your planning team to be responsible for working with each leadership group.

Youth involvement as *peer ministers* on a retreat has been an essential component of youth retreats. Retreat experiences provide a unique opportunity to make a constructive and positive use of peer group influence. Adolescents, who are authentically struggling to find the place of God in their lives and who are willing to communicate their experiences of faith, are very influential witnesses to their peers and can make a solid impact and contribution to the quality of the retreat experience for the participants.

Adult leaders also have a lot to offer and are absolutely essential to a retreat. They provide experience, wisdom, expertise, spiritual direction, information, and stability. Since youth look to the adult world for direction, stability, models of behavior, and authentic faith experience, the greatest contribution adults can make is to share their faith, their prayers, and their love. However, beware of the adults who *need* "the kids," who wind up feeding off them, meeting their own needs, rather than ministering to others.

Peer ministers and adult retreat ministers must receive adequate training for their roles.

STEP FIVE: BUDGETING

Determine the cost and set a definite budget which will allow you to determine a specific cost for the young people participating in the retreat.

Determine what financial subsidy or fundraising options are available to the group. It is a valuable operating principle that the participants in the retreat should pay some, if not all, of the entire cost of the retreat.

Using the questions below estimate your retreat expenses, determine your income sources, and determine the amount to charge the participants.

1. Projected Expenses (Based on estimate of _____ participants)
   Program needs
   Leadership material needs
   Recreation supplies
   Audio-visuals
   Planning team expenses
   Retreat Center:
   > Basic fee
   > Per person fee
   > Other

   Transportation
   > Van/bus
   > Gas for cars
   > Commercial bus
   > Other

   Food (if not included in retreat center charges)
   > # of participants X food cost

   Insurance (if not included in retreat center charges)
   > # of participants X insurance cost

2. Projected Income (Based on estimate of _____ participants)
   Fees from participants
   Income from church/youth ministry budget
   Fund-raising events
   Special scholarship gifts
   Other sources

STEP SIX: PUBLICITY AND PROMOTION

Publicity and promotion are essential procedures which must not be overlooked. Disseminating information, spreading publicity, and seeking support on all fronts is the next crucial step in encouraging the young people to participate in the event. Cooperation from parents should also be elicited. Determine a process of registration that will reflect, wherever possible, this cooperation. Be sure to notify the participants about what they *should* and *should not* bring to the retreat.

Consider the following steps in preparing your promotion plan:

1. Initial announcement. (3 months in advance)

2. Detailed flyer including retreat theme and description, costs, registration information, and permission slip. Send a flyer and invitation to potential participants; send a flyer and letter to parents. (2 months in advance)

3. Personal contacts and telephone contacts. (several weeks after mailing)

4. Reminder announcement. (several weeks before the retreat)

STEP SEVEN: PARENTAL INVOLVEMENT

An important, but often overlooked, step in the planning process is parental involvement. While some parents might be on the planning group, all parents should be kept informed regarding the retreat plans. This may take the form of a pre-retreat meeting for parents (or for parents and youth). Parental involvement might take the form of a special letter or newsletter to the parents explaining retreat policies, goals, etc. It is also important to report back to the parents as a part of the follow-up to a retreat. The parents should know what goals were accomplished. Consult Chapter 12 for family and intergenerational approaches.

STEP EIGHT: EVALUATION

An important part of every retreat experience is a thorough evaluation. An evaluation not only provides a solid check on the achievements of the stated goals, but it also provides a much needed opportunity for debriefing, not only for the participants, but especially for those who were so very much involved in the planning and execution of the retreat. An opportunity to reflect on the significance of the experience they had oftentimes results in an updating and enhancing of that experience by reflecting on its significance and value for individual people. Consult Chapter 14 for evaluation suggestions.

STEP NINE: FOLLOW-UP

The last step in the planning process is really the beginning of a whole new cycle of programming. It is essential that the retreat should not be an isolated event. It is a deeply significant religious experience; it is a time of new beginnings. Adults involved in youth ministry must be keenly aware of this growth and know how and where to lead it to further growth.

It is very important that the retreat be integrated into a comprehensive youth ministry or campus ministry. Any new follow-up programming should be integrated into this broader ministry. Retreat follow-up activities should not be separated programs.

PLANNING RESOURCES

Cooney, Randy. *How to Run Successful Days of Retreat*. Dubuque IA: Wm. C. Brown Company, 1986.

Doyle, Aileen A. *Youth Retreats: Creating Sacred Space for Young People*. Winona MN: St. Mary's Press, 1986.

_____. *More Youth Retreats: Creating Sacred Space for Young People*. Winona MN: St. Mary's Press, 1988.

Harman, Shirley R. *Retreat Planning Made Easy*. Minneapolis MN: Augsburg Publishing House, 1985.

Junior High Retreats. Villa Maria PA: Center for Learning, 1987.

Kamstra, Doug. *The Get-Away Book: A Handbook for Youth Group Retreats*. Grand Rapids, MI: Baker Book House, 1983.

Pastva, S.N.D., Sr. Mary Loretta. *The Catholic Youth Retreat Book*. Cincinnati OH: St. Anthony Messenger Press, 1984.

* Reichter, Arlo, et al. *Group Retreat Book*. Loveland CO: GROUP Books, 1983.

_____, et al. *More Group Retreats*. Loveland CO: GROUP Books, 1987.

Reimer, Sandy and Larry. *The Retreat Handbook*. Wilton CT: Morehouse-Barlow, 1986.

Retreat Models. Villa Maria PA: Center for Learning, 1984.

Senior High Retreats. Villa Maria PA: Center for Learning, 1987.

* highly recommended for retreat planning

Chapter 9

Models For Effective Adolescent Retreats

Reynolds R. Ekstrom

The words "retreat" and "relationship" belong together. While retreats provide times to pull away, to retire, from the stresses and demands of daily routine times to do self-examination and healing re-collection of tattered physical and spiritual fibres, retreats also focus on relationships. When it comes to retreats for adolescents, times are provided, in safe, sacred places set apart, for youth to meet Jesus Christ. The word "sacred" fundamentally implies something or some spot set apart, consecrated and safe, holy, through which God and humanity can relate, can connect.

Care, concern, silence, and trust are essential to communication. They are building blocks for dynamic, healthy relationships. They will be critical to the pace and flow of the individual's relationship with the Word. And they will make or break the quality of the relationships shared by adolescents (among themselves and with adults who minister with them) whenever they gather, particularly when they set sacred time aside for a spiritual retreat.

Recent research in the United States indicates that many, many of us — young and older alike — seek a sense of community, a bonding with and trust in others. About 40% of the U.S. population indicates frequent to periodic feelings of loneliness, intense loneliness. There are great numbers of adolescents standing amidst that lonely crowd. Typically, Americans look to the church for warm feelings of belonging and fellowship. Some have their hungers satisfied, while others come up empty in their efforts. Interestingly, this research also shows that many adolescents and young adults shy away from church, and its activities, because they feel unwelcome, especially if they feel out of synch in their family relationships. (Ekstrom, *Readings*; and Ekstrom, *Growing in Faith* 36-43) The recent book, *America's Faith in the 1990s*, reminds us,

The spiritual dimension Americans want includes helping them to find meaning in their lives and, for Christians, to deepen their relationships to Jesus Christ. It also includes a strong desire for information about the Bible and its meaning. While Americans want spirituality from their churches, they also want practical help. They also want their churches to help them learn how to put their faith into practice; to shed light on the important moral issues of the day; to help them learn how to serve others better and to be better parents. Americans understand that for their faith to be meaningful, it must be real and have a real impact on their day-to-day lives. (Gallup and Castelli 253)

When someone is present to us, cares about us, and takes time to listen well, trust builds. When someone tries to understand our needs and concerns, in a spiritual and compassionate way, enough so as to do something helpful on our behalf, initial trust blooms into a valuable relationship, one we want to see continue, grow, come to full fruit. Trust grows when people work together, in various kinds of relationships, for better, more peaceful lives.

Building a trusting and open dynamic that will lead toward better relationships between all those who participate in a retreat, and between individuals and Jesus, should be a prime consideration whenever you sit down to choose a retreat model and the many activities, events, and spiritual exercises which will put flesh, blood, and breath to the model's bare bones. Developing the activities, situations, and life-sustaining climate, in which trust and relationships can be established, does not always come easily. It takes work and creativity. In her book, *More Youth Retreats*, Aileen A. Doyle reminds us of an underlying principle that should guide us in helping models, relationships, and trusting climates come to life. She uses similes. Youth retreats have a downstream flow. They roll along like rivers, when they are prepared and executed well. For example, she notes

In creating the space for the Lord and the retreatant to meet, it is important to plan activities that take into consideration the trust level of the retreatants. There is a natural flow in the development of trust that takes place in any gathering of people. During the initial gathering there is a limited amount of trust; after a period of interaction the trust level increases and bonds are formed that challenge the retreatants to share. . . This flow is normal and similar to a river flowing downstream. When rocks, fallen trees, and other debris are in the water, the flow of the river is impeded. However, when all of the debris has been removed from the river, the flow is more fluid. The same is true on a retreat. The task of the leaders is to choose activities that enhance the natural flow that is already taking place and to remove any obstacles that might impede the flow. . . At the beginning of the retreat, trust is low. Activities are planned to help the retreatants connect with each other. Activities such as icebreakers, introductions, and goal setting help during this connecting time. When the retreatants begin to share with one another, the trust level begins to increase. Activities that increase the level of trust are appropriate at this time. These activities include structured sharing of personal concerns. (Doyle 12-13)

The pattern of personal risk and interpersonal sharing (through dialogue) described here can be demonstrated symbolically, too. Again, this pattern, an ebb and flow, should be a key concern for retreat leaders. And attention to it should be paramount as a retreat model, plus retreat activities and movements, are selected.

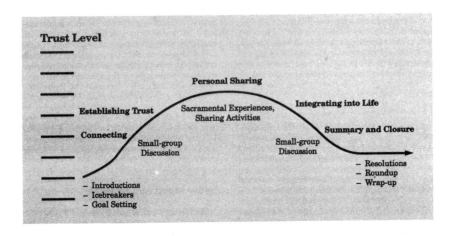

Doyle 12

As you utilize the models which follow, try to integrate the insights offered by this dynamic flow from the everyday to the sacred back to the everyday; from solitude and suspicion to trusting interaction with others; from spiritual unconcern to meaningful prayer and ritual to ongoing spiritual activity; and from a general awareness of (or unconcern for) the Lord to a rich encounter with him that develops into trusting, priority relationships for all who find their ways to your retreat ministry.

THE EVENING FORMAT

6:30	PM	arrival and welcome
		opening prayer
6:45		icebreaker and community building
7:00		barbecue or pizza meal/game(s)
7:30		group activity and discussion
8:00		input/talk or video-presentation
8:30		follow-up activity/discussion(s)
8:50		personal reflection
9:00		artistic activity and/or journaling
9:30		closing prayer
9:45		social time
10:00		conclusion

THE AFTERNOON FORMAT

12:00	PM		arrival and welcome
			opening prayer
12:15			icebreaker and community building
1:00			barbecue or pizza meal/game(s)
1:30			group activity and discussion
2:00			input/talk or video-presentation
2:30			follow-up activity/discussion(s)
2:50			personal reflection
3:00			artistic activity and/or journaling
3:30			closing prayer (or Eucharist)
3:45		(4:15)	social time
4:00		(5:00)	conclusion

A ONE-DAY FORMAT (5 HOURS)

10:00	AM	(1:00)	PM	opening remarks, prayer
10:10		(1:10)		icebreakers
10:30		(1:30)		group activity
10:45		(1:45)		presentation on retreat's theme
11:15		(2:15)		break
11:30		(2:30)		film or video and discussion
12:15	PM	(3:15)		lunch (or snacks)/game(s)
1:30		(4:00)		presentation and activity-response
2:30		(5:00)		Liturgy
3:00		(6:00)		closing/social time or meal optional

A ONE-DAY FORMAT (6 HOURS)

9:00	AM	arrival, welcome, make nametags
9:15		icebreaker(s)
9:30		group activity with discussion
10:00		presentation
10:15		small-group sharing
10:30		large-group sharing/response
11:00		reconciliation experience
12:00	PM	lunch/recreation
1:00		small-group activity
1:30		large-group sharing/discussion
1:45		final talk or presentation
2:15		prayer experience or Eucharist
3:00		conclusion (social time/game(s) optional)

A ONE-DAY FORMAT (10 HOURS)

9:00	AM	arrival, informal welcoming
9:15		introduction and prayer
9:30		icebreaker(s)/ community building phase
10:15		small-group activities

11:00		break
11:15		presentation one
11:35		small-group response
12:00	PM	large-group sharing
12:15		lunch/recreation
1:30		small-group activity
2:00		presentation two
2:25		small-group artwork
3:10		break
3:25		large-group: art display
3:45		Eucharist
4:30		free time (or organized recreation)
5:15		dinner
6:00		presentation three
6:20		group activity
6:45		prayer and wrap-up
7:00		conclusion

A ONE-DAY FORMAT (12 HOURS)

9:00	AM	arrival, informal time
9:15		welcome, introductions, prayer
9:30		Session/Topic One *
11:00		break
11:15		Session/Topic Two
12:45	PM	lunch and recreation
1:30		Session/Topic Three
3:00		games and recreation
4:00		Session/Topic Four
5:30		dinner and relaxation time
6:30		Session/Topic Five
8:00		Eucharist or reconciliation
8:30		social
9:00		closing prayer/conclusion

* Using the terms Session/Topic suggests that you utilize a carefully-planned process which incorporates numerous activities or movements during these blocks of time, for example, shared praxis movements or a process for evangelizing youth. Incorporate a variety of activities and methods in each Session/Topic. These might include audio-visuals, contemporary songs, video, verbal discussions, worksheets, storytelling, Scripture searches, Bible encounters, lecturettes, artwork projects, guest speakers, journaling, simulation games, and many more. (Ekstrom, *Adolescent Catechesis Resource Manual* 80-101) The key here, remember, is to develop a sound, dynamic learning or evangelizing process within each Session/Topic block of 90 minutes. For additional ideas on this particular concern see especially Chapters 6, 7, and 8 in the *Access Guides for Youth Ministry: Evangelization*, edited by Reynolds R. Ekstrom and John Roberto (Don Bosco Multimedia, 1990). Also, consult the comments on catechetical process in Chapter 4B of this book.

THE LOCK-IN FORMAT

9:00	PM	arrival, set-up
9:15		welcome and introductions
9:30		opening prayer
9:45		icebreaker(s) and games
10:30		break
11:00		group activity on retreat's theme; follow-updiscussion process
12:00	AM	pizza
12:15		video movie/discussion
2:00		break
2:15		presentation/response activity
3:00		games and recreation
4:00		video movie (optional sleep time)
5:30		outdoor activity/sports
6:30		breakfast
7:00		housekeeping and clean-up
7:15		presentation/discussion
8:00		Eucharist or closing prayer
8:30	(9:00)	departure

THE OVERNIGHT FORMAT

Evening

7:00	PM	arrival, unpack
7:30		welcome and introduction
7:45		icebreaker(s) and communitybuilding
8:30		small-group activity
9:00		audio-visual or witness talk
9:30		break
9:45		follow-up activities
10:15		large-group sharing
10:30		guided meditation and personal reflection/journals
11:00		healing prayer and reconciliation service
11:30		snacks, games, dance (confessions continue)
1:00	AM	close reconciliation experience with prayer, then lights out
1:00→8:00	AM	sleep time
8:00	AM	wake-up call
8:30		morning prayer and exercise
9:00		breakfast
10:00		icebreaker(s)
10:30		small-group activity
11:00		large-group discussion/sharing
11:15		presentation or witness talk
11:45		sports activity
12:30	PM	lunch/recreation
1:30		small-group tasks to prepare for Eucharist/ journaling time
2:00		Eucharist
2:45		wrap-up activity
3:30		departure

THE 1-1/2 DAY (MODIFIED OVERNIGHT) FORMAT

10:00	AM	arrival, unpack
10:30		welcome and introductions
10:45		icebreaker(s)
11:15		group activities on retreat's theme
12:00	PM	witness talk or audio-visual
12:30		lunch and recreation
1:30		video movie appropriate to retreat's theme
3:15		break
3:30		discussion(s)/artwork activity
4:15		large-group sharing
4:30		prepare for reconciliation/journaling time
5:00		celebrate reconciliation
5:30		dinner and recreation (confessions continue)
6:45		conclude reconciliation service
7:00		games and prizes
7:30		evening Session/Topic (see explanation of Session/Topic process under the One-Day [12 Hour] Format above)
9:00		break
9:15		witness talk by youth with night prayer/journaling time
9:45		snacks/video movie and music option
12:00	AM	lights out
12:00 →8:00	AM	sleep time
8:00	AM	wake-up call
8:30		morning prayer and exercise
9:00		breakfast
9:30		small-group activity and presentation
10:15		prepare for Eucharist/journaling time
10:45		Eucharist
11:30		retreat wrap-up activity
12:00	PM	conclusion

(lunch could be included before 12:30 departure)

A TWO-DAY FORMAT

10:00	AM	arrival, unpack
10:30		introductions and opening prayer
10:45		icebreaker(s) and community/building exercises
11:30		small-group activity
11:50		large-group reports
12:00	PM	presentation one
12:30		lunch/free time
1:45		small-group response activity
2:15		large-group reports and discussion
3:00		recreation and games
4:00		presentation two
4:30		small-group response activity and free time for journaling
6:00		dinner
7:00		preparation for reconciliation
7:30		reconciliation service
8:00		break
8:15		small-group tasks in preparing for Eucharist (confessions continue)
9:15		conclude reconciliation service
9:45		snacks/video movie and music options or indoor sports
11:45		night prayer
12:00	AM	lights out
12:00 →8:00	AM	sleep time
8:00	AM	morning prayer and "aerobics"
8:30		breakfast
9:00		small-group activity
9:30		presentation three
10:00		small-group response activity
10:30		large-group reports
11:00		break

11:15		witness talk by youth
11:30		reflection time/journaling
12:00	PM	Eucharist celebrated
12:45		lunch and recreation
2:00		final small- and large-group activities
2:45		clean-up details and closing prayer
3:00		departure

A WEEKEND FORMAT

Friday

7:30	PM	welcome and introductions; settle in
8:00		opening prayer
8:15		icebreakers and community building
8:45		small-group activity
9:00		presentation one
9:30		small-group discussion
9:50		large-group reports
10:00		break
10:15		video movie/snacks
12:15	AM	night prayer
1:00		lights out

Saturday

8:00	AM	wake-up call
8:30		exercises and morning prayer
9:00		breakfast
9:30		small-group activities
10:00		presentation two
10:30		response activity
11:00		journaling time
11:30		presentation three (on Scripture themes)
12:00	Noon	lunch
		planned recreation events
1:30	PM	preparation of role-plays/skits on Scripture stories

2:15		present role-plays/skits
3:00		large-group discussion
3:15		break
3:45		presentation four
4:15		small groups: artwork projects
5:00		journaling time
5:20		recreation/social time
6:00		dinner and free time
7:00		small groups share on artwork
7:30		presentation five
8:00		prepare for reconciliation service
8:30		reconciliation experience
9:00		break
9:15		party/social time: use music, video movies, games, other options (confessions continue)
11:30		conclude reconciliation service
12:00	AM	everyone in their rooms
12:30		lights out

Sunday

8:00	AM	wake-up call
8:30		exercises and morning prayer
9:00		breakfast
9:30		small groups: prepare for eucharist
10:30		presentation six
11:00		small-group activity
11:30		large-group discussion
11:45		free time
12:00	Noon	lunch and recreation
1:00		journal entries
1:20		presentation seven: sending forth/challenge theme
1:50		move toward Liturgy
2:00		Eucharist
3:00		closing comments, blessings, and clean-up
3:45	PM	departure

A WEEKEND FORMAT
(APPROPRIATE FOR ADOLESCENT CONFIRMATION GROUPS)

Friday

7:00	PM	welcome and introductions
7:30		get settled in rooms
8:00		icebreaker(s) and community-builders
8:30		session/topic one *
9:00		break
9:30		session/topic one concluded
10:00		video movie/snacks
12:00	AM	night prayer
12:30		everyone to dorm rooms
1:00	AM	lights out

Saturday

12:00 →8:00	AM	sleep time
8:00	AM	wake-up call
8:30		exercises and morning prayer
9:00		breakfast
9:30		session/topic two *
11:00		break with refreshments
11:30		session two concluded
12:00	Noon	lunch
		recreation/athletic events planned
1:30	PM	session/topic three *
3:00		break with snacks
3:15		session three concluded
3:45		recreation/social time
4:30		small groups: plan for the reconciliation experience
5:15		journaling time
5:30	PM	dinner and free time
6:30		session/topic four *
8:30		break
8:45		reconciliation service
9:30		party/social time: use music, board games,

		and video options (confessions continue)
12:00	AM	conclude reconciliation service
12:30		everyone in their rooms
1:00		lights out
Sunday		
8:00	AM	wake-up
8:30		breakfast
9:00		morning prayer and eye-opener
		group exercise
9:15		Session/TopicFive *
11:00		break
11:15		session five concluded
11:45		journaling and free time
12:00	Noon	lunch
		light recreation
1:00	PM	clean-up rooms; pack
1:30		Session/Topic Six *
3:00		break
3:15		Eucharist
4:00		journaling/final sharing opportunity
4:30 PM		closing prayer and departure

* Use of the term Session/Topic is described in some detail earlier in this chapter at the conclusion of the outline for the One-Day Retreat (12 Hours).

WORKS CITED

Doyle, Aileen A. *More Youth Retreats: Creating Sacred Space for Young People.* Winona MN: St. Mary's Press, 1989.

Ekstrom, Reynolds R. "Youth Culture and Teen Spirituality." *Readings in Youth Ministry, Volume I.* Washington DC: National Federation For Catholic Youth Ministry, 1986.

_____. "A Survey of Learning Methods." *Adolescent Catechesis Resource Manual.* John Roberto. New York: Sadlier, 1988.

_____. "The American Family: Change and Diversity." *Growing in Faith — A Catholic Family Sourcebook.* Ed. John Roberto. New Rochelle NY: Don Bosco Multimedia, 1990.

Gallup, George and Jim Castelli. *The People's Religion: American Faith in the 90's.* New York: Macmillan Company, 1990.

Chapter 10

Developing Peer Witness and Peer Ministries in Retreats

Pam Heil

TAPPING THE GIFTS AND POWERS OF ADOLESCENTS

Many adults fail to realize that although youth often lack experience and confidence, and sometimes the necessary skills, they can become gifted and powerful ministers under the direction and encouragement of caring adults. When people consider youth a valuable resource for ministry, they become just that. The U.S. bishops have noted, "Youth have a right and duty to be active participants in the work of the Church in the world." (*TTJD* 36)

Sometimes, what is most obvious escapes us. When planning youth retreats, we should not forget the value of youth's insights and abilities. Their input, from beginning to end, will enhance your retreat program and will attract numbers of retreat participants that we, as youth ministers, may have previously considered overly idealistic.

As a campus minister at a Catholic high school (about 900 students), I can attest to the power of adolescents in making retreats successful growth experiences for youth. In the last two years, I have worked with 200 different seniors on 20 different retreat teams. Since I have sought the active involvement of youth in all phases of retreat work, the effects of our retreat program have been acclaimed as the highlight of many students' high school experiences. Numbers for our voluntary, overnight weekend retreats have grown from 7-10 participants to 45-50 participants among the junior and senior classes. Because adolescents have a great impact on each other, retreats work better when youths minister to youth.

We know how essential peer acceptance is to adolescents. We can read what the experts say about developmental theories. Yet, we need only observe and talk with a handful of young people to believe in the power youth have on youth. We hear often about peer pressure, a term which suggests something which it is not. During frank conversations with adolescents, we are quickly informed that they do not, normally, talk peers into doing drugs, having sex, or becoming "party animals." In fact, young people so vehemently desire to fit in that pressures to conform come from within. Adolescents choose to experience or ingest certain things considered undesirable by adults, just to feel accepted by their peers.

Consider the following chart. It drives home how essential it is for us to integrate youth into leadership and ministry within our retreat programs:

ESTIMATED SHIFTS IN THE INFLUENCES UPON 13-19 YEAR OLDS WHICH CHANGE THEIR VALUES AND BEHAVIOR (CLARK, 133-4)

	1960		**1980**
1st	Mother, Father	1st	Friends, Peers
2nd	Teachers	2nd	Mother, Father
3rd	Friends, Peers	3rd	TV, Radio, Records, Cinema
4th	Ministers, Priests, Rabbis	4th	Teachers
5th	Youth club leaders, Counselors, Advisors, Scoutmasters, Coaches, Librarians	5th	Popular heroes, Idols in sports or music
6th	Popular heroes, Idols in sports or music	6th	Ministers, Priests, Rabbis
7th	Grandparents, Uncles, Aunts	7th	Newspapers, Magazines
8th	TV, Records, Cinema, Radio	8th	Advertising
9th	Magazines, Newspapers	9th	Youth club leaders, Counselors, Advisors, Scoutmasters, Coaches, Librarians
10th	Advertising	10th	Grandparents, Uncles, Aunts

A drop to sixth or ninth place in our influence on teenagers may not be good for our egos. But, with the help of the Holy Spirit, we will recognize the many, different gifts bestowed on youth, and we will call each, one by one, to share themselves with their friends.

Choosing adolescents who are willing to risk their time, talents, and traumas may, at first blush, seem difficult. In choosing and inviting them, we must be willing to go out on a limb. You may even think of yourself as a failure if there seems to be no fruit at the end of the branch. However, your success as a recruiter will improve as you trust more, listen better, and gently probe more deeply into the hearts of your young people.

WHERE TO BEGIN

We are all called to discipleship. So, if a youth minister is worried about choosing the right youth to ask to staff a retreat, he or she should first trust in the guidance and wisdom of the Holy Spirit. I then focus on two procedures for recruiting peer ministers: peer selection and personal invitation.

PEER SELECTION AND PERSONAL INVITATION

Peer ministers are given challenging duties and serious responsibilities in our school community. So, I am always determined not to make selection of them a popularity contest. After three years, I still believe the following procedure has been most effective in the selection of youth who truly desire to minister to their peers.

I visit each religion class. I explain what responsibilities peer ministers have and what qualities a candidate for peer ministry should possess. They conduct workshops for younger students, in our feeder schools, and serve in an advisory capacity to me in various situations. Some peer ministers, ones comfortable with groups, facilitate support groups with me. Such groups deal with divorce, death, chemical dependency, eating disorders, insights on responsible decision-making, and making smoother life transitions. Peer ministers are sometimes called on to be mediators in disputes between individuals. The most common responsibility of a peer minister is to be a support person, a caring listener, to a youth who would rather share a concern with a peer than with an adult.

I then describe problem scenarios when the wrong type of person is chosen for peer ministry. For example: A good listener says, "I'm not supposed to tell you this, but because I know I can trust you, and you're my best friend, I'll tell you anyway . . ." That individual should not be a peer minister because the gift of confidentiality must be guaranteed. Another example: Friends who are constantly letting secrets slip should not be burdened with the responsibility of carrying someone's secrets.

After describing more examples of problems and betrayals of confidence, and once a few questions have been fielded, I ask adolescents to answer the following two questions, anonymously, on slips of paper: To whom would you go (in your group or class) if you had a problem? Whom would you trust with your deepest, darkest secrets knowing nobody else would ever know? I stress that the one name written must be the response to both questions. I allow two or three minutes, then I collect the slips from everyone. Usually, many papers are blank. This confirms the seriousness with which the young people considered only trustworthy candidates. I tally the names by myself, so no one else will know who was named.

Next, I make a list of possible candidates. I list all the names nominated, at least, five times. I will then approach each candidate individually, usually 20 to 35 students. I ask each if he or she would be willing to attend and participate in an introductory meeting, five training sessions, and a retreat to prepare for peer ministry. I explain that, often, peer ministers are asked to miss a study hall, to shorten lunch periods, to come to school early, or to stay late to support another student in turmoil. I stress the confidentiality which peer ministers have to maintain and emphasize the responsible position they would hold as peer ministers. I ask each to think it over and let me know, in writing, the next day.

Every year, about five refuse the call to peer ministry for various reasons. As their youth minister, I am often tempted to encourage individuals to change their minds. But, I do not believe this is a good idea. I respect youth's decisions, unless one says he or she just does not feel self-confident enough to do it. In that case, I encourage a young person to go through training sessions and, only then, make a final decision.

TRAINING FOR PEER MINISTRY

When candidates for peer ministry first gather, it is essential to establish trust and comfort levels, plus a warm, open atmosphere. Provide as many introductory activities you think necessary to allow all involved to get to know each other better. There are numerous sources for icebreaker and community building activities. (Rydberg 1985) Trust your instincts. Feel for the youth in your group. Pick the games and activities you believe will work best. Be sure to allow ample time for mixing, since the group newly gathered may consist of young people from different grade-levels.

For the duration of your first meeting, I suggest using with the adolescents a handout which helps them assess their opinions on various issues, then another instrument which helps them get in touch with their feelings. Break them into small groups for sharing opportunities. Have each group write a group reaction to this initial meeting and a summary of their feelings about becoming peer ministers. Offer time for sharing in the large group next. Close with a brief prayer service. Incorporate a Scripture reading about our call to discipleship, an inspirational reading, and, finally, a contemporary song on friendship, which adds a nice touch.

Five 2-hour training sessions should deal with topics of major concern to young people. In assessing my experiences and in surveying adolescents, I find essential topics should include alcohol and other drugs, sexual issues (for example, premarital sex, pregnancy, abortion, AIDS), family troubles and divorce, suicide, the grieving process, fitting-in, and friendship. You could seek professionals, who specialize in each area, to present workshop sessions for your peer ministry candidates.

Begin the first session with a 60-minute workshop on communication skills. Practice active listening, communicating "I" messages, and carefully cover roadblocks to effective communication. A handout, which I particularly enjoy using in this effort, is one called "Rules For Conflict And Resolution." Role-playing opportunities are essential to each session. Youth can take turns being ministers listening to a troubled peer. Critiquing each other, in such workshop groups, works well in later sessions. Use a variety of brief prayer experiences to close your sessions.

There is a growing library of books and resources on how to effectively minister to and with youth. This list of books on adolescent psychology and spirituality, plus excellent publications on each of the particular training topics, listed above, also grows. Trust your judgment. Consult with respected professionals in your area. Ask which resources you should use with your ministry trainees. I do, however, recommend that you always make use of handouts, inspirational readings, and telephone numbers of local crisis hotlines, plus other resource people and agencies.

During the training sessions, stress that all mention of suicide, abuse, or any life-threatening circumstances must cause peer ministers to tell the one(s) sharing that the information will be passed on to a trusted adult. All other conversations should be kept fully confidential, unless a peer minister becomes unduly burdened by a given circumstance. In such circumstances, the same procedure noted above should be followed. The one(s) sharing may be angry, initially, but will not feel lied to or betrayed after help has been sought. In life-threatening situations, peer ministers must recognize one option — get professional help, immediately.

Upon completion of training sessions, peer ministry candidates should participate in a retreat. My retreat design for this includes prayer-time, sharing time, and care-time. Scripture readings about helping one another, seeing Christ in each other, and being Christ to one another are selected. Contemporary musical pieces, especially love songs that are tasteful and appropriate, work really well on these retreats. I suggest that God is a lover, and this links God's unconditional love for us with popular music. Allow ample time for sharing in both small and large groups in your retreat. Finally, provide ministry candidates ways to show their care and support for one another, in their ministry. Use an affirmation activity which symbolizes their unity, with God as their head. I stress to these young people that they will not be alone in their ministry. I inform them that there will be bimonthly support group meetings just for them. After the retreat, a full-school (or full-parish) Liturgy should be celebrated so peer ministers can be commissioned, before their peers, the ones who have called them, and before God, who has called each of us to serve. (Reynolds 1983)

I distribute the list of commissioned peer ministers to the entire school staff. Their names, also, are specially listed in our student directory. Their pictures and names are posted in a display case, so all the students will be able to identify them. I try to collect other information from each of our peer ministers: a) schedules, so I know which periods they have study halls; b) subject areas with which they are most comfortable; c) subjects with which they do not want to deal; d) availability they have each day, before and after school.

Commissioned peer ministers are trained to staff retreats. Most are comfortable doing so. However, although trained in the necessary skills, some prefer not to miss school to work a retreat. It is my belief that if you allow only those adolescents chosen, by their peers, to work your retreats, valuable people-resources will be lost. I have found an effective way to identify other young people who can enhance your retreats.

PERSONAL CALL

Observe the young people around you. Listen to conversations in the halls. Attend extracurricular events. Learn something significant about as many different youth as you can. Be highly approachable. Show kids you are for them unconditionally. Join them on their journeys by meeting them where they are. Listen to their problems. Greet their friends warmly whenever you run into them at a movie or a mall. Compliment them on the big play. Console them about the one that got away. Greet all students as though they are important. This means the jocks, the class officers, the nerds, the leaders, the skaters, the band members, the brains, the clowns, the theater clan, and, yes, even the troublemakers.

Some of my best peer ministry names have been associated with faculty headaches. Usually, young people act-out for a reason. Once I have established a relationship with a misdirected youth, I have usually learned the why's of problem behaviors. When willing to share their growth and struggle stories, these young people can be terrific on retreats.

Anyone can be a potential staff person on a retreat. Do not overlook anybody, automatically. Pray for guidance. Then, personally invite each to share their talents and their stories in your retreat program.

TEAM SELECTION

During a given school year, we conduct five retreats per class. Each underclass retreat brings together a group of 50 students, 10 senior-age team members, one teacher (any subject or department), and me. Intentionally, we mix classes, break up cliques, and strive for a fairly even blending of males and females. In choosing the 10 team-seniors for each retreat, I select young persons from varied interest groups, with different personality preferences, and assorted degrees of popularity.

YOUTH STAFF TRAINING

During the planning of a retreat, I meet first with the 10 team seniors. We brainstorm about feelings in their lives, needs that are not being met, and problems that don't seem to have solutions. I ask them if they recall what their needs, problems, or feelings were when they were freshmen and sophomores. With some guidance from me about adolescent psychological, spiritual, and social needs, we then select a theme for the upcoming retreat. If you can be flexible in your site-selection, have your team help you in this process, too.

Scripture readings, songs, and inspirational readings, which directly relate to your theme should then be selected for prayer services. Some young people have large and varied collections of music. Invite them to consider songs which are unfamiliar to you, but be sure the appropriateness of all songs used can be assessed. Most older youth, also, have poems and prayers which have helped them through tough times. Often, they are eager to share these, if invited to do so.

Gregarious youth can be placed in charge of organizing community builders and icebreakers. Remind your team to choose activities in which all will be able to participate. Delegate all related tasks: gathering necessary equipment, making nametags, etc. With adolescents, it is essential to closely monitor task completion. Schedule all deadlines for at least two weeks before your retreat dates.

Decide with peer ministers the objectives to be accomplished by every retreat. Discuss how they think those objectives can best be accomplished. Provide different kinds of reflective activities for them to critique. Have videos available to preview. Seek volunteers from among peer ministers to deliver those witness talks which they decide will be helpful in fulfilling their purposes. For example, talks could number two or three (or more) presentations, 10-20 minutes each in length, or could be organized as a series of two- or three-minute witnesses by several of the team members.

I prefer that each of the 10 older students talk briefly about the selected topics from their own perspective when addressing much younger groups of adolescents. This increases the chance that each young retreatant will relate to someone speaking. Preparing talks and telling their story helps the adolescents on your ministry team get in touch with their own feelings and their own journeys. Talking publicly provides tremendous growth experiences. Likewise, retreatants undergo powerful growth opportunities when there are various sharings by a teen panel.

Many underclass groups have said they experience a sense of awe that older youth cared enough about them to share their struggles, pains, and failures just to help them make wiser choices, discover different options, and avoid some of the heartaches they have endured. Such lessons are invaluable. Young adolescents see people, whom they often idolize, as ones who have survived crisis, ones who have learned from their mistakes and have grown in their faith commitments. A gift of hope and love, in stories, helps them truly appreciate the peers ministering to them. Often, youth will cry when they share their personal stories. Others cry right along with their role models.

Another very important role, played by each team member, is small group facilitator. To prepare for this responsibility, simple rules are explained to the team and procedures are practiced, with me as facilitator. In this, we stress that everyone in a group should sit in a circle on the same plane. Nobody should be outside the circle during small group dynamics. We remind the team that everything shared in groups should be kept confidential. Entire groups should be focused on the person sharing, and side conversations among group members should be discouraged. Each individual is worthy of the small group's undivided attention. We try to keep our team facilitators aware that sharing should be at a level comfortable to each retreatant. The facilitator should begin with non-threatening group activities or with individuals who are eager to share and address feeling issues, rather than with those retreatants who are not yet open.

The final step to our team preparation is covering the do's and don'ts which apply to our peer ministers throughout the retreat:

Be sincere and honest.

Be sensitive to the loner and reach out to him or her.

Treat each other with respect and support. Your conduct will be emulated by retreatants.

Aid with discipline. Don't raise your voice.

Don't say "Shut up!" at any time.

Don't use any put-downs or name-calling.

Don't show favoritism.

Offer your continued support to retreatants throughout the year.

Assist with all general house-cleaning of the site before departure.

Our peer ministry team members turn in written evaluations of each retreat, plus they offer other comments they wish to share with me within two days. These assessments indicate to me how peer ministers' self-esteem has been enhanced by their service. They seem to appreciate the bonding which occurs among themselves. For many, retreats provide the only times when those ten individuals, of such varied interests, spend together in their years of acquaintanceship.

CONCLUSION

Although my account focuses mainly on the use of seniors in retreat ministries, I believe even younger people can successfully be incorporated as peer ministers on youth retreats. Any adolescent can be encouraged to share his or her gifts with others on retreat. Therefore, many adolescents can be easily trained to staff retreats, for confirmation candidates or early adolescents, using the same procedures suggested above. Young people who share a success story with you, who are survivors of adolescent traumas, or who are coping well with loss in their lives should be invited and encouraged to staff a retreat. This could empower them to teach as Jesus did, by example.

People were drawn to Jesus because they saw love in action. Peer ministers represent a beautiful example of Christ's love in action in our Church. Watching them minister to their own has been one of the most powerful, spiritual experiences of my life. I have no doubt the Holy Spirit is in action when I see adolescents captivate and motivate their peers with their stories. Everybody has a story, and teenagers are eager to listen to those told by peers.

Three common misconceptions held by many youth include: nobody else has my problem, nobody is willing to listen, and nobody really cares. All of these are proved untrue when youths minister to other youth. Adolescents have the same, basic human needs as adults. In ministering through retreats, one becomes a significant person in another's life. One develops, much more, a sense of self-worth. Feeling good about oneself makes one feel lovable. This feeling is essential to the establishment of deep, personal relationships. God's love is experienced relationally by adolescents. Meaningful relationships with peers can help them to better understand God's unconditional love for them. A love they can pass on! What better reason to utilize the gifts of youth in your adolescent retreats?

WORKS CITED

Clark, Dan. *The Missing Link*. Ontario: Humansphere Inc., 1986.

National Conference of Catholic Bishops. *To Teach As Jesus Did*. Washington DC: United States Catholic Conference, 1972.

Reynolds, Brian. *A Chance to Serve: A Peer Ministry Leader's Manual*. Winona MN: St. Mary's Press, 1983.

Ryberg, Denny. *Building Community in Youth Groups*. Loveland CO: Group Books, 1985.

BIBLIOGRAPHY

Bolton, Robert. *People Skills*. New York: Touchstone, 1986.

Brown, Carolyn C. *Youth Ministries: Thinking Big with Small Groups*. Nashville: Abingdon, 1984.

DiGiacomo, James. *Understanding Teenagers*. Allen TX: Argus, 1983.

Doyle, Aileen A. *Youth Retreats: Creating Sacred Space for Young People*. Winona MN: St. Mary's Press, 1986.

_____. *More Youth Retreats*. Winona MN: St. Mary's Press, 1989.

Ekstrom, Reynolds R. "Youth Culture and Teen Spirituality: Signs of the Times." *Readings in Youth Ministry, Vol. I*. Ed. by John Roberto. Washington DC: National Federation For Catholic Youth Ministry, 1986.

_____. *Access Guides for Youth Ministry: Pop Culture*. New Rochelle NY: Don Bosco Multimedia, 1989.

_____ and Roberto, John. *Access Guides for Youth Ministry: Evangelization*. New Rochelle NY: Don Bosco Multimedia, 1990.

Elkind, David. *All Grown Up and No Place to Go*. Reading MA: Addison-Wesley, 1984.

Finn, Virginia. *Pilgrim in the Parish: A Spirituality for Lay Ministers*. Mahwah NJ: Paulist, 1986.

Ianni, Francis A.J. *The Search for Structure: A Report on American Youth Today*. New York: Free Press, 1989.

Leckey, Dolores. *Laity Stirring the Church*. Philadelphia: Fortress, 1987.

Roberto, John. *Access Guides to Youth Ministry: Liturgy and Worship*. New Rochelle NY: Don Bosco Multimedia, 1990.

Shelton, S.J., Charles. *Adolescent Spirituality*. Chicago: Loyola University Press, 1983.

Warrick, Keith et al. *Catholic High School Ministry*. Winona MN: St. Mary's Press, 1986.

Warren, Michael. *Youth ,Gospel, Liberation*. San Francisco: Harper & Row, 1987.

Yaconelli, Mike and Jim Burns. *High School Ministry*. Grand Rapids: Zondervan, 1986.

Chapter 11

Family and Intergenerational Approaches

Rebecca Davis

SACREDNESS OF THE ORDINARY

Since 1980, the Church's Year of the Family, many family spirituality resources have been developed to meet the changing needs of families today. Adopted, extended, merged, nuclear, blended, multi-generational, and enculturated families are words which describe Christian communities, deep in faith and spirituality, good ground for healthy adolescent faith formation. While many changes have occurred in the American family, the family is here to stay. (Ekstrom 29-44)

Catholic tradition affirms that the family constitutes an authentic form of church. Family members, appropriately, may consult their own experiences in the development of a spirituality that fits their family lifestyles. The down-home, ordinary experiences of family living can and do reflect the sacred. (Finley 1984) Family relationships either nourish or inhibit faith-growth in young persons. In relaxed settings, family members have powerful opportunities, teachable moments, to catechize: by showing love, affection, and acceptance; by living Catholic Christian moral beliefs; by responding to the needs of others and working for peace and justice; by facilitating the internalization of moral beliefs; by developing a liberating rather than inflexible faith-life; by sharing stories and experiences of faith; by discussing Scripture and praying with the family; and by reverently receiving the Eucharist and living its spirit. (*Challenge* 6)

Various families give evidence, though, of particular stresses due to separations, divorce, blended-family or single-parent situations, illness, unemployment, over-scheduling, insufficient communication, or an insidious lack of unity. Today, the contemporary family requires helpful directions and new strategies to readily respond to these challenging concerns.

A family is a small group of people who regard themselves bound to each other through abiding links of responsibility for each other's well-being. The family is ". . . a system of interdependent relationships, engaged in change and adaptation, and geared to the growth and support of each member. This is the family's primary function and its main psycho-social task. It is this experience of family which gives us our first sense of who we are and of how we are related." (Durka 79)

The family is the first social sphere a child experiences. To a great extent, family is his or her world. Interaction between family members is the most significant contribution to the child's formation of personality. (Dewey 8). Many parents, and other family members, recognize a need for assistance in fostering faith-growth in adolescents.

When adolescents test their independence from the family, other adults (and family members) may assist parents by serving as Christian role models. A family perspective needs to be woven throughout adolescent catechesis. Acknowledging the importance of the family in catechesis means sponsoring programs for parents around their areas of need, creating parent catechetical experiences that parallel the adolescent catechetical program, sponsoring intergenerational catechetical experiences, and supporting parents in their catechetical ministry. The church of the home needs to reclaim its own mission and task. (Challenge 6)

In an insightful overview of adolescent religious behavior, pollster George Gallup addressed the National Family Life Conference over a decade ago. He advocated that strong support be given to family life because of its centrality in youth's development. (Shelton 7) Gallup highlighted two areas for ministry to adolescents' spiritual formation: Bible study groups and youth retreats. Both activities are enhanced through intergenerational and multicultural approaches. In such settings, adolescents have access to the insights and strengths of different age-groups with varied experience-levels. Such groups are challenged and enriched by participants' accrued wisdom.

After the National Conference of Catholic Bishops' pastoral action plan for family ministry was developed in the 1970s, several pertinent studies were conducted by the Boys Town Center at Catholic University and other research organizations. (Nelson, et al, 1976; Paradis and Thompson, 1976; Thompson, et al, 1976) Among many conclusions, these studies spoke to intergenerational retreats: a) we have and will continue to witness a decline in youth involvement in formal religious education programs; and b) the Church in the past, concerned with erecting schools and church buildings, had precariously neglected the crucial role the family plays in the religious development of young people.

FAMILY SYSTEMS AND FUNCTIONS

As the fundamental social system, family communicates and reinforces religious values, and moral and human values as well. There are no self-sufficient, independent, autonomous family units devoid of social pressures. No one family can meet all the needs of developing adolescents. Like the global, human family, we are interdependent, linked nation to nation, country to country, people to people, heart to heart, and hand to hand. Every decision we make as individuals or as a nation affects the global, family climate. A change in the position, status, behavior, or role(s) of any member, of any family, leads to adaptation in the conduct of other members. A family system is itself an ecological system, in transaction with other systems.

Periods of disequilibrium typify family systems. Systems reform and adapt to cope with changes they experience. Healthy family systems are open to new ideas, outlooks, changes. In contrast, imbalanced families view change as threatening. They rivet themselves in fixed roles and communication patterns.

Each stage in the life cycle of the family is characterized by an average, expectable crisis brought about by the convergence of bio-psychosocial processes which create phase-specific family tasks to be confronted and completed. These family tasks reflect the assumption that developmental tasks of individual family members have an overriding influence or effect on the nature of family life at a given time and present family themes that apply to family members as individuals as well as a group. (Durka 83-84)

INTERGENERATIONAL RETREATS

Intergenerational retreats offer families opportunities to encounter their members as real, multidimensional people. They offer occasions for personal growth and family system replenishment, plus communication, support, companionship, and networking. True companionship in family relationships is often overwhelmed by parenting roles or other role-specific responsibilities. A family's durability and strength depends on the adaptations used to reestablish reasonable balance. Family well-being calls for breakthrough or rediscovery. "Rediscovery refers to intergenerational connectedness as well, with parents and [youth] reinvesting in one another and renegotiating their relationships." (Durka 86)

Intergenerational retreats facilitate the recognition and celebration of Christ present in the dynamics of family life. Such retreat experiences nourish our intimacy with Jesus and with each other. We recover in them a greater sense of the sacredness in ordinary, family interactions and choose to recognize the transcendent, deeper dimensions to even the most prosaic facets of family life. The intergenerational retreat models I include below should offer you some approaches to enrich the health of family spirit.

MODEL I: THE WAY OF THE FAMILY

The Way of the Family is a Lenten Family Day of Reflection designed to develop and support 15 healthy family attributes. It makes use of current, family resources and a contemporary Way of the Cross. You will have to develop a family retreat team to implement this retreat model.

9:00 AM Arrival and Welcome

9:15 Introductions and Opening Prayer

9:30 Family Icebreakers and Focusing Activity

Invite family members to choose a cartoon, TV, song, or movie family that most resembles their own and to share their responses.

10:00 Small Group Parent-Youth Partners

Introduce this activity with words such as these: Lent is a time for renewal and repentance. It is a time to be born again. During Lent, we are invited to examine our lives, to look at and evaluate our relationships with Christ, our friend and Savior, with our families — parents, relationships with our spouses, your children, your friends, and your co-workers. In examining the ways you relate and communicate as a family, you'll also begin to discover the ways you relate to our global, human family.

Arrange family units into varied small groups. Distribute sheets of newsprint and markers to each group. Invite groups to write their definitions of family. Play the song, "We Are Family," by Sister Sledge, over a sound system. Display the groups' definitions by taping them to a prominent wall as they share their responses.

Say, then: In summary, the family is a group of people who consider themselves bound to each other through an enduring commitment and sense of responsibility for each other's well-being, a support system that is central to Church and society.

10:20 Break

10:30 Dyads, Triads, and Me-O-My-Ads

Ask parents and kids to gather in individual family units. Encourage participants to openly share feelings and opinions. Ask all to refrain from critical or corrective responses. The focus of this communication exercise is to cultivate listening skills and to increase understanding. Encourage dialogue.

Youth may choose to share their responses to suggested topics like:

* My most valued possession . . .
* What I believe most deeply in . . .
* The biggest challenge I face right now . . .
* The best part about who I am right now . . .

* A person I really admire a lot . . .
* I like my friends because . . .
* What worries me most . . .
* An area of my life I'd like to improve . . .

Adults may choose then to share their responses to the following:

* How I felt about myself when I was growing up . . .
* The relationship I had with my family and parents when I was living at home . . .
* My most valued possession when I was a teenager . . .
* The best thing I ever did when I was a teenager . . .
* My favorite class and activity when I was growing up . . .
* The number one mistake I ever made when I was a teenager . . .
* The craziest thing I ever did when I was a teenager . . .
* My biggest worry when I was a teenager . . .
* My relationship with God and the Church when I was a teenager . . .

11:00 Enter "The Ways"

A facilitator should say, "Renewal, repentance, and rebirth mandate a willingness to die to self in order that we might rise as new and changed persons. Each of us experiences dyings and risings in everyday routines, with those with whom we share our lives. Often deaths occur through giving to others: giving of our time, of our lives, and of our feelings. It is in and through prayer that we share most deeply in our relationship with God and with one another. By taking a look at the meaning of the Passion of Jesus in our own lives, our families, our relationships will be strengthened and renewed.

Lent is a special time for journeying. The Way of the Cross parallels The Way of the Family. The journey is a life-long process. Today, we are going to create 15 Stations of the Family based on a summary from Dolores Curran's book, *Traits of a Healthy Family*. (Curran 1981) Just as 14 Stations of the Cross cause us to reflect on the meaning, purpose, and example of Jesus' life, we will now explore 15 redemptive, supportive traits of a family's lifeway that give purpose and meaning to each individual family member.

Distribute the handout, "Traits of a Healthy Family: A Summary" (see below 166-167). Also give out copies of Everyone's Way of the Cross to multi-family groups. (Enzler 1986) Invite small-group members to take turns in reading each trait on the healthy family handout. Once each trait is read, invite small-group sharing. Then, encourage groups to identify and discuss how the Way of the Cross relates to the 15 healthy-family traits. For example, healthy family trait #1 says, "The healthy family communicates and listens." Jesus is condemned to death in the first station of the Way of the Cross. Reflect upon how much alone Jesus must have felt when the crowd laughed, shouted, and refused to listen to Him. How do we sometimes do the same with family members? How can we become more loving and accepting toward one another? Allow groups to select a volunteer to record their responses. Play reflective music in the background.

12:00 Noon Lunch and Playtime

1:00 PM Stations of the Way of the Family

Allow groups to share their responses, to the pre-lunch exercise, in the large group. Then, invite multi-family groups to create visual, audio, or written expressions of the 15 Stations of the Way of the Family paralleled with the Way of the Cross. Groups may select one, two, or three Stations to create based on the size of the entire group. Some suggestions include: 1) cut out pictures from various magazines and paste, in collage-fashion, on poster board to show ways in which people today might experience this trait or station; 2) Using markers and sheets of paper, draw ways we may experience this trait or station in our own families; 3) create a modern-day story of the trait or station using a cassette or video recorder; and 4) using clay, make a symbol of this trait or station. A different artistic mode could be used with each trait/station.

2:15 "Trust Them" Exercise; Break

Move participants outdoors, if possible. Divide the large group into smaller groups of five or six. Explain that the purpose of this activity is to develop trust levels and to have fun. Place a chair or other stable object that is at least 3-4 feet high at the end of a double row of small group participants who are facing each other. Ask for a volunteer to stand on the object with his or her arms and hands interlaced and locked over the abdominal area. The volunteer will turn around on signal, close his or her eyes and fall, rigidly, backwards into the double row of extended and interlaced arms of the other small group participants. Invite another volunteer to lie face-up under the "arm-net." Allow everyone an opportunity to experience both roles of falling and watching/praying.

2:45 Family Plans

Invite each family to develop a written resolution to do something practical and possible, as a family, to address the needs and concerns identified in the Stations activity. For example, "This week, we'll be conscious of family members who may feel overwhelmed with challenges they may be facing and do our best to encourage and support them." Then, invite each family member to contribute to writing a family prayer.

3:00   Sharing the "Way of the Family"

In the large group, invite families to share their Stations. They will share their family prayers later.

3:30   Family Reconciliation

Direct all participants to gather informally, in a prepared chapel or church, with lit candles, reflective music, and incense.

Invite one of the retreat team members to say the following: "We have entered into the process of penance and reconciliation. When we do wrong, repent, confess our wrongs to the person(s) we have hurt and to our whole family, we receive pardon and reconciliation, and finally, celebrate that reconciliation. Let's take a look at how a sinner recognized his sin, confessed it, received pardon and reconciliation, and celebrated that experience with his family."

Retreat team, creatively, dramatizes the parable of the Prodigal Son (Lk 15:11-32).

Reflection (by team member): "We prepare for the sacrament of Reconciliation in our daily lives. To recognize sin takes practice. No place is more safe and secure for practicing our sorrow, for the ways we have hurt others, than within a family. Children do this regularly. We are all called to become like children. Admitting that we are wrong, then asking for forgiveness from our own family members, is the ideal preparation for the sacrament. The family needs the warm and wonderful experience that only reconciliation can provide. Without it, old grudges and hurts can tatter the whole fabric of family life. For a holistic family life, expressing sorrow and receiving forgiveness, as we identify it in the rite of reconciliation, is positively essential. As Jesus teaches us, we must forgive, and be forgiven, continually, that is, over and over again."

Distribute small votive candles to every person. Say: "This afternoon, we invite you to take some time to reflect and to receive the sacrament of Reconciliation. Please feel free to go to any of the priests now positioned throughout the chapel (church). Go when you are ready. Also, feel free to go to any of your family members to ask them for forgiveness too. When you are finished, please light your votive candle from our Easter candle. Place it on the family tree next to it."

Place reflective music throughout this period.

4:45   Liturgy Preparation; Break

The retreat team and celebrant should now design pertinent discussion questions for the homily. Incorporate the family prayers at an appropriate time in the liturgy.

5:00   Liturgy

6:00   Family Picnic and Games

8:00 PM Conclusion

Notes: Other intergenerational retreat models will include workshops for youth and adults, simultaneously, which concentrate on matching topics. For instance, a one-day retreat model on teenage sexuality may contain separate and integrated sessions on the subject, for youth and adults. It is important to recognize that the more support and interest a youth receives from an intergenerational system, following a retreat experience, the more effective will be his or her assimilation of the retreat experience.

CHRISTMAS FAMILY RETREAT

(This intergenerational retreat was developed by Rev. Daniel Manger, O.F.M. Conv., Retreat Director, Mount Saint Francis Retreat Center, Mount Saint Francis, IN.)

Friday

7:00 PM	Registration (retreat team)
8:00	Opening orientation and remarks
	Song
8:15	"I Am Joseph, Your Brother"
	(20-minute dramatic portrayal of the Joseph story from Genesis.)
8:45	Adults move to the lounge for discussion; children to activity centers to discuss and do related activities.
9:15	Community time (refreshments, social, etc.)

Saturday

7:30 AM	Rise
8:30	Breakfast
9:30	Morning praise
9:50	"Bethlehem Bake Shop" (in dining room, dress in your work or casual clothes for this one)
12:30 PM	Lunch
1:30	Relaxation time
2:30	Family visitation (in retreat rooms). Each family is visited for some individual ministry by team members. Charade preparation time
4:30	Bible charades

6:00		Dinner
7:30		"Las Posadas: Retracing the Bethlehem Journey"
9:30		Community time; refreshments; storytelling; Christmas carols
Sunday		
8:30	AM	Breakfast
9:30		Morning prayer
9:50		Preparation for Liturgy
10:00		Eucharist
		Stewardship talk and wrap-up
12:30	PM	Dinner
1:30		Conclusion

DRAMA: "I AM JOSEPH, YOUR BROTHER"

Utilize the Old Testament story of Joseph sold off into bondage by his brother; (Gn 37: 39-48). This should be enacted in story form and played out with characters. It is a family story of jealousy and shows how God loves the person who does not give into injustice. Joseph is a symbol of the Dreamer, Reconciler, and Provider. If possible, have a storyteller and dramatize the Joseph story emphasizing these symbols/images (by team members). The actor playing Joseph should pass out flour to each of the families present as the drama ends. The flour should be in sacks (to be used in Saturday's meditation).

"BETHLEHEM BAKE SHOP"

A retreat team member should play God in God's bakery, with other members of the team helping out. God should be in the bakery with three lumps of dough, each with a personality. One personality is shyness (fearful). The second, a real enthusiastic personality. The third is one with a chip on its shoulder, very resistant. God interacts with the three personalities — to mold and convince them to be prepared to be transformed into wonderful pastry. All of the personalities struggle, to a greater or lesser degree, to be shaped by God's hands. The final test will come in being put in an oven, so full transformation can happen. Finally, God manages to coax the most resistant personality into the oven. Out comes the dough transformed into beautiful pastry.

Following this, conduct a kneading party. All of the families should prepare their flour/dough to be baked for Christmas bread. Excess dough from all of the loaves will be used to build a House of Bethlehem Bread, the centerpiece for the meal that evening. (This symbol should continue to connect with the closing Eucharistic Liturgy.) Team members will help on this project. Get the families to participate in bread-shaping and baking — a primary symbol of grace Eucharistic life they share.

This whole activity should be held in a dining room. At first, a team member can be seated behind a large counter. Three other team members, playing the voices or personalities, can be hidden. Then the tables around the dining room can accommodate the kneading part of the activity. Team members give instructions on how much water, yeast, etc., can be used along with other ingredients to make bread. Perhaps a sweet bread can be made. You will need aluminum, recyclable pans for the loaves.

A portion from each family's dough will be needed to construct the manger Bethlehem House of Bread. Then, all build it by shaping a part to be used in the form of a stable. Baking will take place later.

"LAS POSADAS: RETRACING THE BETHLEHEM JOURNEY"

Borrowing from Catholic, Hispanic traditions, a way of luminarios (candles in lunch bags) will line the processional way. Essentially, Joseph and Mary make their journey, with all the retreatants, to the stable. Each station where the retreat team member awaits the arrival of Mary and Joseph represents a particular social problem. The person at the station displays indifference toward Mary and Joseph and, then, a prayer is prayed, by the whole procession, for this world issue. The procession moves on until it arrives at the manger-and-stable setting for conclusion.

The families bring their bread, wrapped, to be placed in the manger when they arrive. Then, a brief homily is given and a song is sung to close the journey. Also, teens could be asked to prepare the lunch bags with sand and candles.

This could be conducted outside. Tents could be set up for the people who are presenting the social problems and the reasons why Mary and Joseph cannot stay there. Supplies needed include votive candles, sand, paper bags, and tents.

SUNDAY LITURGY TO CLOSE THE RETREAT

All of the loaves should be marked with family names, then collected and wrapped. The retreat team will wrap all of the loaves with Christmas wrapping. Before the liturgy, the House of Bread will be placed near the altar of sacrifice, with nicely wrapped bread-presents all around it in the manger. At Communion time, after all have received Communion, St. Nick will show up and kneel in silence before the altar and pray. Then, he will distribute the loaves to families, with an exhortation to share the bread with each other on Christmas to remember Jesus in each other.

SUMMARY: THE PARTS OF A WHOLE

When parts of an intergenerational system are combined effectively, the whole is greater than the sum of its parts. If the family system is to achieve common, mutual goals, it, too, must have a master plan, a blueprint, to sustain individual members in relationship with each other. Building a home can be among the most creative, fulfilling, and challenging tasks of a lifetime. A house is built by fitting together, piece by piece, the foundation, walls, floors, and roof. Building intergenerational relationships, through retreats, also embodies a process of fitting together, person-by-person, until the whole is complete. The ordinary, yet profound, building of the kingdom of God, within youth, is a critical part of the intergenerational weaving of the warp of our faith and the weft of the Spirit.

SUMMARY HANDOUT: TRAITS OF A HEALTHY FAMILY

Trait 1 The healthy family communicates and listens. (mutuality and equality in married relationship, control over TV, listens and responds, recognizes nonverbal messages, encourages individual feelings and independent thinking, recognizes turn-off words and put-down phrases, interrupts, but equally develops a pattern of reconciliation)

Trait 2 The healthy family affirms and supports one another. (parents have good self-esteem, everyone is expected to affirm and support, support doesn't mean pressure, basic mood is positive, supports its institutions but not automatically)

Trait 3 The healthy family teaches respect for others. (respects individual differences within family, respect for self, respect to all groups, not just specifically approved ones, respects individual decisions, shows respect to those outside the family, respects the property of others)

Trait 4 The healthy family develops a sense of trust. (husband and wife trust each other deeply, children are gradually given more opportunity to earn trust, don't play the trust-trap game, doesn't break trust for the amusement of others, broken trust can be mended, all are trustworthy.)

Trait 5 The healthy family has a sense of play and humor. (pays heed to its need to play, recognizes its stress level, doesn't equate play with spending money, uses humor positively)

Trait 6 The healthy family exhibits a sense of shared responsibility. (parents understand relationship between responsibility and self-esteem, understands responsibility means more than doing chores and doesn't necessarily mean orderliness and perfection, gears responsibility to capability, responsibility is paired with recognition, expects members to live with consequences of irresponsibility)

Trait 7 The healthy family teaches a sense of right and wrong. (parents share a consensus of important values and teach clear and specific guidelines about right and wrong, children are held responsible for their own moral behavior, intent is crucial in judging behavior, help children to live morally)

Trait 8 The healthy family has a strong sense of family in which rituals and traditions abound. (treasures its legends and characters, has a person and/or place that serves as locus, makes a conscious effort to gather as a people, views itself as a link between past and future, honors elders and welcomes babies, cherishes it traditions and rituals)

Trait 9 The healthy family has a balance of interaction among members. (does not allow work and other activities to infringe routinely upon family time, actively discourages the formation of cliques within the family)

Trait 10 The healthy family has a shared religious core. (faith in God plays a foundation role in daily family life, religious core strengthens the family support system, parents feel a strong responsibility for passing on the faith, but they do so in positive and meaningful ways)

Trait 11 The healthy family respects the privacy of one another. (looks forward to the teen and separating years, moves from a base of parental rules to one of mutually negotiated rules, does not dole out respect according to age, sex, or any other criterion, respects fads, friends, and confidences, room, privacy, and time to be alone)

Trait 12 The healthy family values service to others. (empathetic and altruistic, serves others in concrete ways, seeks to simplify its life-style, is generously hospitable, keeps its voluntarism under control)

Trait 13 The healthy family fosters table time and conversation.

Trait 14 The healthy family shares leisure time. (keeps collective leisure time in balance, prioritizes activities, prizes time alone with individual members, controls TV, plans how to use its time)

Trait 15 The healthy family admits to and seeks help with problems. (expects problems and considers them to be a normal part of family life, develops problem-solving techniques)

WORKS CITED

The Challenge of Adolescent Catechesis. Washington DC: National Federation For Catholic Youth Ministry, 1986.

Curran, Dolores. *Traits of a Healthy Family.* Minneapolis: Winston Press, 1981.

Dewey, Edith A. *Basic Applications Of Adlerian Psychology.* Coral Springs, FL: CMTI Press, 1978.

Durka, Gloria. "Family Systems: A New Perspective For Youth Ministry." *Readings In Youth Ministry, Volume I.* Ed John Roberto. Washington DC: National Federation For Catholic Youth Ministry, 1986.

Ekstrom, Reynolds R. "The American Family: Change And Diversity." *Growing In Faith — A Catholic Family Sourcebook.* New Rochelle NY: Don Bosco Multimedia, 1990.

Enzler, Clarence. *Everyone's Way Of The Cross.* Notre Dame IN: Ave Maria Press, 1986.

Finley, Mitch and Kathy. "The Sacredness Of The Ordinary." *Family Spirituality.* Kansas City: National Association Of Catholic Diocesan Family Life Ministers, 1984.

Nelson, Hart M., Raymond H Potvin et. al. *The Religion of Children* Washington DC: United States Catholic Conference, 1976.

Paradis, Wilfred and Andrew Thompson. *Where Are The 6.6. Million?* Washington DC: United States Catholic Conference, 1976.

Potvin, Raymond H., Dean Hoge et. al. *Religion and American Youth* Washington DC: United States Catholic Conference, 1976.

Roberto, John, editor. *Growing In Faith — A Catholic Family Sourcebook.* New Rochelle NY: Don Bosco Multimedia, 1990.

Shelton, S.J., Charles M. *Adolescent Spirituality.* Chicago: Loyola University Press, 1983.

Thompson, Andrew A. et. al. *The Next Fifteen Years.* Washington DC: National Catholic Educational Association, 1976.

BIBLIOGRAPHY

Bradshaw, John. *Bradshaw on the Family.* Deerfield: Health Communications, 1988.

Friedman, Edwin. *Generation to Generation: Family Process in Church and Synagogue.* New York: Guilford Press, 1985.

_____ "A Family View of Rites of Passage." *Growing In Faith — A Catholic Family Sourcebook.* New Rochelle: Don Bosco Multimedia, 1990.

Fowler, James. "Faith Development Through The Family Life Cycle." *Growing In Faith — A Catholic Family Sourcebook.* New Rochelle: Don Bosco Multimedia, 1990.

Iannone, Joseph and Mercedes. "The Educational Ministry of the Christian Family." *Living Light* 21:2 (January 1985).

McGinnis, James and Kathleen. "The Social Mission of the Family." *Growing In Faith — A Catholic Family Sourcebook.* New Rochelle: Don Bosco Multimedia, 1990.

Stinnett, Nick and DeFrain, John. *Secrets of Strong Families.* New York: Berkley Books, 1985.

Strommen, Merton and Irene. *Five Cries of Parents.* San Francisco: Harper and Row, 1985.

Chapter 12

Issues to Handle with Care

Robert McCarty

You have a creative schedule. You have even reserved the retreat site. And you have planned for great refreshments. What could possibly go wrong? There are several key factors in developing effective retreat programs that, when ignored or forgotten, can undo the best of planning efforts. There are important issues not readily apparent in retreat planning. These must be addressed prior to a retreat for adolescents. Such issues fall into four general categories:

Participant issues — handling discipline problems and cliques;

Retreat team issues — handling inappropriate behavior by team members; the "counseling trap"; and "my personal opinion versus Church teaching" issues;

Programming issues — developing an appropriate pace for your retreat schedule; emotional manipulation issues; liturgy and prayer concerns; and parental involvement concerns;

Legal issues — use of permission forms; adequate supervision on retreats; volunteer covenants; and transportation issues.

This is not an all-inclusive listing of issues which should be addressed in planning effective adolescent retreats. Nor can each issue be handled here in full. But the issues listed do identify key concerns that sometimes get lost in the planning process. Let us review each issue now and possible responses.

PARTICIPANT ISSUES

DISCIPLINE

One of the most difficult aspects of leading a retreat for young people is handling discipline. It is easy to get frustrated when participants do not behave appropriately, when they break rules, when they, generally, act like adolescents. At one moment, they can be discussing very relevant and critical issues of faith, belief, and values. Then, in the next moment, they cover a room with shaving cream, sneak off to drink, or break curfew. "What's wrong with them? How could they do this to me?" you wonder. "I thought they were so mature!"

Adolescents are at a point in life in which they borrow behaviors from both adult years and junior high. They are capable of both types of behavior. This is not a contradiction for them. In fact, aren't we adults capable of the same? We rationalize. We say it is the adolescent in us coming out! The key to effective retreat discipline is identifying clear guidelines and consequences, then making sure retreat participants know them.

Response: Pre-Retreat

It is important that participants have a clear understanding of the retreat's goals and purpose, the expectations, and the rules. Is this retreat for fun? For community building? Does it have a theme? Is there free time? All participants need to know what the retreat is meant to accomplish. They can begin, then, to internalize expectations and appropriate behavior. This can be made clear during pre-retreat meetings with all. Expectations can be outlined, the schedule reviewed, and questions and concerns addressed.

Use of a written Code of Conduct is always very important for adolescent retreats. This Code of Conduct should list expectations about retreat behavior. It is often signed by both participants and their parents in advance of retreats. The Code lists that which is not allowed (e.g., alcohol, drugs, large radios perhaps,. . .) as well as what is expected. For example, a Code could incorporate a statement like: "Given the nature of this retreat, it is expected that the participants will commit to being fully involved in the various activities. . . ."

It is a good practice to send this Code to retreatants' parents. It might be helpful to list, on the Code, the "going home offenses," the GHOs, you will enforce. GHOs might include drinking, possessing or doing drugs, malicious damage to the retreat facility, and flagrant, out-of-bounds activity (e.g., leaving the retreat center's property or being in the room of a person of the opposite sex). Whatever your list might include, a good practice is to describe the consequences of certain things (e.g., parents will be called and asked to pick up their child). Having parents and youth sign your Code, hopefully, will ensure that they have read it.

Response: Opening Session

As the retreat begins, the director should review the Code of Conduct, program objectives, and all expectations with retreat participants. Spell rules and regulations out clearly. That is the only way accountability can be expected.

Response: Resolving Problems During A Retreat

Whenever a problem arises, the retreat director should sit down with participants involved and ask the right questions.

* What was going on?

* Who was involved?

* What are the rules which apply?

* What does the Code of Conduct state?

* What were you told about the consequences?

Certainly, it is never so easy! Keep the discussion focused on agreed-upon expectations. Discipline problems and dialogues can be opportunities for personal growth and mature decision-making, for choice of appropriate behaviors, and even for reconciliation. Importantly, retreat directors must not see problem behavior as a personal affront ("How could you do this to me?"). In keeping some personal distance, a director can walk a retreat participant through situations and point out other options, decisions, and unforeseen consequences. The director has to follow through in terms of the stated consequences.

Not every discipline issue during a youth retreat is a GHO. So, appropriate consequences will vary. It may be helpful for a retreat director to talk over problem situations, and possible responses, with his or her retreat team before confronting a difficult matter. This will give perspective, other viewpoints, and time to vent emotions. In summary, it is important for a retreat director to confront discipline issues, rely on a Code of Conduct, and determine appropriate responses.

CLIQUES

It is natural for people in new situations to want to hang around their friends. Thus, cliques are normal. They are common in any type of youth retreat, parish, school, or diocesan-sponsored. While perhaps providing a sense of security, cliques can be annoying or harmful to a retreat when they prevent youth participants from interacting with the whole group. Cliques require a both-and response.

Response: Rather than trying to break up every clique ("What? We are not a clique. We're just friends."), develop opportunities within your retreats for mixed groupings. Encourage participants to meet and work with others. Throughout each adolescent retreat, use activities which ask participants, at times, to be with their friends (e.g., get with any two other people to. . .) and which, on the other hand, help them meet new people (periodically use one-to-one activities or pre-assigned small groups). It is normal to want to be with our friends. We do it all the time! But, a retreat offers a special opportunity to move out from the security of our personal circle. Retreats which give youth time for both friends and new relationships will encounter greater cooperation and less resistance from participants.

RETREAT TEAM ISSUES

It is not always the participants who cause difficulties on a retreat. Whether a team is composed of adolescent peer ministers, young adults, older adults, or some combination of these, there are several key issues that should be considered.

INAPPROPRIATE BEHAVIOR

Sometimes, the retreat team creates problems. Disruptive behaviors, drinking, doing drugs, inappropriate relationships with retreat participants... the list could go on.

Response: The key to dealing with staff is very similar to the key in dealing with retreat participant discipline. Instead of a Code of Conduct for your team (which may be appropriate), job descriptions for retreat team members are very important. Have clear expectations, mutually agreed upon, by both team and director. It is a good idea for retreat teams to devote a planning session to the development of job descriptions. (Or they could review and revise already existing descriptions.)

The retreat director, also, should ask his or her retreat team about consequences. What should be the GHOs for team members? What are fair expectations about team members' behavior? Whenever a situation arises, a director will have to meet with a team member, during a retreat, to confront a problem, just as if it were a participant issue.

THE COUNSELING TRAP

Commonly, on a retreat, a young person will confide in a team member. The retreat experience fosters sharing and openness. It helps participants confront personal issues. It is important, though, for team members to avoid the counseling trap. Quite simply, retreat team members are not (usually) trained counselors. This does not mean they can do nothing. It does mean they must know their limits. They should identify the roles they can play and they have to avoid trying to save a young person experiencing crisis.

Response: Often retreat team members are effective listeners. They are relational friends. It is appropriate for team members to help youth clarify concerns and give them an opportunity to ventilate their feelings. In the case of a parish retreat, during which a parish team has been involved, it may be appropriate to follow up with a call or visit after the retreat. In most cases, though, the role of the team member is to connect and refer.

When retreat team members are not from the participants' parishes or schools, it is important to connect hurting youth with their youth group advisor, youth minister, school moderator or counselor, or other significant adults or parents. One need not violate confidentiality. Simply tell the significant adult that you have some concerns about a certain young person; then ask that someone to make contact with that adolescent as a follow-up to the retreat.

Sometimes the issues involved prove more serious. These call for a referral to a professional. The parish, school, or diocese should be able to find a suitable counselor or youth-serving agency for an adolescent in crisis. Serious family, substance abuse, and personal problems require long-term care. It is a disservice to young people whenever team members do not connect them with more professional, consistent care. It is important for every retreat team member to say, "I am really concerned about this issue, but I do not have the skills to really help you. Let's find someone who is better able to handle this."

Retreat directors and team members should check state laws. Know what needs to be reported. In most states, suspicion of child abuse must be reported to local authorities. This is a good topic for a retreat team training session. Teams might want to role-play ways to handle such situations.

"MY OPINION VERSUS CHURCH TEACHING"

It is common for young people to probe retreat team members about their values and beliefs. However, what if a team member holds a view contrary to official Church teaching? Mass attendance, sexual morality, and Church doctrine are areas ripe for discussion among young people. How does a retreat team minister respond when challenged with "I know what the Church teaches, but what do you believe?"

It is very difficult for any team member to share the entire process of decision-making and reflection that has led him or her to a view which differs from Church teaching. In fact, it is not fair to the team member nor the participants to try to share it all. A young person, simply, might be looking for confirmation of something he or she already believes, "Well, the retreat team said it was okay to. . ." This could prove very embarrassing to a team.

Response: Remember, at all times, the retreat team represents the Church. A retreat team is always "on." Therefore, members must articulate the Church's teachings on sensitive topics. The retreat team enables retreatants to incorporate Church tradition and teaching as their own. Yet, the task of fostering critical thinking skills should not be neglected. Adolescent retreats provide excellent opportunities for young people to search out personal values and beliefs. A retreat team must ask good questions. It should enable participants to give birth to their own freely-chosen beliefs and faith.

It is not avoidance to turn participants' questions back to them. What do you think? How did you come to believe that? How do you understand this Church teaching? How would you handle this argument or situation? But, it is also inappropriate for a team to use a retreat to push its own, personal agendas. Retreat teams should discuss this "My opinion versus Church teaching" issue, and then role-play possible responses.

PROGRAM ISSUES

PACE

Retreat teams should understand that a variety of personality types and learning styles is present in any group of individuals, retreat groups included, so attention should be paid to the kinds of activities planned during retreat programs.

Response: Youth retreats ought to incorporate large group and small group discussions, individual reflection sheets, quiet-time, various forms of prayer and worship, fun, and other activities in order to accommodate a variety of personality types. Pay attention to each retreat group's responses to activities. Care should be shown to participants who are uncomfortable with writing and/or reading exercises due to learning disabilities. Balance and flexibility should prevail. It is not necessary to pack every minute of a youth retreat. Social time is very valuable to adolescent participants. It is essential for community building.

MANIPULATION OF EMOTIONS

Never evaluate the effectiveness of your retreat by the number of tears shed. Though not as common today, due to a better understanding of retreats in youth ministry, there was a tendency in the past to evaluate retreats on the expression of emotions by participants. This amounted to manipulation by retreat directors and teams.

Response: Make sure your youth retreat schedules include sufficient breaks for relaxation and fun, plus enough time for sleep. Appropriate curfews should be set for all participants. The more tired participants become, the more prone they are to emotional outbursts. Remain conscious of session topics and activities, too. Recall the objectives of youth retreats. They are not meant to be therapy groups.

PRAYER AND WORSHIP

Retreats offer opportunities for creativity in prayer experiences, Eucharist, and the celebration of reconciliation. Worship should be the highlight of your adolescent retreats. It should be a genuine celebration of shared faith in Jesus.

Response: Plan carefully! Prayer and Liturgy should flow from the topics and activities of your retreats. Participants tend to remember prayer and liturgical celebrations more than any particular topic of a retreat. So, give these celebrations appropriate energy and attention. Try to be conscious of multicultural dimensions in your planning of prayer and worship. Draw from the richness of various cultural and ethnic traditions, as well as the richness of youth culture — their music, their symbols, etc.

PARENTAL INVOLVEMENT

Incorporating the family into retreat programs will provide support and follow-up for adolescents. It is not essential that every youth retreat be an intergenerational or family experience. Yet, there are ways to connect parents to adolescent retreat experiences.

Response: Consider sending parents a letter explaining the objectives of a youth retreat, along with a Code of Conduct, discussed previously, and a permission form. (See notes on permission forms below.) Parents could be invited to write letters of support to their children. These letters, then, could be delivered during your youth retreat. Participants could be encouraged to write letters of thanksgiving, or even "state of the union" (here's how I am doing) letters to their parents. The retreat team members could mail them. If the situation is right, invite parents to your closing Liturgy.

Other ideas: A short prayer service could be sent to families for use when retreat participants get home. This could connect some theme from a youth retreat with back home. A follow-up letter to parents could also offer some ideas on how to support adolescents following their retreats.

LEGAL ISSUES

There are several legal and paralegal issues which retreat directors and planners should address. These lead to procedures which need to be instituted.

PERMISSION FORMS

These forms perform a number of important functions. They serve as information sheets for parents. They list the basic facts of a retreat: departure times, locations, emergency phone numbers. Permission forms can include a "Waiver and Hold Harmless Agreement." This informs parents of potential risks and asks for acceptance of responsibility. Permission forms should also include basic medical and insurance information. Include a permission for treatment clause. These forms do not make retreat sponsors immune to civil suits in cases of negligence. But, they spell out levels of responsibility. Always use permission forms and information sheets for overnight activities and for activities outside-the-parish/school boundaries. A sample parental agreement and permission form is included at the conclusion of this chapter.

TRANSPORTATION

Chartered bus is the preferred mode of transportation to and from many youth activities. When adult advisors or parents provide transportation in personal vehicles, your young people's parents should all be informed. Appropriate insurance should be required of each driver. At no time should adolescents be allowed to provide their own transportation to and from youth activities. At the end of any program, the director (or parish youth minister) has the responsibility to wait until all participants have been picked up.

SUPERVISION

The duties of supervision fall to the youth retreat director. He or she acts *in loco parentis* — in the place of parents. The director is expected to provide appropriate supervision and to protect retreat participants from harm.

VOLUNTEERS

Screen volunteers carefully before placing them in positions of responsibility and authority. Any volunteer guilty of sexual abuse must be terminated immediately. Any volunteer suspected or accused of sexual misconduct should be suspended and provided due process. A volunteer who acts irresponsibly should not be given further responsibilities.

CRISIS MANAGEMENT

Each retreat team member needs to give some thought to how crises will be handled during retreats. Medical emergencies, emotional outbursts, suicidal threats, and other personal traumas can easily arise. Retreat teams should consider procedures for handling emergencies. Decide who will handle first aid, who will be the primary contact(s) with parents, and if or how retreat participants will be told of problems at hand. The team should encourage any adolescent in crisis to make parental contact. The retreat director should communicate directly with parents, too, whenever necessary.

CONCLUSION

It was not my intention to overwhelm anyone responsible for planning and implementing retreats for young people. Retreats are integral to our youth ministry. They provide opportunities for adolescents to reflect on their faith, to consider their relationships with others, and to experience a genuine sense of community. Careful planning allows all retreat objectives to be accomplished. It enhances our efforts in fostering the faith-maturing process in youth.

PARENTAL AGREEMENT AND PERMISSION SLIP

Name   Home Phone

Address   Parent's Work Phone

(Street)(City)(Zip)

In consideration of the wholesome recreation and/or learning experience in which my son/daughter will participate, I/we, as parent(s) or guardian(s) of   allow my/our son/daughter to accompany the youth group to their organized group trips, or activities during   .

By so permitting my/our son/daughter to participate, I/we expect reasonable and adequate supervision of my child. It is thus agreed that I/we will hold   , and all their agents, servants, and employees harmless from all liability and all legal proceedings arising from this trip or activity, unless caused by or due to the gross negligence.

* * * * *

I hereby grant permission to the youth group's adult advisor in charge to obtain medical care from a licensed physician, hospital, or medical clinic for my/our son/daughter in the event that I cannot be reached.

I am covered for hospitalization and medical care under policy #   , issued by   .

Father (Guardian-Responsible Party)

Mother (Guardian-Responsible Party)

Date   , 19   .

Add any other medical information concerning medication, allergies, dietary restrictions:

Chapter 13

Evaluating Adolescent Retreats

Jeffrey Kaster

A pastor came up to me at the conclusion of a parish confirmation retreat. He asked, "How did it go?" My mind raced. I remembered the opening session, 46 tenth grade youths giving me that look, "How boring will this be?" Then, the image of a small-group session in which a young person admitted, honestly, "I'm really not sure what I believe in." I recalled a powerful drama about Jesus mending a wounded heart. A fourth image came back — the reconciliation service during which a number of those in the back of the church talked and laughed during the examination of conscience. Finally, I remembered tears from a few youth after they had received a surprise letter from their parents, telling them of their love. Given this mix of images, how could I say, accurately, how the retreat had gone?

For some, the retreat had seemed like a very positive, perhaps powerful experience. To others, it seemed like a waste of time. I answered the pastor. "We took evaluations at the end of the retreat. I will send you the results in a few days." Here are a few responses from adolescent participants concerning that retreat:

"This retreat was excellent. I guess I really didn't want to come. But I'm very glad I did. I kind of wish it was longer. I really liked the skits you put on. They were effective."

"Some of the stuff was uncomfortable and sappy. I was practically forced to come here as was almost everyone else. Get off our backs. If we don't participate, that is why."

"Everything was great. Reconciliation was a great part because I haven't opened up my problems for a long time."

What is striking is that these adolescents attended the same retreat, yet they had such different reactions to it. Effective retreat evaluations can give you the information necessary to answer, objectively, the question, "How did it go?"

This essay is about the process of evaluating retreats, and about the process of forming retreat teams. It will focus on several questions.

1) How are diocesan retreat teams formed?
2) How can evaluation process be used simply yet effectively?
3) Can evaluation actually prove to be a key to successful retreats?

I hope to show that evaluations are keys in building excellent and credible retreat programs. As we begin, though, one word of caution. Experiences of God, during retreats, are not easily evaluated. God can be experienced in many ways. If someone were to shed tears on a retreat, would that mean he or she has experienced God? If someone were to get angry about something said during a retreat for youth, would that mean he or she has not experienced God? Experiences of God are deeply mysterious and very diverse. Keep in the forefront of your retreat ministry that God is at work. Our God has been known to throw us curveballs when we expect a fastball.

FORMING DIOCESAN RETREAT TEAMS

I was hired in 1989 by the Diocese of St. Cloud, MN, as its consultant for youth. The first item on my job description read, "Recruit and train teams to conduct retreats for youth." This was a new position in the diocese. These retreats for adolescents would be a new service offered through the diocesan Bureau of Education. My main goal, in beginning the St. Cloud Diocesan Retreat Teams, was to provide excellent retreat experiences. I wanted our retreat teams to build an excellent reputation within the diocese. I started slowly. I wanted to build the highest quality program possible. From the start, I realized that a primary task would be to enable teams to offer effective retreats, independently. I believed that if I did this well, then, I would not need to attend each youth retreat. Our first year focus was confirmation retreats. That was the need most often expressed in a diocesan youth ministry survey, conducted the year before, by the diocesan pastoral council.

THE FIRST TASK: In forming retreat teams, set overall goals for your retreats and your teams. I set four goals:
1) establish two or three teams of six adults who will be willing to present up to two youth retreats per month;
2) enable each retreat team, through training and use of their gifts, to present effective retreats;

3) create retreat environments which allow young persons the opportunity to experience the personal love, forgiveness, and call of Christ; 4) provide a positive experience of Church and retreats to young people.

THE SECOND TASK: In forming retreat teams, recruit prospective members. I set certain qualities for retreat team membership:

* a person of faith, committed to Christ and the Church;

* a person of prayer;

* a person who likes and enjoys youth;

* a person willing to use his or her gifts in the service of youth;

* a person willing to commit himself or herself to work (at most) two retreats a month during the school year.

I had two major concerns about prospective members. I wondered if I could find mature, faithful, fun-loving, theologically-balanced adults to serve on these teams. I was concerned, also, about liability and abuse issues. These concerns prompted me to screen, thoroughly, all candidates for these teams.

I screened applicants using this process. I recruited team candidates through recommendations from the campus ministry offices of three colleges in the area, from the central Minnesota TEC (Teens Encounter Christ) program, and from two Catholic college student service programs. Another recruitment method you might use is invitation to adults who are already active in parish youth ministries or retreat ministries.

Experience has shown that we, also, should include high school-age youth on our retreat teams. We will recruit these adolescents through recommendations from parish coordinators of youth ministry, from youth who attend a summer, regional leadership camp, and from the diocesan youth council. A key in the screening process: retreat team candidates should be recommended for team membership by a responsible person.

Next, I sent each retreat team candidate an application form. I checked their references and their backgrounds. Then, I set up a personal interview with each prospect. During the interviews, I tried to determine each candidate's maturity, his or her ability to make commitments, motivation to be on these teams, ability to reach out to youth, and his or her basic theology.

I believe the critical factor in forming successful retreat teams is adequate screening. Having now observed our teams in action, the personal qualities I see as most indicative of effective retreat ministers are: spiritual vitality; prayerfulness; joyfulness; ability to take risks; deep respect for youth; willingness to listen to adolescents' opinions; cooperation; dependability; and desire to share one's faith journey with others.

Eleven young adults were accepted for the St. Cloud Diocesan Retreat Teams. Three others were willing to substitute when needed. Two retreat teams were formed. Each team member was willing to do up to two youth retreats per month.

TRAINING DIOCESAN RETREAT TEAMS

Training was designed to enable retreat team members to give effective youth retreats. This training consisted of two evening sessions and one weekend session.

EVENING ONE:
1) Introductions and sharing of faith stories. Discussion: "How did you become aware of God's presence in your life?"

2) History, purpose, and goals of retreat teams

3) Input on evangelization

4) Retreat team guidelines

EVENING TWO:
1) The needs of youth

2) Theology of confirmation

3) Incorporating sacramental experiences on adolescent retreats

WEEKEND RETREAT:
1) Community building

2) Dividing into teams

3) Review the retreat format
   a. goals and objectives
   b. scheduling
   c. components — talks, small groups, icebreakers, dramas, music, liturgical options

4) Teams practice giving parts of retreat

5) Closing liturgy: "Empowerment through the Holy Spirit"

During our third training session, each team actually practiced presenting parts of a retreat before others. After these practice sessions, suggestions were made on possible improvements. The training sessions bonded our team members together. A sense of community, mission, and service developed.

THE RETREAT EVALUATION PROCESS

Before you can evaluate something accurately, you should have very clear statements on what you wanted to accomplish. These statements are called goals and objectives. Effective retreat evaluations should always focus on the goals and objectives of your retreat. Evaluations simply determine if a retreat accomplished what it set out to do. They answer the basic question: How well did the retreat meet its goals and objectives?

What if a retreat does not accomplish that which it set out to do? This question addresses the basic fear in evaluation process. The fear of failure. I believe it is acceptable to fail. If we put forth good effort, yet something just doesn't work, it is okay. It is not okay to make the same mistake twice. Evaluations can inform us about what, exactly, did not work and can give us insights into why. We can learn to not repeat the mistakes we have made.

I went along as an observer on the first retreats our diocesan teams implemented. After each retreat, we dialogued about strengths and weaknesses. Also, we asked each person who had attended the retreats to complete an evaluation form. Usually, we read through these immediately to get a general sense of what youth had thought. A few days later, I compiled the results of the retreatants' evaluations, then wrote my specific comments concerning retreat strengths and weaknesses.

Once I no longer attended parish youth retreats, I made contact with the pastor, religious education coordinator, or coordinator of youth ministry for feedback. I would include their comments with retreatants' evaluations on a written form sent to each team member and to parish contact persons. The specific information on this form included the name of the parish, its location, retreat date, time, number of participants, team members present, summary of retreatants' written evaluations, general observations about the retreat, and specific suggestions for improvement. These were dated by me, signed, then mailed. Here are some examples of the general observations and suggestions for improvement on the first retreat a team gave:

General Observations

I thought the retreat team did an excellent job! I believe the retreat accomplished what it was designed to do. For the very first retreat, I was very pleased. I especially thought the following were excellent:

1) opening session;

2) the dramas;

3) the large-group game;

4) Alan's talk;

5) prayer with youth.

Suggestions for Improvement

1) watch sight lines in the dramas; make sure the audience can see your actions;

2) short witness talks should spend more time on "the story"; give details of what happened in your life to bring you to Christ;

3) watch the time!; a break before the reconciliation service would have helped;

4) use liturgical music which is "live" in the reconciliation service;

5) have more lighting during the reconciliation service.

An important lesson I have learned is that new problems surface constantly. It is better to be direct and clear about these, rather than indirect and general, in fear of hurting someone's feelings. A case in point: our teams did an overnight confirmation retreat for six rural parishes. I joined the teams for the first day of this retreat. But, I was unable to stay overnight. I came back the next morning. While having a cup of coffee with an adult chaperone from one of the parishes, she mentioned her concerns about a male team member doing some counseling with an adolescent female. She said they had talked for some time, after lights were out, and that they had been alone in a small room. I listened to her concerns and said I would follow up.

I was nervous about how to handle this. I decided to talk, privately, with the retreat team member about it once the retreat had been completed. I told him directly about the concerns the chaperone had expressed. He said the female retreatant had been sharing so deeply about so many hurts in her family, he just could not stop her. I listened. Then, I explained that it had been inappropriate for him to be alone with the girl after lights out. I discussed the liability issues involved. At the same time, I tried to reassure the team member that listening to adolescents can be very healing for them. I was surprised that he did not get defensive. He understood the problem, and he assured me that it would not happen again. On the retreat evaluation form, I wrote later, under specific suggestions for improvement,

The team has to be very careful about getting all students to their rooms by lights out. The team needs to be clear about the inappropriateness of listening to students in a one-to-one session after the time lights are to be turned off.

In following-up in a direct way, a potentially damaging situation was dealt with honestly, fairly, and professionally.

ADOLESCENT EVALUATIONS OF RETREATS

A key element in a retreat evaluation process is asking adolescents on a retreat what they thought about it. Compile their responses on a summary statement. What should be asked on youths' evaluation forms? Again, I remind you that evaluations, to be effective, must be linked to a retreat's goals and objectives. This is the one place at which the majority of evaluations go wrong. I teach a pastoral ministry course on retreat work. This is the one area in which my students have the most trouble. Their retreat evaluations, typically, include only two questions. First: Did you have fun on this retreat? Second: What did you like or dislike about this retreat? Now these are fine questions. But, they do not tie the evaluation process directly to the goals and objectives of a retreat (unless the only goal established for their retreats was to have fun).

Look at the goal and the objectives for the retreat that our retreat teams have facilitated.

Goal: Retreatants will experience God's love and forgiveness in a personal way.

Objectives:

1) Retreatants will leave the retreat saying it was a positive experience.

2) Retreatants will hear the gospel that Jesus loves them, proclaimed through talks, dramas, small groups, and friendly outreach.

The evaluation form we have used to determine if we have met this goal and objectives includes:

Retreat Evaluation

1) Do you think that this retreat was a positive experience?

Yes   No   Unsure

2) Did you hear the gospel proclaimed that Jesus loves you?

Yes   No   Unsure

3) Did this retreat help you experience God's love and forgiveness in a personal way?

Yes   No   Unsure

4) Overall, how would you rate this retreat?

Excellent Good Fair Poor

5) Comments

What could be improved?

What did you especially like?

The first three questions are linked, directly, to the goal and the objectives of the retreat. We wanted to hear what youth thought, if they believed that the retreat team had accomplished what it set out to do. Question four has given us general perceptions about what they have thought. This question, therefore, is related to the general goal of the retreat team: give excellent retreats. The final comments we have elicited have given us specific information about strengths and weaknesses of our retreats.

INTERPRETING EVALUATION RESULTS

The data from evaluations we have implemented tell us that our retreats have gone quite well. For the majority of adolescent retreatants, the retreat has met its objectives. Not all thought it was excellent, but that continues to be a goal for which our retreat teams strive. I find most interesting, in evaluating retreats, the instant credibility often given to negative responses. When a team reads through written evaluations, initially, one response that affects it most is a negative one. For example, one student wrote: "I was practically forced to come here as was almost everyone else. Get off our backs." Our teams, often, have been deeply affected by negative comments from a few retreatants. But, in looking at all evaluations, we have been continually amazed that so many youth have felt the retreat experience was positive, that they had heard the gospel proclaimed, and that they had had a personal experience of God's love and forgiveness.

At the end of our teams' first year, I added all evaluation responses into a year-end report. This report has been used to evaluate the first year of the St. Cloud Diocesan Retreat Teams. It will be used, again, in future years for comparisons. The results include:

* 12 retreats given
* 19 parishes participating
* Types of retreats
  confirmation: 8
  youth groups: 2
  junior high: 2
* Number of youth attending retreats: 475
* Summary of youth evaluations
  Question 1 — Positive experience: Yes 94%; No 1%; Not sure 5%
  Question 2 — Gospel proclaimed: Yes 90%; No 1%; Not sure 9%
  Question 3 — God's love experienced: Yes 86%; No 4%;
    Not sure 10%
  Question 4 — Overall ratings: Excellent 50%; Good 42%; Fair 7%;
    Poor 1%

I have shown these results to my supervisor and he was pleased. He was even more pleased, though, to see some data which give accurate insight into our retreat ministry's successes. Too often, evaluations within church settings are based, solely, on complaints or praises of one or two persons. Written evaluations provide a much broader base from which we can assess the effectiveness of any program. I mentioned earlier that I wanted to build a reputation of excellence for these retreat teams within the diocese. Statistics give solid evidence that our retreat teams are developing an excellent record. It is also important to note that effective marketing means informing the public about successes. Our results were published in our diocesan newspaper in an article about the retreat teams.

I believe we can trust responses from those present on adolescent retreats. If they don't like something they will tell us so. We have a chance, then, to fix problems before the next retreat. Evaluations, also, put into perspective the amount of value we should give to negative remarks. If half of all participants indicate that a retreat was poor, a strong statement about a retreat has been made. If one or two say a retreat was poor, a different type of statement gets made. Building successful retreat ministries demands we know what those who attended retreats have thought. Remember the story of the pastor who asked me, at the conclusion of a youth retreat, "How did it go?" I hope this essay will continue to help us answer such questions more objectively.

I conclude with a few cautions concerning evaluations within a ministry perspective. I do not believe that God is an accountant. I do not believe God judges the successes or shortcomings of a retreat on how positive an experience it was for those participating. Second, I believe the challenge of the Gospel actually should make us uncomfortable at times. Like all ministries of the Church, retreat ministry must be challenging. Third, I am constantly amazed by those who end up in ministry. Often, I have heard stories from youth ministers, priests, religious education coordinators, and members of religious communities who tell us that when they were young, they were the ones who caused much trouble on retreats and in their religion classes. God has very strange ways, especially with the troublemakers on our retreats. Finally, I believe evaluations are useful tools which affirm the high quality of ministry for which we strive in the Church.

Chapter 14

Follow-up Programming for Adolescent Retreats

Rebecca Davis

Oh, my God, it was so unreal! Here I was so excited. I was so high on God. I had this tremendous love for everybody. I felt like I could even be nice to my little sister, until she ran out to my car, flapping her arms. Before I could even slam the door shut, she was telling me Mom and Dad had moved all my stuff out to the garage, disinfected my room, and now she had it. I couldn't believe it! I was feeling so good, and she just dumped her usual garbage all over me. She said Mom and Dad kinda liked me being gone for three days and that they were thinking about asking me to move out for good. The next day, at school, I tried to tell my friends what it was like. After a while, they started razzing me. They were saying I'd better give up Jill and enter the priesthood. They just don't understand what happened.

Mike's frustration and confusion reflect the reality many youth encounter after a dynamic, life-changing retreat experience. Eager to share intense experiences with family and friends, they often find the opposite of what they expect. Instead of support, enthusiasm, and joy, some face isolation, ridicule, and complacency. When they do not have an opportunity to keep retreat experience alive, their social environments, everyday routines, and pre-retreat attitudes can choke the blooms from their new-life experiences and smother the awakening roots of faith.

Youthworkers' services are equated, often, with those of midwifery. We assist young people in reflecting upon their life experiences and in giving birth to interpretations of those experiences in light of Christian faith. Another image for our ministry is that of sowers. Those who plant the seeds of God's Word should undertake proper soil preparation. Central to our mid-wifing and sowing ministry is a key question about healthy, adolescent faith-development: What do we do once the child is born anew or the seedling has broken ground in the garden?

Should adolescents reach an "aha" moment on a retreat, how can we follow-up on it, enabling a continuing, resounding "Amen?" How do we cultivate further opportunities for the Spirit to do what the Spirit does best? What types of tools and resources can we hand our young people to combat the typical, incessant garden weeds of post-retreat loneliness, misunderstanding, doubt, and feelings of being unappreciated?

Left unattended, gardens grow weeds. That is why retreat follow-ups, like medical check-ups for the body, are essential to the ongoing spiritual health of post-retreat adolescents. The following guidelines and examples may offer some insights on how retreat ministers, like weekend gardeners, cultivate in youth the fruits of the spirit in all seasons.

A HOLISTIC RETREAT PROCESS

Often relegated to the fine-print in retreat manuals, the retreat follow-up typically is tacitly assumed, completely overlooked, or nonexistent. The contributing factors to this type of critical, gardener's neglect range from lack of experience and resources among retreat teams to overburdened schedules and physical exhaustion — occupational hazards inherent in the art of ministry, as Joanne Cahoon points out in her Chapter 6 essay. As every good ministry gardener soon learns, each seedling is different. Some require extra amounts of TLC, tender loving care. A comprehensive approach to youth retreats will stress that it is absolutely essential to prepare young people for post-retreat, Monday morning Jesus experiences. (Moore 1984)

Negative, post-retreat feelings, identified earlier, are sometimes part of the total experience of a youth retreat. While not completely bad nor to be completely avoided, they can produce adverse, even devastating effects when they catch adolescents unprepared, totally by surprise. We can encourage youth to face these feelings head-on, with the support of others. We can help them understand that we cannot maintain forever the intensity of a "mountaintop" retreat experience. We can show them the power in crossing the barren desert on our Christian journey and to experience the presence of Christ through faith alone.

After a fine retreat experience, youth will feel a renewed energy, a love for living, yet they may be tired, wiped out, emotionally and physically. It is important for youth to rest and to bask in positive feelings of self-worth, warmth, friendship, and appreciation for closeness to Jesus at such times. They may need to be reminded that it is normal to anticipate feelings of drudgery in returning to daily routines, and they should be urged to be patient with themselves as they readjust. Adolescents normally want to continue to indulge in the wonderful experience of retreat time (much like a vacation or excellent party). Often, retreatants may fear slipping into old patterns of behavior, even though they would like to change. They may feel anxious because they have allowed other people to see their true selves. Encourage them to be patient with themselves and, if they notice such responses in other retreatants, to likewise be patient and supportive with them. Assure them of Jesus' attentive guidance when they pray after the retreat. (Tyme Out)

A retreat allows youth time and space to back off from their everyday, busy lives. In the absence of typical distractions, they can concentrate on their encounter(s) with God. Henri Nouwen has spoken of the benefits of Christian solitude: "A life without a lonely place, that is, a life without a quiet center, easily becomes destructive."

> In solitude we can slowly unmask the illusion of our possessiveness and discover in the center of our own self that we are not what we can conquer, but what is given to us. In solitude we can listen to the voice of him who spoke to us before we could speak a word, who healed us before we could make any gesture to help, who set us free long before we could free others, and who loved us long before we could give love to anyone. (Nouwen 21-22)

Throughout retreats, youths reflect, alone and in small groups, upon their daily lives and the choices they make. They examine their deepest feelings. They think and talk about who they really are. They pray to get in touch with themselves, with Jesus, and with others, especially family and friends. They experience affirmation and healing from their community, and grow and change, trusting together in God's Word. The chief purpose of a retreat is to allow youth opportunities to realign their own decision-making processes, in light of Gospel values, in order to better live their daily lives.

Through retreats they can become a little wiser, a little closer to each other, and to God. Hopefully, when they return to their schools, jobs, families, and friends, they are a little holier, too, a little healthier, and a little happier with who they are in Christ.

LISTEN TO YOUTH

Post-retreats, we should listen to youth, to hear their stories, to share in their experiences, to attend to their questions, to laugh with their zaniness, and to weep with them in joy.

In pastoral terms, we must help adolescents after retreats consider the values in their lives and how retreat experiences have helped them clarify those values. It is pivotal that adolescents understand that faith commitments require nurture. Adolescents need to reflect on how they will provide for this in daily life. Retreat ministers, as spiritual gardeners, could show young people a variety of gardening tools like books, articles, Bible studies, skill-building resources, leadership training programs, service projects, or catechetical texts, community builders, athletic activities, and prayer and worship opportunities.

Questions also could facilitate processing of adolescents' retreat experiences:

* Since your retreat experience, how have you experienced Jesus in your life?

* Who is Jesus to you now?

* What was your most significant experience on the retreat? The least significant?

* Do you now feel a need to spend more time with the Lord?

* Do you feel that God may be inviting you to do something specific as a result of your retreat?

* How will you continue to nourish the seed(s) the Holy Spirit has planted in you?

In his book, *Adolescent Spirituality*, Charles Shelton identifies the relationship between a youth's reflective experience and his or her call to appropriate action. So, reflect with the adolescent on where this experience now leads him or her, or how this (retreat) exercise can lead to actions that are more Christian.

This reflection is very important for the adolescent. The adult needs to aid the adolescent in seeing the relationship between the contemplative life and the active life (a favorite Ignatian theme). How does prayer (or a retreat) lead the adolescent to act to further the reign of God, the kingdom, in this world? The ideal Ignatian vision is found in the term "contemplative action." For our day, this phrase describes prayerful men and women who minister and labor in the world to bring about God's reign of peace and justice. (Shelton 134-135)

Retreat responses have their ultimate test in the arena of daily life. How a youth retreat has enhanced or diminished adolescent faith-development is determined in daily interactions. "Ultimately the worth of reflective responses cannot be decided in the mind but must be decided on the basis of experience." (Bolton 76)

POST-RETREAT ACTIVITIES IN THE SPIRIT

Retreats are multiform activities, the chief agent of which is the community gathered. The community is the prime embodiment of an adolescent retreat's message. In a sense, the community is the message. (Durka 138-39) The young person returning from a retreat may want to become more involved in his or her parish community. Retreat follow-up programs offer adolescents times to gather, again, as Christian community. The outcomes of these gatherings can be: 1) recall of retreat experiences; 2) renewal of friendships; and 3) discussion of progress on retreat resolutions. A retreat follow-up program is most potent when it happens within four weeks after a retreat. Knowing when a retreat follow-up is appropriate and which types of activities to provide during the follow-up(s) will help determine a retreat's overall viability.

Perhaps follow-through is a term more applicable than follow-up. It conveys an ongoing focus or direction. After a retreat, youths often will gravitate naturally into already existing programs, for example, youth ministry teams and commissions, which help facilitate the total youth ministry in a parish; youth faith-sharing groups; religious education workshops; communication, publicity, or resource development campaigns; parish, deanery, or diocesan retreat teams; outreach and rally teams; Bible studies and various support groups; athletic activities; confirmation programs; youth liturgy teams; service projects; and other apostolic opportunities.

Follow-up programs can be as varied as the environments to which retreatants return. These may provide youth, therefore, with opportunities to develop their own spirituality and, likewise, meet parish/community needs. Retreat follow-up programs presented here provide you with some material you can adapt and customize for needs found among your adolescents.

A HARVEST HOMECOMING

A Harvest Homecoming is a two-hour experience designed for an afternoon or evening meeting of retreatants. Choose a time when most youth can attend. Many times after-school activities will compete with other schedules. Perhaps a Saturday morning meeting or night-time meeting would work better for you.

SCHEDULE

10:00 AM	Gathering
10:15	Introduction and prayer
10:30	Post-retreat small-group discussions

11:00	Large-group discussion
11:45	Closing Prayer
12:00 Noon	Celebration

Detailed Schema:

10:00 AM — Gathering. The retreat team welcomes retreatants. Light refreshments are served.

10:15 — Introduction and prayer. Hand out copies of the retreat schedule for review. Mention some memorable and humorous incidents (or insights) from the retreat. Invite input from the group. Use a prayer handout and an appropriate song from the retreat which will help the retreatants recall the theme of the retreat experience.

Introduce the meeting, then, with something like the following: We've come together for "A Harvest Homecoming" to recall our retreat experience and to pray together again as a Christian community. Our schedule will follow a two-hour track, and the train will be full. Let's begin by reviewing the activities of our retreat experience. As you review the retreat schedule, try to recall the thoughts and feelings that you had then. Now come forward, choose one of these markers, and write or draw on the blank newsprint mural, the one we have taped on the wall, something you remember from the retreat: an event, a prayer, a song, a talk, whatever stands out as most significant for you. After you finish, we'll have some time to talk about your recollections.

Play some music, used during the retreat, in the background.

10:30 — Post-retreat small-group discussions. Creatively arrange youth into small groups. Explain that the next activity will give the retreatants an opportunity to discuss retreat and post-retreat experiences. Distribute the questions below on a handout. Encourage each small group to give each member an opportunity to respond to each question.

1) How do you feel about being here today?

2) What were your thoughts and feelings immediately following the retreat?

3) What were your thoughts and feelings just now while we reviewed the retreat schedule?

4) Did you have a retreat resolution or post-retreat plan of Christian action? How have things been going with this since our retreat?

5) What have been the most challenging post-retreat experiences for you?

6) What have been the most positive post-retreat experiences you have had?

Gather the small groups together in one large group. Proceed with the following.

11:00 — Large-Group Discussion. Invite the retreatants to share their personal responses in the large group. Review retreat and discussion guidelines first. All should adhere to confidentiality, respect, no putdowns, trust, honesty, and an attempt to include everybody. Invite a response from everyone. Ask the reflection questions below, pointing out similarities and differences in the responses.

1) What thoughts and feelings did you get in touch with in your small group?

2) Has the retreat made a difference in your life? Explain.

3) How can you actively support other retreatants?

4) How can we support you?

11:45 — Closing Prayer. Choose another appropriate retreat prayer and song which highlight the theme of the retreat. Encourage retreatants to pair off as prayer partners and to pray for each other during this time.

12:00 Noon — Celebrate. Go out to lunch together or have a pre-arranged, pitch-in lunch planned.

CREATIVE REMINDERS TECHNIQUE

Whenever a youth retreat format does not allow retreatants time to create a letter, a prayer, a poem, a picture, or some other form of expressive memento to symbolize and summarize a significant retreat experience, you may wish to include your own technique like this within the retreat itself. Then, put it to practical use in a follow-up.

Three to six weeks after your retreat(s), mail the mementos to retreatants, like a business mails catalogues after a purchase. You could insert these items mailed in a parish youthletter which also features pictures, articles, and first-person narratives about the retreat(s). Make sure every parish youth who has participated gets recognized.

Then, invite several retreatants to help plan an informal, social activity or a Day of Reflection for other parish youth who were on the retreat(s). Display retreat pictures on parish bulletin boards. Publish notices in bulletins. Invite the parish community to continue praying for your retreatants. These are positive ways to "keep the seeds alive."

YOUTH LITURGIES

Since 1980, the New Albany Deanery, in southern Indiana, has sponsored deanery retreat reunions in the form of deanery youth liturgies. You could adapt this concept in your area. Special rituals help youth nourish their retreat-growth through mutual support and help them stay in touch with other people who have shared in their retreats. In these liturgies, youth gather to participate in a celebration of the Eucharist and, then community building activity.

To help each of 19 parishes in the deanery host a deanery youth Mass in their community, the New Albany Deanery Youth Ministry Activities Team, through its committee on liturgy and spirituality, has compiled and distributed a packet of information. It includes guidelines for planning one of the monthly Masses, as well as handouts for youth who will be lectors, Eucharistic ministers, and liturgy planners. There is even a recipe for Eucharistic bread and a parish host schedule showing dates and post-liturgy activities. The deanery youth liturgies are held, usually, on the last Sunday of the month, from 6:00-9:00 PM. Parish youth and adults are encouraged to be creative, in a spirit of prayer and reverence for the Eucharist. Activities which follow liturgy range from Super Bowl parties, to dances, to scavenger hunts and games. Adult involvement is integral. Most parishes car-pool or bus participants to the various parishes.

CATECHETICAL FOLLOW-UP MODULES

Some ideas on how catechesis can be utilized within the scope of retreat ministry follow-ups will appear below. Other suggestions can be gleaned in consulting Chapter 4B by John Roberto on catechesis within youth retreats.

(A) Full Day of Catechesis

This brings youth from a retreat together for an extended period, again, for six to eight hours. Include a meal, a liturgical celebration, informal socializing, plus two or three learning sessions lasting two hours each. Full-day ministry programs call for much planning. A retreat team should meet to preview resource materials; select a date (avoid scheduling conflicts); choose a pleasant environment; plan snacks and meals; assign catechists/facilitators; prepare liturgy and prayer services.

(B) Week of Catechesis

First option: a weeknight program for three to five nights, two hours per night. This takes the weekly model (below) into one-week. The big advantage: concentration and continuity. Use careful planning, especially in selecting post-retreat weeks which do not conflict with community or school events, or with exams or special tests. Clear dates with school and parish administrations so that nothing else will be scheduled during these special week-long post-retreat ministries.

Second option: full days (for a whole week, Monday through Friday for example, or most of one week) during school vacations or summers. Many parishes have adapted this concept to their young adolescent program. With morning and afternoon learning sessions each day, there is time also scheduled everyday for recreation and socializing. A variation on this is similar to summer camp. Young people spend several days at a retreat or campsite. One or two catechetical faith-themes could be addressed during a week-long program such as this.

(C) Weekly Catechesis

Catechetical sessions (1-2 hours per week) are scheduled after a youth retreat (on weeknights or Sunday evenings). Organized like short-term mini-courses, in post-retreat blocks, or seasons (Fall-Winter-Spring-Summer), these allow retreatants to enroll each time they are offered after a youth retreat.

EVANGELIZATION FOLLOW-UP MODELS

Follow-up ministry activities can further support and enrich evangelizing efforts undertaken within a retreat for adolescents. These follow-ups carry on the outreach and relationships already established. They re-invite youth, as retreats themselves do, to examine their relationship with Jesus and with the community which follows him. Typically, evangelizing follow-ups will deepen an initial proclamation and sharing of the Good News. The person of the Lord, stories from both the Hebrew and Christian Scriptures, and challenges to live lives faithful to the Gospel will be central to evangelizing follow-up ministries.

A few simple models for such retreat follow-up approaches can be found here. Yet, for some specific ideas on evangelization of Catholic youth, and for some particular tips on developing and designing activities and story-based experiences which share the Good News in vibrant and attractive ways, see especially Chapters 6-10, and 14 in the *Access Guides to Youth Ministry: Evangelization*.

(A) Evangelization Evening

6:30	PM	arrival and welcome
		opening prayer
6:45		icebreaker and community-building
7:00		barbecue or pizza meal/game(s)

7:30		group activity and discussion
8:00		input/talk or video-presentation
8:30		follow-up activity/discussion(s)
8:50		personal reflection
9:00		artistic activity and/or journaling
9:30		closing prayer
9:45		social time
10:00		conclusion

(B) Follow-Up Evangelization Day I

10:00 AM	(1:00 PM)	opening remarks, prayer
10:10	(1:10)	icebreakers
10:30	(1:30)	group activity
10:45	(1:45)	presentation on retreat's theme
11:15	(2:15)	break
11:30	(2:30)	film or video and discussion
12:15	(3:15)	lunch (or snacks)/game(s)
1:30	(4:00)	presentation and activity-response
2:30	(5:00)	liturgy
3:00	(6:00)	closing/social time or meal option

(C) Follow-Up Evangelization Day II

9:00 AM		arrival, welcome, make nametags
9:15		icebreaker(s)
9:30		group activity with discussion
10:00		presentation
10:15		small-group sharing
10:30		large-group sharing/response
11:00		reconciliation experience
12:00 PM		lunch/recreation
1:00		small-group activity
1:30		large-group sharing/discussion
1:45		final talk or presentation
2:15		prayer experience or Eucharist
3:00		conclusion (social time/game(s) optional)

REVOLVING-SEASONS RETREAT MINISTRY

Nearly every retreat can have a follow-up. And nearly every follow-up can have a retreat. In revolving seasons of spiritual planting and harvesting, youth become increasingly sensitive to the movement of God in their lives. As their abilities to reflect develop, adolescents are empowered to sort out movements, inclinations, and impulses, and identify those that come from the Lord. Only then can a personal response follow. In their book, *Christian Life Patterns*, Evelyn E. and James D. Whitehead describe religious growth as "one's ability to discern patterns of God's presence within human life and to respond in an increasingly open way to this presence." (Whitehead 36)

Discerning Christians are always in need of growth. St. Paul reminded the people of Corinth to remain vigilant and to guard against foolishness in thinking they possessed all wisdom. In retreat environments, youth have opportunities for discernment. They reflect on their lives in ever-deeper ways so they can hear the Lord's call. This process is boundless. Youth are always encountering new experiences that challenge them to follow the Lord. Shelton points out that "we must respond to this call through our helping and sustaining responses to others." (Shelton 338)

CONCLUSION

Retreat follow-ups help youth define their personal commitments to Jesus and to Jesus' message. "During the adolescent years, these values are no doubt often realized and expressed in a seesaw fashion. At times, the values surface, but at other times they disappear." (Shelton, 338) Yet, adolescents gradually experience a deepening commitment to the beliefs and priorities in their lives. As Fr. Shelton also notes, "These growing, but often tentative assertions and reflections become the seeds from which maturing commitments are harvested in the later years of Christian adulthood." (Shelton 339) Follow-up gardening in retreat ministry requires responsible, loving, caring attention to empower youth's discovery of the "Come, follow me" challenge.

WORKS CITED

Bolton, Robert. *People Skills*. New York: Simon and Schuster, 1979.

Durka, Gloria. "Youth Ministry: Models for Personal and Social Transformation."
    Faith Maturing: A Personal and Communal Task. Ed. John Roberto.
    Washington DC: National Federation for Catholic Youth Ministry, 1985.

202   ACCESS GUIDES TO YOUTH MINISTRY

Ekstrom, Reynolds R. and John Roberto, editors. *Access Guides to Youth Ministry: Evangelization.* New Rochelle NY: Don Bosco Multimedia, 1989.

Moore, Joseph. *Monday Morning Jesus.* Ramsey NJ: Paulist, 1984.

Nouwen, Henri J.M. *Out of Solitude.* Notre Dame IN: Ave Maria Press, 1975.

Shelton, S.J., Charles M. *Adolescent Spirituality.* Chicago: Loyola University Press, 1983.

Tyme Out Center. "Turning Your Retreat Into Everyday Living." Milwaukee: Tyme Out.

Whitehead, Evelyn E. and James D. *Christian Life Patterns.* Garden City NY: Doubleday, 1979.

Appendix

Resources for Youth Retreats

FOUNDATIONAL UNDERSTANDINGS

Campolo, Anthony. *Growing Up in America - A Sociology of Youth Ministry*. Grand Rapids: Zondervan, 1989.

Ekstrom, Reynolds, R. *Access Guides to Youth Ministry: Pop Culture*. New Rochelle: Don Bosco Multimedia, 1989.

Ng, David. *Youth in the Community of Disciples*. Valley Forge PA: Judson Press, 1984.

Rice, Wayne. *Junior High Ministry*. Grand Rapids: Zondervan, 1987.

Roberto, John, editor. *Readings in Youth Ministry - Volume 1*. Washington DC: NFCYM, 1986.

_____, editor. *Readings in Youth Ministry - Volume 2*. Washington DC: NFCYM, 1988.

Roehlkepartain, Eugene C. *Youth Ministry in City Churches*. Loveland: Group Books, 1989.

Shaheen, David. *Growing a Junior High Ministry*. Loveland: Group Books, 1986.

Shea, John. *Stories of Faith*. Chicago: Thomas More Press, 1981.

_____. *An Experience Named Spirit*. Chicago: Thomas More Press, 1983.

_____. *Spirit Master*. Chicago: Thomas More Press. 1988.

_____ and John Nelson. *Perspectives on Catholic Identity*. Network Paper #29. New Rochelle: Don Bosco Multimedia, 1990.

Shelton, S. J., Charles. *Adolescent Spirituality.* New York: Loyola University Press, 1983.

_____. *Morality and the Adolescent.* New York: Crossroad, 1989.

Steinberg, Laurence, and Ann Levine. *You and Your Adolescent — A Parent's Guide for Ages 10-20.* New York: Harper & Row, 1990.

Vision of Youth Ministry. Department of Education. Washington DC: USCC, 1976.

Warren, Michael. *Youth, Gospel, Liberation.* San Francisco: Harper and Row, 1987.

Warren, Michael. *Faith, Culture, and the Worshipping Community.* New York: Paulist Press, 1989.

Zanzig, Thomas. "Youth Ministry: Reflections and Directions." *PACE 11.* (Also in: *Readings and Resources in Youth Ministry.* Edited by Michael Warren. Winona MN: St. Mary's Press, 1987.

EVANGELIZATION

Bausch, William. *Storytelling: Imagination and Faith.* Mystic: Twenty-Third Publications, 1984.

Ekstrom, Reynolds R., and John Roberto, editors. *Access Guides to Youth Ministry: Evangelization.* New Rochelle: Don Bosco Multimedia, 1989.

Kimball, Don. *Power and Presence - A Theology of Relationships.* San Francisco: Harper and Row, 1987.

Hater, Robert J. *News that is Good.* Notre Dame: Ave Maria Press, 1990.

Ng, David. *Youth in the Community of Disciples.* Valley Forge: Judson Press, 1984.

Nolan, O.P., Albert. *Jesus Before Christianity.* Maryknoll: Orbis, 1977.

Shea, John. *An Experience Named Spirit.* Chicago: Thomas More Press, 1983.

_____. *Spirit Master.* Chicago: Thomas More Press. 1988.

Walsh, John. *Evangelization and Justice.* Maryknoll: Orbis Books, 1982.

Warren, Michael. "The Evangelization of Youth." *Readings and Resources in Youth Ministry.* Edited by Michael Warren. Winona: St. Mary's Press, 1987.

_____. "Youth Evangelization - Ten Years Later." *Readings and Resources in Youth Ministry.* Edited by Michael Warren. Winona: St. Mary's Press, 1987.

CATECHESIS
The Challenge of Adolescent Catechesis. Washington DC: NFCYM, 1986.
Groome, Thomas. *Christian Religious Education.* San Francisco: Harper & Row, 1980.
Little, Sara. *To Set One's Heart.* Atlanta: John Knox Press, 1983.
Roberto, John. *Adolescent Catechesis Resource Manual.* New York: Sadlier, 1988.

PRAYER AND SPIRITUAL DEVELOPMENT
Broccolo, Gerard. *Vital Spiritualities.* Notre Dame: Ave Maria Press, 1990.
Cully, Iris V. *Education for Spiritual Growth.* San Francisco: Harper & Row, 1984.
Fischer, Kathleen. *Reclaiming the Connections.* Kansas City: Sheed and Ward, 1990.
Finn, Virginia. *Pilgrim in the Parish - A Spirituality for Lay Ministers.* New York: Paulist Press, 1986.
Johnson, Susanne. *Christian Spiritual Formation in the Church and Classroom.* Nashville: Abingdon, 1989.
Kovats, Alexandra. *Prayer - A Discovery of Life.* San Francisco: Winston Press, 1983.
Pennock, Michael. *The Way of Prayer.* Notre Dame: Ave Maria Press, 1987.
Schmidt, Joseph. *Praying our Experiences.* Winona: St. Mary's Press, 1989.
Shelton, S.J., Charles. *Adolescent Spirituality.* New York: Crossroad Publishing, 1983.
Warren, Michael. *Faith, Culture and the Worshipping Community.* New York: Paulist Press, 1989.

PRAYER RESOURCES
Black, Barbara, et al. *Pentecost, Peanuts, Popcorn, Prayer — Prayer Services for High School Students.* Villa Maria: Center for Learning, 1988.
Bergan, Jacqueline and S. Marie Schwan. *Forgiveness — A Guide for Prayer.* Winona: St. Mary's Press, 1985.

_____. *Love — A Guide for Prayer.* Winona: St. Mary's Press, 1985.

_____. *Birth — A Guide for Prayer.* Winona: St. Mary's Press, 1985.

Carroll, James. *Wonder and Worship.* New York: Paulist Press, 1970.

deMello, Anthony. *Sadhana: A Way to God.* New York: Doubleday, 1984.

_____. *The Song of the Bird.* New York: Doubleday, 1984.

_____. *Wellsprings.* New York: Doubleday, 1985.

_____. *The Heart of the Enlightened.* New York: Doubleday, 1989.

Dolores, Curran. *Family Prayer.* Mystic: Twenty-Third Publications, 1983.

Halpin, Marlene. *Imagine That!* Dubuque: Wm. C. Brown, 1982.

Hays, Edward. *Prayers for the Domestic Church.* Easton KS: Forest of Peace Books, 1979.

_____. *Twelve and One Half Keys.* Easton KS: Forest of Peace Books, 1981.

_____. *Prayers for the Domestic Church.* Easton KS: Forest of Peace Books, 1979.

_____. *Prayers for Planetary Pilgrims.* Easton, KS: Forest of Peace Books, 1988.

Hesch, John B. *Prayer & Meditation for Middle School Kids.* New York: Paulist Press, 1985.

Junior High Liturgy, Prayer, Reconciliation. Villa Maria: Center for Learning, 1987.

Link, Mark. *Challenge.* Allen, TX: Tabor, 1988.

McDonnell, Rea. *Prayer Pilgrimage through Scripture.* New York: Paulist Press. 1984.

Prayer: Journey to the Mountain. Villa Maria: Center for Learning, 1979.

Prayer Forms. Mystic: Twenty-Third Publications, 1987.

Prayer Service Models. Villa Maria: Center for Learning, 1984.

Roncolato, David. *A Prayer Journal: To Notice the Lord.* New York: Sadlier, 1988.

Schaffran, Janet. *More than Words.* Oak Park: Meyer Stone Books, 1988.

Winter, Miriam Therese. *Woman Prayer, Woman Song.* Oak Park: Meyer Stone Books, 1987.

Zanzig, Thomas. *Learning to Meditate.* Winona: St. Mary's Press, 1990.

WORSHIP

Benson, Dennis. *Creative Worship in Youth Ministry*. Loveland: Group Books, 1985.

Bailey, Betty Jane and J. Martin. *Youth Plan Worship*. New York: Pilgrim Press, 1987.

Black, Barbara, Karen Jessie and John Paulett. *Pentecost, Peanuts, Popcorn, Prayer — Prayer Services for High School Students*. Villa Maria: Center for Learning, 1988.

Cassa, Yvonne and Joanne Sanders. *Groundwork — Planning Liturgical Seasons*. Chicago: Liturgy Training Publications, 1982.

Center for Learning. *Seasonal Liturgies*. Villa Maria: Center for Learning, 1989.

Duck, Ruth C. and Maren C. Tirabassi. *Touch Holiness — Resources for Worship*. New York: Pilgrim Press, 1990.

Fischer, Kathleen. *The Inner Rainbow - The Imagination in Christian Life*. New York: Paulist Press, 1983.

Fleming, Austin. *Preparing for Liturgy — A Theology and Spirituality*. Washington DC: Pastoral Press, 1985.

Guzie, Tad. *The Book of Sacramental Basics*. New York: Paulist Press, 1981.

Hock, Mary Isabelle. *Worship through the Seasons*. San Jose: Resource Publications, 1987.

Huck, Gabe, editor. *Liturgy with Style and Grace: A Basic Manual for Planners and Ministers*. Revised Edition. Chicago: Liturgy Training Publications, 1984.

_____ et al. *Hymnal for Catholic Students: Leader's Manual*. Chicago: GIA Publications and Liturgy Training Publications, 1989. (Includes the *Directory of Masses with Children*, background essays, and 20 celebrations.)

Johnson, Lawrence. *The Word and Eucharist Handbook*. San Jose: Resource Publications, 1986.

Kovats, Alexandra. *Prayer - A Discovery of Life*. San Francisco: Winston Press, 1983.

Krier, Catherine H. *Symbols for All Seasons — Environmental Planning for Cycles A, B, & C*. San Jose: Resource Publications, 1988.

Marchal, Michael. *Adapting the Liturgy — Creative Ideas for the Church Year*. San Jose: Resource Publications, 1989.

McBride, William and Jeffrey Smay. *Liturgy Models*. Villa Maria: Center for Learning, 1984.

Mick, Lawrence. *To Live as We Worship*. Collegeville: Liturgical Press, 1984.

Mick, Lawrence. *Understanding the Sacraments Today*. Collegeville: Liturgical Press.

Neary S.J., Donal. *Masses with Young People*. Revised Edition. Mystic: Twenty-Third Publications, 1987.

Nelson, Gertrud Mueller. *To Dance with God — Family Ritual and Community Celebration*. New York: Paulist Press, 1986.

Ostkiek, Gilbert. *Catechesis for Liturgy — A Program for Parish Involvement*. Washington DC: Pastoral Press, 1986.

Reeves S C , Sister John Maria and Sister Maureen Roe, R.S.M. *Junior High Liturgy, Prayer, Reconciliation*. Villa Maria: Center for Learning, 1988.

Roberto, John, editor. *Access Guides to Youth Ministry: Liturgy and Worship*. New Rochelle: Don Bosco Multimedia, 1990.

_____, editor. *Readings in Youth Ministry - Volume II*. Washington, DC: NFCYM Publications, 1989.

Searle, Mark. *Liturgy Made Simple*. Collegeville: Liturgical Press, 1981.

Walden, Carol, editor. *Called to Create — Christian Witness and the Arts*. San Jose: Resource Publications, 1986.

RETREAT RESOURCES

Carotta, Mike. *Junior High: Growing Selves, Emerging Faith*. Minneapolis: Winston Press, 1985.

Clark, Keith. *Make Space, Make Symbols*. Notre Dame: Ave Maria Press, 1979.

Coleman, Lyman. *Youth Ministry Encyclopedia*. Littleton: Serendipity House, 1985.

Cooney, Randy. *How to Run Successful Days of Retreat*. Dubuque: Wm. C. Brown Company, 1986.

Doyle, Aileen A. *Youth Retreats: Creating Sacred Space for Young People*. Winona: St. Mary's Press, 1986.

_____. *More Youth Retreats: Creating Sacred Space for Young People*. Winona: St. Mary's Press, 1988.

Harman, Shirley R. *Retreat Planning Made Easy*. Minneapolis: Augsburg Publishing House, 1985.

Junior High Retreats. Villa Maria: Center for Learning, 1987.

Kamstra, Doug. *The Get-Away Book: A Handbook for Youth Group Retreats.* Grand Rapids: Baker Book House, 1983.

New Games Foundation. *New Games.* Garden City: Doubleday & Company, Inc. 1976.

New Games Foundation. *More New Games.* Garden City: Doubleday & Company, Inc., 1981.

Pastva, S.N.D., Sr. Mary Loretta. *The Catholic Youth Retreat Book.* Cincinnati: St. Anthony Messenger Press, 1984.

Reichter, Arlo et al. *Group Retreat Book.* Loveland: Group Books, 1983.

_____ et al. *More Group Retreats.* Loveland: Group Books, 1987.

Reimer, Sandy and Larry. *The Retreat Handbook.* Wilton: Morehouse-Barlow, 1986.

Retreat Models. Villa Maria: Center for Learning, 1984.

Rice, Wayne, Denny Rydberg, and Mike Yaconelli. *Fun N Games.* Grand Rapids: Zondervan Publishing House, 1977.

Rice, Wayne, John Roberto, and Mike Yaconelli, editors. *Creative Resources for Youth Ministry* (6-volume series). Winona: St. Mary's Press, 1981.

Senior High Retreats. Villa Maria: Center for Learning, 1987.

Sawyer, S.S.N.D., Sr. Kieran. *The Jesus Difference.* Notre Dame: Ave Maria Press, 1987.